THE
OXYRHYNCHUS PAPYRI

VOLUME LI

THE
OXYRHYNCHUS PAPYRI

VOLUME LI

EDITED WITH TRANSLATIONS AND NOTES BY

J. R. REA

Graeco-Roman Memoirs, No. 71

PUBLISHED FOR
THE BRITISH ACADEMY
BY THE
EGYPT EXPLORATION SOCIETY
3 DOUGHTY MEWS, LONDON WC1N 2PG

1984

PRINTED IN GREAT BRITAIN
AT THE UNIVERSITY PRESS, OXFORD
AND PUBLISHED FOR
THE BRITISH ACADEMY
BY THE EGYPT EXPLORATION SOCIETY
3 DOUGHTY MEWS, LONDON WC1N 2PG

ISSN 0306-9222
ISBN 0 85698 086 2

PREFACE

ALL the items in this volume are documentary. They have been chosen for their individual interest and therefore touch on a great variety of topics, but the largest section, that of Official Documents, is concerned with the government and administration of Roman and Byzantine Egypt. Starting our selection at the highest level we may mention Chosroes II, 'king of kings', the recipient of the taxes in gold concerned in **3637**, an official letter dating from AD 623, when Egypt was occupied by the Persians. Next come a rescript of Valerian and Gallienus about the emoluments of victors in sacred games (**3611**), a record of a judgement of Septimius Severus (**3614**), delivered in Alexandria in AD 200 in Latin ($\tau\hat{\eta}$ $\pi\alpha\tau\rho\acute{\iota}\omega$ $\phi\omega\nu\hat{\eta}$), and a very fragmentary official letter concerned with the accession of Gordian I and/or Gordian II in AD 238 (**3607**). With these we can associate a group of sworn undertakings to assist in arrangements to supply pack animals during Caracalla's visit to Egypt in AD 215 (**3602–5**). The chronology of the changes of reign in AD 250 and 251 is affected by the date-clauses of **3608–10**. As for consuls, the fragment of a roll with declarations of prices (**3624–6**) has revealed the *nomen* of a consul of AD 358, Censorius Datianus. Perhaps the most interesting contribution to the history of the provinces is the first documentary confirmation of the existence of the province of *Aegyptus Iouia*, hitherto known only from a single mention in a seventh-century manuscript; **3619** is a bilingual record of proceedings before a *praeses Aegypti Iouiae*. From **3636**, one of several fragments of a roll containing lists of commodity prices and tax accounts, we get the first unambiguous evidence that the province of Arcadia contained a nome called the Theodosiopolite, to be distinguished from the Upper Theodosiopolite nome in the Thebaid. We learn of one new prefect of Egypt, Ti. Flavius Laetus, of AD 326 (**3620**). Three other prefects have contributed a letter (**3612**), an edict (**3613**), and a record of a judgement (**3627**). By way of sad contrast we can read the unflattering descriptions of runaway slaves in **3616** and **3617**.

Dr Rea edited the texts and compiled the indexes. He would like to thank Dr Coles and Mr Parsons for help and support at every stage, and Dr I. Gershevitch for his specialist advice on Persian in connection with **3637**. It is a pleasure to acknowledge again the skill and efficiency of the Oxford University Press and of their Reader, Dr L. A. Holford-Strevens.

P. J. PARSONS
J. R. REA
General Editors,
Graeco-Roman Memoirs

September 1983

CONTENTS

TABLE OF PAPYRI

I. OFFICIAL DOCUMENTS

[1] All dates in this table are AD

LIST OF PLATES

NUMBERS AND PLATES

NOTE ON THE METHOD OF
PUBLICATION AND ABBREVIATIONS

THE method of publication follows that adopted in Part XLV. As there, the dots indicating letters unread and, within square brackets, the estimated number of letters lost are printed slightly below the line. The texts are printed in modern form, with accents and punctuation, the lectional signs occurring in the papyri being noted in the *apparatus criticus*, where also faults of orthography, etc., are corrected. Iota adscript is printed where written, otherwise iota subscript is used. Square brackets [ ] indicate a lacuna, round brackets () the resolution of a symbol or abbreviation, angular brackets 〈〉 a mistaken omission in the original, braces {} a superfluous letter or letters, double square brackets ⟦ ⟧ a deletion, the signs ` ´ an insertion above the line. Dots within brackets represent the estimated number of letters lost or deleted, dots outside brackets mutilated or otherwise illegible letters. Dots under letters indicate that the reading is doubtful. Lastly, heavy arabic numerals refer to Oxyrhynchus papyri printed in this and preceding volumes, ordinary numerals to lines, small roman numerals to columns.

The use of arrows (→, ↓) to indicate the direction of the fibres in relation to the writing has been abandoned for reasons put forward by E. G. Turner, 'The Terms Recto and Verso' (*Actes du XVe Congrès International de Papyrologie* I: Papyrologica Bruxellensia 16 (1978) 64–5), except when they serve to distinguish the two sides of a page in a papyrus codex. In this volume most texts appear to accord with normal practice in being written parallel with the fibres on sheets of papyrus cut from the manufacturer's roll. Any departures from this practice which have been detected are described in the introductions to the relevant items.

The abbreviations used are in the main identical with those in E. G. Turner, *Greek Papyri: an Introduction* (2nd edn., 1980). It is hoped that any new ones will be self-explanatory.

ADDITIONS AND CORRECTIONS TO PAPYRI PUBLISHED BY THE EGYPT EXPLORATION SOCIETY

I   **14.** A. S. Hollis, *CQ* NS 32 (1982) 117-20.

     32. P. Cugusi, *ZPE* 42 (1981) 137-40; H. Cotton, *Documentary Letters of Recommendation in Latin from the Roman Empire* 15-23.

     43 *verso* (= W. *Chr.* 474). 7. M. Del Fabbro, *Stud. Pap.* 21 (1982) 15-17.

     105 22. After Ἀδριανοῦ add Cεβαcτοῦ, which is present on the papyrus. P. J. Sijpesteijn, *ZPE* 45 (1982) 181.

     106 (= M. *Chr.* 308). 6. For cτρ(ατηγὸν) Δημήτριον read cτρ(ατηγήcαντα) Δ., cf. P. Oxy. Hels. 19. 1, where Apolinarius is now attested as strategus on 14 March 134. Demetrius will be the strategus of 118-21, in which period the will in question was originally made. Correct *ZPE* 29 (1978) 173, Nos. 40, 46, and 47. J. E. G. Whitehorne.

     146 3. For εὐμάνου read ἐν μόνον. See LI **3640** 5 n.

     147 2. For εὐμά(νου) read ἐν μόνῳ. See LI **3640** 5 n.
          3. For the era date cλα καὶ c read cλβ καὶ cα = AD 555/6 = indiction 4; the date of the document is 7 April 556. See LI **3640** 5 n.

     172 (description). Edition by R. Pintaudi, *ZPE* 46 (1982) 263-5, with Taf. XV b.

II   **331** (description). Edition by A. Martin, *CE* 56 (1981) 299-303.
          15-16. For [± 6] ‚‚κοιρ‚‚, τῶν read and restore probably [καὶ τῶν] cυγκοιρόγ|¹⁶των (= cυγκυρόντων). J. R. Rea.

III   **420.** W. Luppe, *Philologus* 125 (1981) 181-7.

     574. F. Montanari, *ZPE* 48 (1982) 89-92.

IV   **663.** E. W. Handley, *BICS* 29 (1982) 110, 114.

VII   **1021.** M. G. Schmidt, *ZPE* 49 (1982) 45-50.

VIII   **1110** 18. For Ἰδιοκ‚ [read probably ἰδιόκτ[ητος. See L **3555** 5 n.

IX   **1174.** E. V. Maltese, *Sofocle, Ichneutae* (Papyrologica Florentina, Vol. X, 1982).

     1197 29-30. For Cαραπίῳ[ν ....] ἐγ [ραψα read Cαραπίῳ[ν .... ου] ἐγ[γυῶμαι, cf. 17-19 with the correction recorded in XLIII, p. xv. For a similar guarantor's subscription see e.g. XLVII **3344** 30-3. The traces at the beginnings of **1197** 31-2 are too uncertain to support any further restoration of the text. P. J. Sijpesteijn.

X   **1293** 5, 33, 39. A. M. Tromp, *Stud. Pap.* 21 (1982) 39-40.

     1317 (description). Transcription in J. Bingen *et al.*, *Au temps où on lisait le grec en Égypte*. Catalogue de l'exposition de papyrus et d'ostraca (1977), p. 14, No. 31.

XI   **1394** (description). Edition by W. E. H. Cockle, *ZPE* 45 (1982) 166-8.

XII   **1407** 21-2. On a possible version for the restoration of the titulature of Aurelian see P. J. Sijpesteijn, *ZPE* 45 (1982) 194, n. 53.

     1454 12. For [Καίcαρος Νερούα Τρα]ιαν[ο]ῦ read probably [Καίcαρος Νέρουα Τραιανοῦ Ἀρ]ίcτ[ο]υ. P. J. Sijpesteijn, *ZPE* 45 (1982) 179.

     1560 13. For]υρι‚ω Αὐρηλίῳ Ὡρείωνι read Καλπο]υρνίῳ κτλ. See L **3564** 1 n.

XIII   **1611** ² 124-30. L. Leurini, *QUCC* 38 NS 9 (1981) 155-61.

XIV   **1627** 29. The notary Diogenes appears also in XLIII **3146** 26, where restore δι' ἐμο[ῦ Διο]γένους, and in PSI VIII 882. 14. K. A. Worp.

     1635. For the date (44-30 BC) see XLIX **3482** introd. para. 3.

1648   13. For Αὐρηλίῳν read probably Αὐρηλίου. P. J. Sijpesteijn, *ZPE* 45 (1982) 185.

1695   14. M. Del Fabbro, *Stud. Pap.* 21 (1982) 15–17.

1703. This is to be dated *c.* 260/1, see P. Upps. Frid 5, which mentions the same cosmetes Aurelius Apion alias Ptollion in this year.

1704   11. For μοι (l. μου) ἀ[ν]τλετικου (l. ἀντλητικοῦ) read μοιλ[αίου] ἀλετικοῦ. See LI **3639** 10–11 n.

1776   11. For Ϲεμψαύ read Παψαύ. See L **3556** 14–15 n.

XV **1807.** Cf. P. Köln IV 185, another fragment of the same manuscript, containing Aratus, *Phaenomena* 918–29, with scholia.

XVI **1843.** This is perhaps to be dated to 6 November 623. See LI **3637** introd.

1878   1. For *heṃọl*( ) read *Heracl*(*eopoli*). See LI **3619** introd., p. 48.

1890   8. For ϲτεγικόϲ read ἀλετικόϲ. See LI **3639** 10–11 n.

XVII **2106**   1. This line of *ed. pr.* is actually two lines in the original. J. R. Rea, *JRS* 54 (1964) 205.

2153   4–5. For (τετρά)χ(ορα?) Ἑρλβ, διπ(λᾶ) ρκα, δίχο(ρα?) λζ read (τετρά)χ(οα) Ἑρλβ, δι(πλο-κέραμα) ρκα, δίχο(α) λζ. See L **3595** 10–12 n.

XVIII **2162.** D. F. Sutton, *GRBS* 22 (1981) 335–8.

2193, 2194. A related letter has been published in P. Köln IV 200.

XX **2256** [9(a), 9(b)]. D. F. Sutton, *ZPE* 51 (1983) 19–24.

XXI **2288**   18–19. M. Parca, *ZPE* 46 (1982) 47–50.

XXII **2310** [1] i 9. Restore perhaps ἀμφὶ δὲ ψ[όγων. C. Carey, *LCM* 6 (1981) 247–8.

XXVII **2455** [6]. W. Luppe, *Studi classici e orientali* 32 (1982) 231–3.

[14] 233–45. W. Luppe, *ZPE* 51 (1983) 25–8.

[107(+57?)]. W. Luppe, *ZPE* 49 (1982) 15–19.

[24, 84, 95, 111, 123]. Ibid. 19–21.

[48, 125]. W. Luppe, *Philologus* 126 (1982) 313–15.

2457. W. Luppe, *Philologus* 126 (1982) 10–18.

2470. L. Robert, *REG* 94 (1981) 446–7, No. 479; K. Weitzmann, *The Age of Spirituality*, No. 86.

XXIX **2506** [26] i 12–16. S. West, *ZPE* 47 (1982) 6–10.

XXX **2513.** R. Janko, *ZPE* 49 (1982) 25–9.

XXXI **2586**   7, 12, 17, 38, 44; XXXVIII **2875** 10, 12, 14, 16, 18, 23, 25, 29. In these third-century documents the apprentice's master, in one case a weaver and in the other a builder, is called ἐπιϲτάτηϲ. Compare A. Thierfelder, *Philogelos der Lachfreund* 100–1, 261 (§ 199), 102–3 (§ 200). These are two jokes about barbers' apprentices whose masters are called ἐπιϲτάτηϲ. Evidently it was a technical term of the institution of apprenticeship. J. R. Rea.

XXXIII **2660.** J. Kramer, *Glossaria Bilinguia* 63–6.

2660a. Ibid. 67–8.

2673. E. Wipszycka, *ZPE* 50 (1983) 117–21.

XXXIV **2723**   18. Restore probably ἃϲ κ]αὶ [ἐν]τεῦθεν προφέρε[τ]α[ι ἀποχαρίζ]εϲθαι. See LI **3638** 16–17 n.

XXXV **2735.** L. Carmignani, *Athenaeum* 60 (1982) 172–9.

2737   34–51. W. Luppe, *ZPE* 46 (1982) 147–59.

44–51. G. Mastromarco, *ZPE* 51 (1983) 29–35.

XXXVI **2783**   29. Perhaps read τὸν Τύφλον, which would in that case be the name of a slave rather than the description of an animal, see BGU XIV 2425. 24, cf. *RHDFE* 60 (1980) 124.

XXXVII **2803** [1] back. M. L. West, *ZPE* 48 (1982) 86.

2806. E. W. Handley, *BICS* 29 (1982) 109–17.

2812. J. S. Rusten, *HSCP* 84 (1980) 339.

XXXVIII **2845**   8. For .εọ.. [read perhaps Δεọντ[αϲ. J. E. G. Whitehorne, *ZPE* 45 (1982) 254–5.

2847. D. Bonneau, *JJP* 19 (1983) 131–53.

2857. L. Migliardi-Zingale, *Anagennesis* 2 (1982) 114–17.

2875. See above under XXXI **2586**.

XXXIX 2889. L. Rossetti, C. Lausdei, *Rhein. Mus.*, NF 124 (1981) 154–65.

XL 2933   2. M. Del Fabbro, *Stud. Pap.* 21 (1982) 18–19.

XLII 3016. A. Biscardi, *Labeo* 27 (1981) 331–4.

XLIII 3094   40 n. On θαλλοί at temples of Sarapis see also P. Nautin, *REG* 90 (1977) xii; A. Thierfelder, *Philogelos der Lachfreund* 56–7, 224–5 (§ 76), where the textual problem may perhaps be solved by emending to πα⟨ιδα⟩ρίῳ.

3096   18. The suggestion by P. Mertens, *Bibliotheca Orientalis* 38 (1981) 607 that we should read ιγϛ (= τρεικαιδεκαετεῖϲ) for ι. ϛ does not appear to suit the remains. J. R. Rea.

3105   11 n. For '12 June' read '24 June' (cf. **3104**). P. Mertens, *Bibliotheca Orientalis* 38 (1981) 607.

3111   5–6. On the title of the legion, λεγιῶνοϲ . . . Οὐαλερι(αν)ῶν καὶ Γαλλιηνῆϲ, see C. Zaccaria, *Quaderni di storia antica e di epigrafia* 2 (1978) 75–6 n. 45.

3114   2–3. This φύλαρχοϲ of AD 267, Aurelius Diogenes alias Hermias, has appeared also as λαογράφοϲ in XXXVIII **2855** (AD 291) and as ϲυϲτάτηϲ in P. Cornell 18 (AD 291) and XLIV **3183** (AD 292). P. Mertens, *Bibliotheca Orientalis* 38 (1981) 608.

3123   7–8 n. For δημοϲία ἐπιϲτήμη as a translation of *publica disciplina* compare also Eusebius, *HE* viii 17.6 κατὰ τοὺϲ ἀρχαίουϲ νόμουϲ καὶ τὴν δημοϲίαν ἐπιϲτήμην τὴν τῶν Ῥωμαίων, 9 μηδὲν ὑπεναντίον τῆϲ ἐπιϲτήμηϲ, which is very like **3123** 7–8. These phrases occur in an edict of Galerius, translated from Latin, see 11, ταῦτα κατὰ τὴν Ῥωμαίων φωνήν, ἐπὶ τὴν Ἑλλάδα γλῶτταν κατὰ τὸ δυνατὸν μεταληφθέντα. J. R. Rea.

3127   6. For κατ]αρομποῦ other possibilities are πρ]ορομποῦ or προ]ρομποῦ. See L **3576** 6 n.

3129   margin. For]l( ) read *Al*]*ex*(*andriae*). See L **3577** introd. (p. 195).

3146   26. See above under XIV **1627** 29.

XLIV 3154   heading. As the first element of the inventory number for '26' read '21'.

3160.   F. Montanari, *Studi classici e orientali* 31 (1981) 101–10.

3178   heading. As the third element of the inventory number for '16' read '76'.

3187   heading. As the last element of the inventory number for 'a' read 'c'.

XLV 3238   heading. As the third element of the inventory number for '1' read '12'.

XLVI 3272   introd., para. 1. In the titulature of Nero Κλαυδίου is indispensable and must have stood at the beginning of l. 3. P. J. Sijpesteijn.
      This leaves more space in the lacuna at the beginnings of ll. 1–2 than was envisaged in *ed. pr.* There can be no certainty about supplements, but there may have been a longer name in 1. L. 2 might have been indented or might have contained a short verb plus the article τό to go with κατ᾽ ἄνδρα. J. R. Rea.

3285.   E. Bresciani, *Egitto e Vicino Oriente* 4 (1981) 201–15, with the remarks of J. M. Modrzejewski, *RHDFE* 60 (1982) 472–3.
      32–7. For Egyptian roof gutters cf. H. E. Winlock, *Models of Daily Life in Ancient Egypt from the Tomb of Meket-Rēʿ* 18–19, pls. 6, 9, 11. 15. W. J. Tait.

3310   heading. As the fourth element of the inventory number for '2' read 'B'.

3315.   J. Kramer, *Glossaria Bilinguia* 69–70.

XLVII 3317   R. Scodel, *ZPE* 46 (1982) 37–42.

3319.   J. N. O'Sullivan-W. A. Beck, *ZPE* 45 (1982) 71–83.

3328   heading. As the first element of the inventory number for '34' read '35'.

3332   heading. As the last element of the inventory number for 'd' read 'a'.

3338   heading. As the third element of the inventory number for '76' read '46'.
      7–9. D. Hagedorn, P. Köln IV 188 introd. n. 2 (p. 178).

3352   heading. As the fourth element of the inventory number for 'H' read 'K'.

XLVIII 3368   A 40, **3369** A 40. E. G. Turner, *ZPE* 46 (1982) 113–16.

XLIX 3462   introd. para. 3 (pp. 109–10). Contrary to what was stated there the word διάζωμα, not yet in the papyrological dictionaries, has appeared in the papyri, in BGU IV 1188. 7, cf. M. Schnebel, *Landwirtschaft* 44 n. 1, although Wilcken suggested that we should read διαχώματοϲ in place of διαζώματοϲ (BL VI 15; *APF* 6 (1920) 282). No doubt διαζώματοϲ is right. Although the text of BGU 1188 is obscure, it clearly shows that the διάζωμα is an irrigation channel. J. R. Rea.

3501 heading. For 'Third/fourth century' read 'Third century', because the institution of epicrisis disappeared during the reforms of Diocletian. J. M. Modrzejewski, *RHFDE* 61 (1983) 161.

Index I (*a*), p. 259. For ἄριϲτοϲ read ἄριϲτον. E. G. Turner.

L **3533** 7–8 = **3532** ³ 9–10. Restore e.g. αἰϲχρῶν [ἀπέχεται]|[οὐδ᾽ ὧντινω]ν. L. A. Holford-Strevens.

3541 3. Restore e.g. ἀνὴρ δ᾽ ἀπει]πὼν οὐδὲ ϲυμβουλὴν ν[οεῖ. 'The man who gives up can't even offer good advice.' L. A. Holford-Strevens.

P. Ant. II   102. The date is perhaps AD 445 rather than AD 390. R. S. Bagnall, K. A. Worp, *ZPE* 46 (1982) 239–40.

III   190. (a) 10, 30; (b) 33. For ἐξ(ῆϲ) read ἐξ (ὧν). P. J. Sijpesteijn, P. Mich. XV 740. 18 n.

O. Fay. 21.3. For ϲάκ(κον) ᾱ read ϲαργ(άνην) ᾱ. C. Gallazzi.

P. Fay. 243 verso (description). Edition by L. C. Youtie, *ZPE* 50 (1983) 51–5; Taf. IIa.

P. Hib. II 186. J. S. Rusten, *HSCP* 84 (1980) 339.

P. Tebt. I 8. T. C. Skeat, *BASP* 18 (1981) 141–4.

II 543 (description). Edition by R. Pintaudi, *Aegyptus* 72 (1982) 162–4; pl. opp. p. 162.

560 (description). Edition by R. Pintaudi, *ZPE* 46 (1982) 265–6; Taf. XVc.

P. Turner 12. F. Montanari, *ZPE* 50 (1983) 21–4.

I. OFFICIAL DOCUMENTS

3601. DECLARATION TO AN ACTING STRATEGUS

43 5B.69/B(1–3)a   13 × 36 cm   29 October or 16 November 202

An Oxyrhynchite woman, daughter of a citizen who had served as strategus of the Small Diopolite nome, sent this declaration to the acting strategus of her own district to prove that her father had, contrary to what was alleged, duly handed on the official papers of his term of office to his successor. Probably the father was dead, though she did not explain why he did not write himself. His name, Hierax son of Dionysius, and that of his successor, Apollonius, are additions to the list of the strategi of the Small Diopolite nome. Both were out of office by 3 August 195, which is the date of the letter quoted as proof of the due transmission of the papers. It is quite possible that IV **708** (= W. *Chr.* 432), which contains texts of two letters sent to an unnamed strategus of this nome in 188, relates to Hierax. It may, therefore, give us one date in his term of office, 27 October 188.

The allegation, which had seemingly been refuted in 195, arose again at a review of the administrative affairs (διαλογιϲμόϲ) of the Oxyrhynchite nome held by the prefect of Egypt Maecius Laetus in 202, and was embodied in a report to or by the acting eclogistes of the nome. This report was 'sent up', εἶδοϲ ἀναπεμφθέν, which probably means that it was sent upstream from Alexandria, where the eclogistae normally functioned, to the acting strategus of the Oxyrhynchite nome, who then probably instructed the daughter of Hierax to enter a defence to the allegation or to pay the fine for negligence of this kind, see 33 n.

The writer of the letter cited as proof of the transmission of the records was a *procurator usiacus*, Alpheius, previously unknown, who was in office on 3 August 195, but out of office by the date of this declaration, 29 October or 16 November 202. He may be identical with a procurator named in an inscription from Sparta, see 15 n.

The recipient of the declaration looks likely to have been the Ammonianus who was royal scribe and acting strategus on 27 March 199 (XII **1473** 20, 23) and on 22 May 199 (VI **899** 34, 36), although a full strategus, Diophanes, intervenes, see J. E. G. Whitehorne, *ZPE* 29 (1978) 177. He was here represented by a deputy of his own, named Ptolemy.

The back is blank.

Ἀμ]μωνιανῷ βασιλ(ικῷ) γρ(αμματεῖ) δια[δεχ(ομένῳ) τὴν στρ(ατηγίαν)
διὰ] Πτολεμαί[ο]υ διαδόχο[υ   c. 10 letters
πα]ρ[ὰ . . . .]. ια[.]. ϲ τῆϲ [κ]αὶ Ἱερακιαίνηϲ ᾿θ[υγατρὸϲ ῾Ἱέρακοϲ
γε]νομέν[ο]υ στρα[τ]η[γοῦ] Δ[ι]οπολε̣ί̣τ[ου Μι]κ[ροῦ

5   Θηβ[α]ΐδοϲ. προϲ εἶδοϲ ἀναπεμφθὲν ὑπὸ
τοῦ διέποντο[ϲ] τὴν ἐγλογιϲτίαν τοῦ ν̣[ομ]οῦ
ἀπὸ διαλογιϲμοῦ Μαικίου Λαίτου τ̣ο̣[ῦ λα]μ-
προτάτου ἡγεμόνοϲ περί τινων [ἐϲτρα-
τηγ[η]κότων ὡϲ μὴ μεταβαλομ[ένων

10   τὰ ἐγβατικὰ βιβλία, ἐν οἷϲ καὶ ὁ ἐμὸϲ πατὴρ Ἱέραξ Διονυϲίου ϲτρατηγήϲαϲ
τοῦ Διοπολείτου, δηλῶ τὰ τῆϲ τάξεωϲ
βιβλία μεταβεβλῆϲθαι τῷ μετ' αὐτὸν [ϲ]τρ[α-
τηγήϲαντι ἀκολούθωϲ τῇ γραφείϲῃ

15   ἐπιϲτολῇ ΄ὑπὸ΄ Ἀλφειοῦ το[ῦ] κρατίϲτου γενομένου ἐπιτρόπου τῶν ο̣ὐϲιακῶν ἐξ[.]ν̣τ̣[
. . . .] ἧϲ ἐϲτιν ἀντίγραφον   (vac.)
Ἀλφειὸ]ϲ ϲτρατηγῷ Ὀξυρυγ[χίτου·
τῆϲ γρα]φ̣εί[ϲηϲ] μοι ἐπιϲτολῇ[ϲ] . [. . . . . . .

20   . [.]ων Ἱέρακοϲ ϲτρατηγή[ϲαντοϲ τοῦ
Διοπολ[εί]του Μεικροῦ Θηβ[α]ΐ[δοϲ τὸ
ἀντίγρ(αφον) πεμφθ[ῆ]ναί ϲοι ἐκέλ[ευϲα
ὅπωϲ, ἐ[π]ε̣ὶ παρέθ̣ετο [γ]ράμματα
τοῦ μετὰ τὸν Ἱέρακα ϲτρατηγήϲα[ν-

25   τοϲ Ἀπολλωνίου ὁμολογοῦντοϲ
τὰ βιβλία τῆϲ τάξεωϲ μετειλη-
φέναι, φροντίϲηϲ μηδὲν κεν[ί-
ζεϲθαι περὶ τὰϲ προϲόδουϲ αὐτῶν ἐκ τῶν πρότερον ἐπιϲτα-

30   λέντων. (vac.) ἐρρῶϲθαί ϲε εὔχομαι.
(ἔτουϲ) γ΄΄ Μεϲορὴ ῑ.   (vac.)
(vac.) ἕωϲ τούτου ἡ ἐπιϲτολ(ή). ἵν᾽ οὖν εἰδῇϲ

1 βαϲ̀γρ𝈷   3 ϊερακιαινηϲ   4 l. Διοπολίτου   5 θηβ[α]ΐδοϲ   6 l. ἐκλογιϲτίαν
10 l. ἐκβατικά   11 ϊεραξ   12 l. Διοπολίτου   15 ϋπο   20 ϊερακοϲ   21 l. Διοπολίτου
Μικροῦ   22 αντιγρ𝈷   24 ϊερακα   27 l. καινίζεϲθαι   31 ∟γ΄΄   32 επιϲτ∂

καὶ τῷ μεταδοθέντι εἴδει αὐτὰ ταῦ-
34   τα παραθῇ, φανερόν coι ποιῶ.
(m. 2)   (ἔτουc) ια Αὐτοκρ[α]τόρων Καιcάρων Λουκίου
    C]επτιμίου Cεουήρου Εὐcεβοῦc Περτίνακοc
    Ἀραβικοῦ Ἀδιαβηνικοῦ Παρθικοῦ Μεγίcτου
    καὶ] Μάρκου Αὐρηλίου Ἀντωνί[νο]υ Εὐcεβοῦc Cεβαcτῶν
    κ]αὶ Πουβλίου Cεπτιμίου Γέτα Καίcαροc Cεβαcτοῦ,
40   Ἀθὺρ β̄.

35 ∟ ια

'To Ammonianus royal scribe administering the office of the strategus, through Ptolemy his deputy, from
. . . alias Hieraciaena, daugher of Hierax former strategus of the Small Diopolite nome of the Thebaid.

'In response to a report sent up by the acting eclogistes of the nome as a result of the administrative review of
Maecius Laetus, the most glorious prefect, concerning certain former strategi alleged not to have passed on their
records on leaving office, among whom was my father Hierax son of Dionysius, former strategus of the Diopolite
nome, I declare that the records of the office were passed on to the person who served as strategus after him
according to the letter written by Alpheius, *vir egregius*, former *procurator usiacus*, . . . , of which this is a copy:'

'Alpheius to the strategus of the Oxyrhynchite nome. I have ordered the copy of the letter written to me
(by our colleague?) Hierax former strategus of the Small Diopolite nome of the Thebaid to be sent to you so
that, since he annexed a letter of Apollonius, who served as strategus after Hierax and acknowledges that he
has taken over the records of the office, you may see to it that no new steps are taken in regard to their revenues
as a result of the previous official communications. I pray for your health. Year 3, Mesore 10.'

'Thus far the letter. For your information, therefore, and so that you may add these same matters to the
report that was delivered (to me), I make this declaration to you.'

(2nd hand) 'Year 11 of Imperatores Caesares Lucius Septimius Severus Pius Pertinax Arabicus
Adiabenicus Parthicus Maximus and Marcus Aurelius Antoninus Pius, Augusti, and Publius Septimius Geta
Caesar Augustus, Hathyr 2 (or 20?).'

2 The end of the line was probably blank, cf. e.g. XVII **2113** 2; **2114** 2.

3 The first name may have been Cαρα]πιά[δ]οc.

4 Μι]κ[ροῦ. Cf. 21. The trace appears to be the top of an upright without a ligature and therefore most
suitable for kappa. The writing must have been very compressed; or alternatively the kappa may have been
raised to indicate abbreviation, i.e. Μι]ᶜ or Μει]ᶜ.

5 εἶδος ἀναπεμφθέν. See introd. para. 2, and N. Lewis, *BASP* 18 (1981) 126–8. Another papyrus referring
to εἴδη connected with the διαλογιcμόc of 202 was published by J. Mathwich, *ZPE* 15 (1974) 69–78, cf. H. C.
Youtie, *Scriptiunculae Posteriores* ii 697–8.

7 διαλογιcμοῦ. There is an implication that Maecius Laetus reviewed the matters concerned here shortly
before the date of the document, 29 October or 16 November. This does not correspond well with the dates of
the so-called *conventus*, the tours of inspection by prefects which took place usually in the period December to
April, see G. Foti Talamanca, *Ricerche sul processo;* I. *L'organizzazione del 'conventus'* 52–78, 204–12. We should
therefore hesitate to translate διαλογιcμόc with *conventus*, as is usually done. For the disappearance of the use of
the word in this sense about the end of the second century, see ibid. 165–7.

Λαίτου. Cf. *ZPE* 17 (1975) 304; 38 (1980) 85. Add XLVII **3340, 3343.** The date of **3601** falls inside his
known term of office.

10 ἐγβατικά (= ἐκβατικά). For εγβ- = ἐκβ- cf. F. T. Gignac, *Grammar* i 175. The word ἐκβατικόc does not
appear in LSJ or Suppl., though the formation is normal. It presumably refers to departure from office, at
which time Hierax had handed his official records over to his successor, see 23–7.

15 Ἀλφειοῦ. Presumably this is the Greek name Ἀλφειόc and not the Roman Alfius, since an official is
normally referred to by *cognomen*, not by *nomen*, if only one name is employed. The Greek name is also more
suited to the indications that the *procurator usiacus* was usually a freedman, see XLIII **3089** 6 n.

There is a strong possibility that this man is to be identified with the *procurator Augustorum*, Aurelius Alpheius, who figures in an honorific inscription from Sparta (*CIG* I 1328 = *IG* V i 546; Ἀλφειοῦ inscr.: Alphius *PIR*[1] i 194 (A 1201): Alfius *PIR*[2] i 294 (A 1442), wrongly). The argument given in *IG* V i plausibly sets the date of the inscription before 212; the *terminus post quem* would then be the date of Caracalla's appointment as Augustus, 198. H.-G. Pflaum, *Les Carrières* iii 1071, gives the limits as 198 and 209 without argument.

16–17 What springs to mind is ἐξ [ἀ]ντ[ι-]|[17][γράφου], but the grammar is then sufficiently odd to raise doubt. The meaning would be that the text of the letter of Alpheius is not taken from the original but from a copy. Easier would have been ἐξ ἀντιγράφου οὗ ἐϲτιν ἀντίγραφον or ἧϲ ἐϲτιν ἀντίγραφον ἐξ ἀντιγράφου. For the last three words cf. XXXI 2558 1a.

Alternatively the syntax would not be disturbed by a second title for Alpheius, on the lines of ἐξ [ἀ]ντ[αρ-]|[17] [χιερέων], which is not, however, attested; cf. XLII 3026 19.

19–20 Most probably the writer of the letter to Alpheius was Hierax himself. The argument is as follows. Since παρέθετο (23), though somewhat damaged, is virtually certain, and since the subject of it is the writer of the letter to Alpheius, ὑπὸ κληρονόμων, or the like, is excluded, and if the writer was not Hierax, there hardly appears to be room to specify who was and also to say that the letter was about Hierax, e.g. περὶ πραγμάτων Ἱέρακος. The best stopgap might be ὑ[πὸ τοῦ ἀδελ(φοῦ)]|[20] ἡ[μ]ῶν, 'by our colleague'.

21 For the nome see *JEA* 50 (1964) 141–3. A search of the recent *Sammelbuch* indexes allows us to add to the references on p. 141 (n. 4) at least P. Med. II 25a (= SB VIII 9857 A). 4, which, if rightly dated from the hand, carries the attestations of the Small Diopolite nome back from 74 BC (SB V 8666) into the third century BC, while **3601** carries them forward from the reign of Vespasian (BGU III 981) to AD 202. Add also XLVII **3362** (= SB XII 11045). 6–7 (ii AD).

31 The date is equivalent to 3 August 195, see also introd., para. 1.

33 It is not entirely certain what μεταδοθέντι means here, but the verb is regularly used of the service of summonses, which included copies of the documents originating the action. Probably, therefore, the report was sent up (ἀναπεμφθέν 5, cf. introd., para. 2) from Alexandria to Oxyrhynchus, where the acting strategus embodied a copy of it in the summons sent to the daughter of Hierax. The penalty for not filing official papers properly was a fine, cf. I **57, 61** (with BL I 312–13).

40 Ἀθὺρ β̄. The traces, though meagre, are enough to make it certain that the month is not Mecheir, the only other ending in rho. The figure is virtually undamaged, but is of the ambiguous cursive form which is often indistinguishable from a cursive kappa. The date is therefore equivalent to 29 October or 16 November 202.

3602–3605. Undertakings on Oath

The evidence which the papyri offer for imperial visits to Egypt has been collected conveniently, and discussed in connection with other evidence for imperial journeys, in F. G. B. Millar, *The Emperor in the Roman World*, 28–40, esp. 34–5. These four documents are sworn undertakings to assist in the public duty of supplying donkeys in connection with Caracalla's infamous visit to Egypt. It may be that we should deduce from one of them that Caracalla had not yet reached Pelusium on the Egyptian border by late November 215, somewhat later than is usually supposed, but there are various considerations which prevent us from regarding this as certain, see **3602** 9 n.

The documents were drawn up not in the Oxyrhynchite but in the Arsinoite nome, as appears from the mention of the village of Cynopolis, see **3602** 23 n. They are of a type which is usually addressed to the strategus of the nome, see E. Seidl, *Der Eid* i 79–80. Unfortunately the tops are missing, but there is a probability that they were addressed to Aurelius Calpurnius Isidorus alias Harpocration as strategus of the departments of Themistes and Polemon in the Arsinoite nome, since we have other papers from his term in this office, namely XLV **3243** (without Aurelius; late 214?) and **3263** (with Aurelius;

shortly after 29 August 215). The inventory number of **3243**, which is 14 1B.202/L(b), indicates that it was found in close proximity to **3602–5**. Calpurnius Isidorus also served as strategus of the Memphite nome, probably early in the sole reign of Caracalla, see **XXXVIII 2876** 14–16n. He can be presumed to have been an Oxyrhynchite who brought home some of his official papers, like his predecessor in the same strategiate of the Arsinoite, Sarapion alias Apollonianus, cf. *Aegyptus* 49 (1969) 149–50.

All the backs are blank, except for some flecks which are probably offsets or stray ink.

3602

14 1B.202/L(c)   10 × 19 cm   24 November 215

.   .   .   .   .

......]. [

ὀμνύω τὴν Μάρκο[υ Αὐρηλίου Cεουήρου
Ἀντωνίνου Παρθικοῦ Μεγίcτου
Βρεταννικοῦ Μεγίcτου Γερμανικοῦ
5   Μεγίcτου Εὐcεβοῦc Cεβαcτοῦ τοῦ
κυρίου τύχην cυνπαραλαβῖν
καὶ cυνπαραδοῦναι τοῖc αἱρεθεῖcι
ἄρχουcι τὰ πεμπόμενα κτήνη
εἰc Πηλούcιον πρὸc τὴν εὐκταίωc
10   γεινομένην ἐπιδημίαν τοῦ κυρίου
ἡμῶν καὶ θεῶν ἐμφανεcτάτου
Ἀντωνίνου ἢ ἔνοχοc εἴην
τῷ ὅρκῳ. παρὼν δὲ Αὐρήλιοc
Ἑρμίαc Μύcτου τοῦ Πετενούφε ὡc′
15   ἀπὸ τῆc αὐτῆc κώμηc ἐνγυᾶται
τὸν Αὐρήλιον Ὀννῶφριν ἐπὶ
πᾶcι τοῖc προκειμένοιc. ἐγρ(άφη) ἐπακολ(ουθοῦντοc)
Αὐρηλίου Μαμερτίνου τοῦ καὶ Πτολ(εμαίου)
ὑπηρέτου.
20   Α(ὐρήλιοc) Ὀννῶφριc ὡc (ἐτῶν) λβ οὐλ(ὴ)
ὑπὸ γόνυ ἀριcτ(ερόν).
(vac.)

6 l. cυμπαραλαβεῖν   7 l. cυμπαραδοῦναι   10 l. γινομένην   14 l. Μύcθου; cf. 22
15 l. ἐγγυᾶται   17 εγρ∫επακδ   18 πτδ   20 α′, ωc⌐ λβοῦ   21 αριcτ

/ (m. 2)   Αὐρήλιος Ἑρμίας Μύcθου τοῦ Πετενο(ύφεως)
          ἀπὸ κώμης Κυνῶν πόλεωc ἐνγυῶμαι
          τὼν Αὐρήλιον Ὀννῶφριν Cαραπίωνος
25   ἐπὶ πᾶcι τοῖc προκιμένοιc.
(m. 1)   (ἔτουc) κδ Αὐτοκράτοροc Καίcαροc Μάρκου
          Αὐρηλίου Cεουήρου Ἀντωνίνου Παρθικοῦ
          Μεγίcτου Βρεταννικοῦ Μεγίcτου Γερμανικοῦ Μεγίcτου
          Εὐcεβοῦc Cεβαcτοῦ, Ἀθὺρ κζ.

22 πετενο)?   23 l. ἐγγυῶμαι   24 l. τόν, Ὀννῶφριν   25 l. προκειμένοιc   26 ∟ κδ

'. . . I swear by the fortune of Marcus Aurelius Severus Antoninus Parthicus Maximus Britannicus Maximus Germanicus Maximus Pius Augustus, the lord, to assist the selected magistrates in receiving and delivering the animals being sent to Pelusium for the visit, which is taking place in answer to our prayers, of our lord and most manifest of gods Antoninus, or may I be liable to the penalty of the oath. Being present, Aurelius Hermias son of Mysthes, grandson of Petenuphis, from the same village, guarantees Aurelius Onnophris upon all the conditions aforesaid. Written under the supervision of Aurelius Mamertinus alias Ptolemaeus, assistant.

'Aurelius Onnophris, about 32 years old; distinguishing mark below the left knee.'

(2nd hand) 'I, Aurelius Hermias son of Mysthes, grandson of Petenuphis, from the village of Cynopolis, guarantee Aurelius Onnophris son of Sarapion upon all the conditions aforesaid.'

(1st hand) 'Year 24 of Imperator Caesar Marcus Aurelius Severus Antoninus Parthicus Maximus Britannicus Maximus Germanicus Maximus Pius Augustus, Hathyr 27.'

9 Πηλούcιον. There was a village of this name in the department of Themistes, see P. Tebt. II, p. 395, which fell inside the same strategiate as the village of Cynopolis, see below 23 n. Nevertheless, it seems more likely that the place meant was the well-known city, cf. XLIII **3090**, in which the cattle were to have gone to Alexandria. If this is correct, there is an implication that Caracalla was still expected on the north-east frontier of Egypt at the date of this document, 24 November 215. However, even if the city were certainly meant, the deduction could not be taken as certain, since there might possibly have been a need for baggage animals at Pelusium in connection with the visit even after Caracalla himself had gone on to Alexandria. Unfortunately, firm dates for Caracalla's visit are lacking, see *Ét. Pap.* 7 (1940) 31-2, though we know that he was back at Antioch by 27 May 216 (*SEG* xviii 759). The *responsum* of Caracalla published in Alexandria in January 216 (P. Flor. III 282. 8) may well have been posted in the course of his visit, if the tentative deduction made above is correct, cf. *Ét. Pap.* 7 (1940) 32 n. 1. The interpretations suggested in that note tend to set Caracalla's presence in Alexandria at a slightly earlier date. On P. Strasb. 245, which presents another problem connected with Caracalla's visit, see J. E. G. Whitehorne, *CÉ* 57 (1982) 132-5, cf. **3603** 11-12 n.

εὐκταί̣ωc. The writing is extremely rapid. Because αι seems relatively clear, this word has been preferred to εὐτυχῶc. See also εὐκταιοτάτην in **3603** 11-12, **3604** 11, and **3605** 4.

11 θεῶν ἐμφανεcτάτου. Cf. XXXVI **2754** 4 (Trajan). Correct P. Yale inv. 1394 verso i 2-3 to θεῷ[ν] (instead of θεό[c]) ἐνφανέcτατοc (Hadrian), see *ZPE* 13 (1974) 23.

14 Μύcτου = Μύcθου, cf. F. T. Gignac, *Grammar* i 86-7, cf. 64(7).

Πετενούφε ὼc'. The superscript writing is very confused. It looks somewhat like a monogram with sigma and omega imposed one on the other, but there is also an unexplained upright. The name is common.

17-19 ἐπακολ(ουθοῦντοc) . . . ὑπηρέτου. Cf. *JJP* 11-12 (1957-8) 141-66, esp. 163-6. Presumably the assistant served the strategus, as so often. The addressee was probably a strategus, see introd. The same assistant appears in **3604** 20-1, **3605** 13-14, a different one in **3603** 22-3.

22 There is a short oblique stroke running up from the left to the top of the first letter. Probably the clerk marked in this way the point where the guarantor was to place his subscription. Probably there would have been another copy with a subscription by, or on behalf of, the declarer himself.

23 κώμης Κυνῶν πόλεωc. This village was in the department of Polemon, see P. Tebt. II, p. 385. See introd. for the connection between this location and the conjectured identity of the addressee.

3603

14 1B.202/L(d) 10 × 19 cm 24 November 215

· · · · ·

κ.[..]....[...]..[*c.* 15 letters
ἀθροῖϲαι καὶ καταϲ[ϲτῆϲαι τὰ ἐπιβλη-
θέν[τ]α τῇ κώμῃ κτή[νη ἅμα τοῖϲ ἐξ ἀρχόντων αἱρεθεῖϲ[ι ὀμνύω τὴν

5   Μάρκου Αὐρηλίου Ϲεο[υήρου Ἀντωνίνου
Παρθικοῦ Μεγίϲτου Β[ρεταννικοῦ Μεγίϲτου
Γερμανικοῦ Μεγίϲτου [Εὐϲεβοῦϲ Ϲεβαϲτοῦ
τοῦ κυρίου τύχη[ν ϲυναθροῖϲαι καὶ ϲυγ-
ϲαταϲτῆϲαι κα..[*c.* 10 letters   τὰ ἐπι-

10   βληθέντα τῇ κώμῃ [κτήνη   *c.* 5 letters
ὅπου ἐὰν κελευϲθῶ ἰϲ τὴν εὐκ[τ]αιο[τά-
την πᾶϲιν ἡμῖν ἐπιδημίαν τοῦ
κυρίου ἡμῶν ἀηττήτου Αὐτοκράτοροϲ
Μάρκου Αὐρηλίου Ϲεουήρου Ἀντωνίνου

15   Εὐϲεβοῦϲ Εὐτυχοῦϲ Ϲεβαϲτοῦ ἰϲ τὸ ἐν
μηδενὶ μεμφθῆναι—παρὼν δὲ Αὐρήλιοϲ
Ἀγχορίμφιϲ μητρὸϲ Τερμούθεωϲ
ἀπὸ τῆϲ αὐτῆϲ κώμηϲ ὤμοϲα τὸν
προκίμενον ὅρκον ἐγγυώμενοϲ

20   τὸν προκίμενον Ἀκῆν ἐπὶ τοῖϲ προκι-
μένοιϲ πᾶϲι—ἢ ἔνοχοι ἴημεν τῷ ὅρκῳ.
ἐγράφη ἐπακολουθοῦντοϲ Αὐρηλίου
Ἀχιλλᾶ ὑπηρέτου.
     (vac.)
    Αὐρήλιοι Ἀκῆϲ ὡϲ (ἐτῶν) νε οὐλ(ὴ) ‾.....

25   δακ(τύλῳ) μ(ικρῷ) χει(ρὸϲ) δεξ(ιᾶϲ).
    Νεῖλοϲ ὡϲ (ἐτῶν) ν οὐλ(ὴ) ἀντικ(νημίῳ) ἀριϲτ(ερῷ).

11 l. εἰϲ   15 l. εἰϲ   19, 20 l. προκείμενον   20–1 l. προκειμένοιϲ   21 l. εἴημεν
24 ⌐νεοͧύ   25 δακμ‾χειδεξ′   26 ⌐νοῦἀντικαριϲτ‾

(ἔτους) κδ′ Αὐτοκράτορος Καίσαρος Μάρκου
Αὐρηλίου Σεουήρου Ἀντωνίνου
Παρθικοῦ Μεγίστου Βρετανικοῦ Μεγίστου
30   Γερμανικοῦ Μεγίστου Εὐσεβοῦς Σεβαστοῦ,
Ἀθὺρ κζ.

(m. 2)   Αὐρήλιος Ἀν...............

27 ⌐κδ′

'... (having been appointed?) to collect and present the animals assigned to the village along with persons selected from the magistrates I swear by the fortune of Marcus Aurelius Severus Antoninus Parthicus Maximus Britannicus Maximus Germanicus Maximus Pius Augustus, the lord, to assist in collecting and presenting ... the animals assigned to the village ... wherever I may be ordered, for the visit, which is the answer to the dearest prayers of us all, of our lord the unconquered Imperator Marcus Aurelius Severus Antoninus Pius Felix Augustus, so as to incur no blame in any respect—being present, I, Aurelius Anchorimphis, mother Termuthis, from the same village, swore the oath aforesaid, guaranteeing the aforesaid Aces upon all the conditions aforesaid—or may we be liable to the penalty of the oath. Written under the supervision of Aurelius Achillas, assistant.

'Aurelius Aces, about 55 years old; distinguishing mark (...?) on the little finger of the right hand.
'Neilus, about 50 years old; distinguishing mark on the left shin.
'Year 24 of Imperator Caesar Marcus Aurelius Severus Antoninus Parthicus Maximus Britannicus Maximus Germanicus Maximus Pius Augustus, Hathyr 27.'
(2nd hand) 'I, Aurelius Anchorimphis (?) ...'

9 καὶ.[or κατα[would suit the remains. The other items offer no parallel.

11-12 This passage provides some more support for the suggestion of J. E. G. Whitehorne, *CÉ* 57 (1982) 134, that we should restore P. Strasb. 245. 10-12 as πρ]ὸς τὴν [εὐκταιο]τάτην [ἡμῖν ἄνο]δον rather than π. τ. [εὐτυχες]τάτην [ἐπάνο]δον, which implies that Caracalla intended to pay yet another visit to Egypt.

15 Εὐτυχοῦς. *Felix* seems rather intrusive here, since it does not appear in any of the other versions of the titulature found in this group of documents. It does occur elsewhere among Caracalla's titles for the last years of his reign, see P. Bureth, *Titulatures* 103-5, but its use is infrequent and seemingly inconsistent.

24 The rapid writing at the end of the line is puzzling, because nothing is expected between οὐλ(ή) and δακ(τύλῳ), see Alessandra Caldara, 'I connotati personali nei documenti d'Egitto dell'età greca e romana', *Studi della Scuola papirologica* (Milan, 1924-6) iv 2. 123-4. Possibly it should be read as {δạκ.́μ.}, i.e. substantially the same as the beginning of 25, but less carefully written. A similar problem arises in **3604** 22-3, see n.

32 Evidently this is the subscription of the guarantor named in 16-17, cf. **3602** 22-5. The name may have been spelt Ἀνχερύμφις, cf. F. T. Gignac, *Grammar* i 289-90 (ε for o), 270 (υ for ι). No decipherment of what follows has been made. It seems short if this is the last line, cf. **3602** 22-5. The foot is irregular enough to allow the possibility that 32 was not the last line, but not much can have been lost.

3604

14 1B.202/L(e)　　　　　　　9.5 × 19 cm　　　　　　　27 November 215

. . . . .

ạ[

ἀπὸ κώ(μης) . ϛ . [

ε . . ονων ὀμνύω [τὴν Μάρκου

Αὐρηλίου Ϲεουήρου [Ἀντωνίνου

5　Παρθικοῦ Μεγίϲτου Βρε[ταννικοῦ

Μεγίϲτου Γερμανικοῦ [Μεγίϲτου

Εὐϲεβοῦϲ Ϲεβαϲτοῦ τ[ύχην ἅμα τοῖϲ

ἐξ ἀρχόντων α[ἱρεθεῖϲι

εἰϲ τοῦτο ϲυνεξελέϲθαι καὶ ϲυν-

10　καταϲτῆϲαι ὄνουϲ πεμπομ(ένουϲ) εἰϲ

τὴν εὐκταιοτάτην ἐπιδημ(ίαν)

τοῦ κυρίου ἡμῶν Αὐτοκράτοροϲ

Ϲεουήρου Ἀντωνίνου, οὓϲ καὶ

ἀποκαταϲτήϲω καὶ παραδόϲω

15　εἰϲ τὸ ἐν μηδενὶ μεμφθ(ῆναι) ἢ ἔνοχοϲ

εἴην τῷ ὅρκῳ. παρέϲχον δὲ

ἐνγυητὴν εἰϲ τοῦτο Αὐρήλιο⟨ν⟩

Πωλίωνα Λ . . . τοϲ ἀπὸ ⟨τῆϲ⟩

α(ὐτῆϲ) κώ(μης) παρόντ[α] κ[α]ὶ εὐδοκ(οῦντα)

20　ἐπὶ πᾶϲι τοῖϲ προκ(ειμένοιϲ). ἐγρ(άφη) ἐ(πακολουθοῦντοϲ) Α(ὐρηλίου) Μαμερτί-

νου τοῦ καὶ Πτολεμ(αίου) ὑ(πηρέτου).　　καί εἰϲι

Α(ὐρήλιοι) Πακλῆϲ (ἐτῶν) μ οὐ(λὴ) . . . .

ἀντικ(νημίῳ) δεξ(ιῷ),

Πωλίων (ἐτῶν) με οὐ(λὴ) ἀν(τικνημίῳ) ἀριϲτ(ερῷ).

25　(ἔτουϲ) κδ Αὐτοκράτοροϲ Καίϲαροϲ

Μάρκου Αὐρηλίου Ϲεουήρου Ἀντωνίνου

Παρθικοῦ Μεγίϲτου Βρεταννικοῦ Μεγίϲτου Γερμανικοῦ

Μεγίϲτου Εὐϲεβοῦϲ Ϲεβαϲτοῦ, Ἁθὺρ λ⁻.

2 κω[⁻]?; cf. 19　　9–10 l. ϲυγκαταϲτῆϲαι　　10 πεμπο̸μ　　11 ἐπιδη̸μ　　14 l. παραδώϲω
15 μεμφθ̸　　17 l. ἐγγυητήν　　19 α′κω̄, ευδοκ̄　　20 προκ̄εγρ∫ε)α′　　21 πτολεμ̄υ)
22 α′, ∟ μ ου) . . . .　　23 αντικ̄δεξ′.　　24 ∟ με ου)αν̣‾αριϲτ　　25 ∟ κδ

'. . . from the village of . . . (having been placed in charge of donkeys?) I swear by the fortune of Marcus Aurelius Severus Antoninus Parthicus Maximus Britannicus Maximus Germanicus Maximus Pius Augustus to assist the persons selected from among the magistrates for the purpose in picking out and presenting donkeys being sent for the visit, which is the answer to our dearest prayers, of our lord Imperator Severus Antoninus. These I shall return and deliver so as to incur no blame in any respect, or may I be liable to the penalty of the oath. I have presented as guarantor for this purpose Aurelius Pollio son of L. . . from the same village, who is present and consenting upon all the conditions aforesaid. Written under the supervision of Aurelius Mamertinus alias Ptolemaeus, assistant. And they are:

'Aurelius Pacles, 40 years old; distinguishing mark . . . right shin.

'Aurelius Pollio, 45 years old; distinguishing mark on the left shin(?).

'Year 24 of Imperator Caesar Marcus Aurelius Severus Antoninus Parthicus Maximus Britannicus Maximus Germanicus Maximus Pius Augustus, Hathyr 30.'

2 Read perhaps Θεα[δελφείας. This was in the department of Themistes, see P. Tebt. II, p. 379, and therefore in the appropriate strategiate, cf. Introd. and **3602** 9, 23 nn.

3 Read perhaps ἐπὶ ὄνων, 'in charge of donkeys', which might have been preceded by a participle meaning 'having been appointed', e.g. κατασταθείς.

7 Perhaps omit the preposition from the restoration, cf. **3602** 7. In **3603** 3 a preposition is needed, because the verbs are simple, not compounds of ςύν. In **3605** 1–2 τῶν ἐξ [ἀρχόντων αἱρε]θέντων implies that μετ[ά] precedes.

22–3 Nothing seems to be required between οὐ(λή) and ἀντικ(νημίῳ), see Caldara, op. cit. (**3603** 24 n.), 126–7.

3605

14 1B.202/L(f)   10.5 × 18.5 cm   27 November 215

> · · · · ·
>
> . . . [.] τῶν ἐξ [ἀρχόντων αἱρε-
> θέντων ςυνεξ[ελέςθαι καὶ ςυγκατα-
> ςτῆςαι ὄνους π[εμπομένους εἰς τὴν
> εὐκταιοτάτ[ην ἐπιδημίαν τοῦ κυρίου
> 5   ἡμῶν Α[ὐτοκράτορος Ϲεουήρου
> Α]ντωνείν[ου, οὓς καὶ ἀποκαταςτήςω
> καὶ] παραδώς[ω εἰς τὸ ἐν μηδενὶ μεμ-
> φθῆναι ἢ ἔνοχος εἴην [τῷ ὅρκῳ.
> παρέςχον δὲ ἐμαυτοῦ εἰς τοῦτο ἐ[γ-
> 10   γυητὴν Αὐρήλιον Πελῶριν . . . [. .
> τεως { . } α . . . . [. .] . . παρόντα καὶ εὐ-
> δοκοῦντα ἐπὶ πᾶςι τοῖς προκειμένοις.
> ἐγρ(άφη) ἐπακολ(ουθοῦντος) Αὐρηλίου Μαμερτείνου τοῦ [καὶ
> Πτολεμαίου ὑ(πηρέτου). καί εἰςιν Αὐρήλιοι

6 l. Ἀντωνίνου   13 εγρ∫επακὸ   14 υ)

15 Βελλῆς ὡς (ἐτῶν) . . οὐλ(ὴ) ἀντι. ( ) ἀριϲτ(ερ-),
    Πελῶριϲ ὡς (ἐτῶν) νε οὐλ(ὴ) ἀντίχιρι ἀριϲτ(ερῷ).
    (ἔτουϲ) κδ´ Αὐτοκράτοροϲ Καίϲαροϲ Μάρκου
    Α[ὐ]ρηλίου Ϲεουήρου Ἀντωνείνου Παρ[θικοῦ
    Μεγίϲτου Βρεταννικοῦ Μεγίϲτου
20 Γερμανικοῦ Μεγίϲτου Εὐϲεβοῦϲ
    Ϲεβαϲτοῦ, Ἀθὺρ λ¯.

15 ωϲL . . οὐ αντι. αριϲτ   16 ωϲL νε οὐ, αριϲτ; l. ἀντίχειρι   17 L κδ   18 l. Ἀντωνίνου

'. . . to assist, along with the persons selected from among the magistrates, in picking out and presenting donkeys being sent for the visit, which is the answer to our dearest prayers, of our lord Imperator Severus Antoninus. These I shall return and deliver so as to incur no blame in any respect, or may I be liable to the penalty of the oath. I have presented as guarantor of myself for this purpose Aurelius Peloris son of . . . from . . . who is present and consenting upon all the conditions aforesaid. Written under the supervision of Aurelius Mamertinus alias Ptolemaeus, assistant. And they are:

'Aurelius Belles, about . . . years old; distinguishing mark on the left shin(?).
'Aurelius Peloris, about 55 years old; distinguishing mark on the left thumb.
'Year 24 of Imperator Caesar Marcus Aurelius Severus Antoninus Parthicus Maximus Britannicus Maximus Germanicus Maximus Pius Augustus, Hathyr 30.'

1 The traces allow μετ[ά]. One other item had a preposition governing the dative, i.e. ἅμα or ϲύν, see **3603** 3–4; in **3604** 7–8 the endings are lost; in **3602** 7–8 there is a dative depending on the ϲυν- in the compound verbs.

10–11 After the name we expect a patronymic, or μητρόϲ, in full or abbreviated, with the name of the mother. Evidently -τεωϲ is the end of this element. Then comes a short upright which looks like the abandoned beginning of an unwanted letter. Next must be ἀπὸ τῆ[ϲ α(ὐτῆϲ)] κώ(μηϲ), or some other version of the same words, cf. **3603** 18, **3604** 18–19, or ἀπό with a village name, cf. **3602** 23.

15 Probably understand ἀντικ(νημίῳ) ἀριϲτ(ερῷ), since ἀντίχ(ε)ιρι is written in full in the next line.

3606. MUNICIPAL RECORD

48 5B.26/A(1–3)a   8.5 × 23 cm   *c.*230–5

The birthday of Severus Alexander, Phaophi 4 = 1 October, which was already known from the calendar of Philocalus (*CIL* I² pp. 255, 274), is mentioned here, and the document adds to the evidence on the prytaneis of Oxyrhynchus.

The top and the foot of the sheet are lost. Most of what was contained in the first two surviving lines is damaged and incomprehensible and there is a short endorsement along the fibres of the back, the purpose of which is uncertain (25). The rest of the document (2–24) comprises three virtually complete entries each introduced by a number, 8, 9, and 10, followed by a double curve and two oblique strokes, raised and rising to the right. These symbols are very often attached to numbers indicating regnal years and in some cases require actually to be expanded as (ἔτουϲ) or some other case of ἔτοϲ. If the numbers here do denote regnal years of Severus Alexander, they are equivalent to 228/9, 229/30, and 230/1.

After the numbers and symbols in the second and third entries comes the word
πρυτανείας followed by the name of the prytanis in the genitive case. In the first entry, the
day, Phaophi 4, intervenes (4); this is omitted in the second entry (17–18), and post-
poned till after the name of the prytanis in the third (22). In spite of these slight
inconsistencies, this method of introducing the entries is very similar to that of P. Berol.
inv. 11314, published by Z. Borkowski in *CÉ* 43 (1968) 326-31 and fig. 1, p. 327—so
similar, in fact, that without changing the sense we may expand πρυτ( ) there in ll. 3, 6,
9, 12, and 15 to πρυτ(ανείας) instead of πρυτ(ανεύοντος?), as was tentatively suggested by
the editor. Purely formal differences are that there no day is mentioned and the numbers
are followed only by the double curve and not also by oblique strokes.

There the successive figures 3 to 7 were interpreted as denoting regnal years of
Probus and the entries seem to record annual disbursements to two persons who drew
and heated water for some baths. Each year was also designated by the name of the
prytanis because, presumably, the disbursements were made from the funds of the town
council.

In **3606** each entry continues with a reference to a column of some record of the
town council (κολλήματος α⁻ 12, cf. 18; lost from 22), which is followed by a copy of a
signed declaration in the form, 'I, So-and so, made the registration (ἀπεγραψάμην)'.

In spite of the obscurity of the details it appears that a registration of some kind had
to be made each year on 1 October and recorded in a council record. It is most likely that
this registration was connected with the commemoration of the emperor's birthday.
Compare W. *Chr.* 41 iii 8-16, an entry from the official day-book of a strategus, which
records that he attended celebrations in connection with Severus Alexander's birthday
on 1 October 232. The festivities included a banquet (εὐωχήθη 15), attended also, it is
suggested in the note, by the municipal office holders.

A difficulty immediately arises when we compare the names and dates in this
document with the list of known prytaneis of the reign in A. K. Bowman, *Town Councils*
131:

1	221/2	Gaius Calpurnius (Lucius?)	XLIV **3173**
2	222/3	Aurelius Ammonius	I **77**
8	228/9	Aurelius Theon alias Maximus	XLV **3244**
14	234/5	Aurelius Pecyllus alias Theon	P. Osl. III 111

In **3606** we have:

8	228/9	Calpurnius Gaius
9	229/30	Aurelius Theon alias Maximus
10	230/1	Aurelius Pecyllus alias Theon

The office of prytanis was annual, see Bowman, op. cit. 61–5, but now we have two
names for 228/9. The figures here are all clear to read and so is the year number in XLV

3244 27, which has been checked again from the original. We must suppose that the year began with Calpurnius Gaius in office and that he was replaced by Aurelius Theon alias Maximus, who continued to hold the post in the next year. The combined data produce the following list:

1	221/2	Gaius Calpurnius (Lucius?)	XLIV **3173**
2	222/3	Aurelius Ammonius	I 77
8	228/9	Calpurnius Gaius (1. 10. 228)	**3606**
		Aurelius Theon alias Maximus	XLV **3244**
		(3. 12. 228)	
9	229/30	Aurelius Theon alias Maximus	**3606**
10	230/1	Aurelius Pecyllus alias Theon	**3606**
14	234/5	Aurelius Pecyllus alias Theon	P. Osl. III 111

This fairly clear case of two persons serving as prytanis in a single year eases the difficulty raised by P. Flor. I 63, where Aurelius Apollonius alias Dionysius appears as prytanis in the fifth regnal year of an unnamed emperor. His known career would induce us to assign this year to Probus (279/80) or Aurelian (273/4), both years already occupied by other prytaneis, see the more detailed statement in *CÉ* 46 (1971) 153–4, and we may now feel more comfortable about accepting that there were two prytaneis in one of these years. See also N. Lewis, *BASP* 14 (1977) 155, No. 52, where it is pointed out that XLIV **3202,** an invitation to the crowning of a prytanis in the middle of the Egyptian year, may mean that the man first appointed had for some reason to be replaced in the course of the year.

Since the formula of ll. 6–9 indicates that Severus Alexander was considered to be alive at the time of writing, the date of **3606** must fall between 1 October 230, mentioned in 20–2, and the time when news of the emperor's death reached Oxyrhynchus. His successor Maximinus was recognized in Rome by 25 March 235 (*CIL* VI 2001), but not yet in Oxyrhynchus on 3 May (PSI VI 733. 66–70). The news must have arrived soon after that and was known in the Arsinoite nome by 12 May, cf. X. Loriot, *ZPE* 11 (1973) 150.

.   .   .   .   .

$$\ldots\ldots]. [\ldots]\xi\alpha[\ldots\ldots$$
$$\ldots\ldots].\phi\ldots\delta\omega.\ \eta\varsigma''$$
  Φαῶφι δ⁻ πρυτανεί-
  ας Καλπουρνίου Γαΐου
5 γενεθλίου οὔςης
  τοῦ κυρίου ἡμῶν
  Αὐτοκράτορος Μάρκου
  Αὐρηλίου Ϲεουήρου
  Ἀλεξάνδρου Καίϲαρος
10 τοῦ κυρίου. ἔϲτι δέ
   οὕτωϲ. (vac.)
  κολλήματοϲ α⁻.
  Αὐρήλιος Ἀριϲτίων
  ἔναρχος ἀρχιερεὺς
15 βουλευτὴς ἀπεγραψά-
  μην. (vac.)
    (vac.)

(m. 2) θϲ''πρυτ[α]γίας Θέωνος τοῦ
   καὶ Μαξίμου. κολ(λήματος) δ⁻.
  Αὐρήλ(ιος) Θέων γυμ(ναϲιαρχ-) βουλ(ευτὴς) ἀπεγρ(αψάμην).
    (vac.)

20 (m. 1) ιϲ''πρυτανείας Πεκ[ύλ-
  λου τοῦ καὶ Θέωνο[ϲ
  Φαῶφι δ⁻. [κολ(λήματος) . .
  Αὐρήλιος Θέ[ων γυμ(ναϲιαρχ-)
  βουλ(ευτὴς) ἀπεγ[ραψάμην.

.   .   .   .   .

25 Back. (m. 3?)]ϲ βουλ(ευτ-)

17 l. πρυτανείας 18 κδ̄ 19 αυρή̣, γ̈β̈ο̈ϋαπεγρ∟ 25 βού̈

'. . . 8th year, Phaophi 4, in the prytany of Calpurnius Gaius, being the birthday of our lord emperor Marcus Aurelius Severus Alexander Caesar, the lord, viz., as follows: Column 1: I, Aurelius Aristion, chief priest in office, councillor, made the registration.'

(2nd hand) '9th year, in the prytany of Theon alias Maximus: Column 4: I, Aurelius Theon, (ex-?) gymnasiarch, councillor, made the registration.'

(1st hand) '10th year, in the prytany of Pecyllus alias Theon, Phaophi 4: Column *n*.: I, Aurelius Theon, (ex-?) gymnasiarch, councillor, made the registration.'

1–2 Since the year-number is not at the beginning of a line and in other respects too the remains do not parallel the subsequent entries, it is probable that these two lines were part of a heading, which, properly interpreted, might have told us the nature of the document as a whole. It is therefore particularly unfortunate that they are so difficult to interpret.

In 1 the first trace is a mere dot;]ξα[calls to mind Ἀλεξάνδρου in 9, but this idea leads no further and countless other possibilities exist. In 2 the first group of traces consists of a ligature descending at a shallow angle to the middle of the roundel of phi, with a tiny spot of ink on the edge of the papyrus below the beginning of the ligature. After phi there are (1) traces of a vertical, (2) a narrow gap, (3) traces which may represent the top of a vertical cut at the mid-height level by a horizontal (1 + 3 = η?), (4) the top half of a vertical (ι?). Between this and the delta is the tail of xi from l. 1 above. After omega the most likely close seems to be nu or sigma. Neither is strongly suggested, but either would do as well as anything else. Perhaps something like (ἀπο-?)γρ]αφὴ (or -ῇ) ἰδῶν (= εἰδῶν), 'list (or registration?) of goods in kind (or documents?)'. This is not helpful, and it is not very likely to be a correct reading of the remains.

4 Καλπουρνίου Γαΐου. Dr Bowman has suggested that Γαΐῳ Καλπουρνίῳ Λογ[κ]ίῳ (*cognomen* uncertain), prytanis in 221/2, see XLIV **3173** 1 n., was the same as the L. Calpurnius Gaius who appears in XXXIV **2723** as prytanis in an unknown year of the third century and as the father of L. Calpurnius Firmus, a minor. Both Gaius and Lucius were used by Greek-speakers as personal names and could therefore become *cognomina* when bearers of them adopted the *tria nomina*. The identification, consequently, is not compelling. On the other hand, the repeated prytanies of Aurelius Theon alias Maximus and Aurelius Pecyllus alias Theon, see introd., show that there was no objection at this period to the office being held a second time with little or no interval.

Persons called Calpurnius Firmus appear in three undated papyri from Oxyrhynchus, PSI XII 1252 (Aurelius Calpurnius Firmus; year 2 of an emperor later than Caracalla), 1255 (Calpurnius Firmus), 1256 (L. Calpurnius Firmus), and in one dated to 225 but referring to a loan made previously to the city by a Calpurnius Firmus, XXXVIII **2848**. It is not clear to me whether any of these is to be identified with the minor son of L. Calpurnius Gaius in **2723**. The suggestion in **2848** introd. that the Calpurnius Firmus there might be related to two prefects of Egypt with the same *cognomen* but different *nomina* is utterly unconvincing, see also L **3564** 1 n., where the relationships of yet more Calpurnii are considered.

12 κολλήματος α¯. See N. Lewis, *Papyrus in Classical Antiquity* 79–83, H. C. Youtie, *Scriptiunculae* ii 718, 720, 722. Originally κόλλημα meant a sheet of papyrus glued into a roll and was distinguished from cελίc, the column of writing, which could easily run over the joins. The distinction was not maintained in the official language of the papyri, so that references of this sort may normally be taken to indicate column numbers, though they might also refer to the sheet numbers of a τόμος cυγκολλήcιμος, i.e. a file of separate documents glued together into a roll.

13 Ἀριστίων. Since the next two registrations (19, 23–4) were made by Aurelius Theon, (ex-?) gymnasiarch and councillor, there is a possibility that Aristion and Theon should be identified with a father and son who appear in XXVII **2473** of 11 September 229. That document refers to a purchase of property, dated in Hathyr (28 October–26 November) 228, from Aurelius Theon gymnasiarch and councillor, son of Aristion former exegetes, grandson of Tiro. Here Aristion is described as 'chief priest in office'. This post did not occupy a fixed place in the municipal career, see F. Oertel, *Liturgie* 336. The title 'former exegetes' indicates the highest rank attained in that career. Unfortunately it is not clear whether the titles in **2473** relate to the date of that document, 229, or to the date of the purchase mentioned in it, 228. The Aristion here was clearly chief priest in office on 1 October 228.

17–19 This entry is in a smaller and more rapid hand than the rest. This, together with the abbreviations, suggests that it was written later and inserted into a rather inadequate space left for it. Perhaps there was, say, a roll for each year, and the roll for year 9 was not to hand when this document was being compiled, so that this entry had to be skipped over until the roll for year 9 was located or fetched.

19 γυμ(ναcιαρχ-). It is not clear whether we should expand to γυμ(ναcίαρχοc) or γυμ(ναcιαρχήcαc). If the identifications suggested in 13 n. are right and the titles given in **2473** relate to AD 229/30, γυμ(ναcίαρχοc) is probably right here. The same abbreviation may well have occurred in the lost part of 23, which relates to the next year, 230/1. If so, it might be that there it should be expanded to γυμ(ναcιαρχήcαc).

20–1 Πεκ[ύλ]λου τοῦ καὶ Θέωνο[c. See XLII **3048** 13 and n.

23 The restorations depend on the very likely, but not completely certain, assumption that $\Theta\epsilon$[is identical with the person in 19.

25 The first trace is a curving descender, probably part of a mark of abbreviation in the normal form of a double curve. This may be another mention of Aurelius Theon $\gamma\nu\mu](\nu\alpha\sigma\iota\alpha\rho\chi\text{-})$ $\beta\sigma\upsilon\lambda(\epsilon\upsilon\tau\text{-})$.

3607. COVERING LETTER FOR AN ACCESSION EDICT

9 1B.170/J(e)   6.5 × 15.5 cm   Before 13 June 238

The short reign of Gordians I and II is attested here, for only the third time in the papyri, cf. XLIII **3107** 12–15 and n., P. Yale inv. 156 (in *AJP* 51 (1930) 62–6).

The text of **3607** is contained on a patch pasted on to a fragment of a roll. The recto of the roll has been used for an official-looking land register, full of abbreviations, among which areas measured in aruras are conspicuous, and the verso has farming accounts probably of a private nature, including payments to a vine-dresser and a cowherd. These texts on the fragment of roll, which measures *c.* 13 × 32.5 cm, are too damaged to repay transcription.

The patch was glued to the recto of the roll, over much of the original writing and upside down in relation to it. Very probably the register was old and damaged and the patch was stuck on to the roll to strengthen it before the farm-accounts were copied on to the back. On the patch the ends of about nineteen lines of practised official cursive survive. They are fairly legible except where they are badly abraded near the top edge of the text, which coincides with the bottom edge of the register on the recto. Of course the back of the patch is concealed and the papyrus is too fragile to allow it to be removed in safety.

Lines 7–19 contain the remains of an open letter from a deputy strategus, presumably of the Oxyrhynchite nome. As can be deduced from parallels, the letter was intended to accompany the publication of an edict relating to the celebration of an accession. The loss of the beginnings of the lines makes the detail of the interpretation difficult. Probably a joint accession is meant, but the text could be restored to refer to a separate accession of Gordian II later than his father's, see the reconstructions below.

It is very regrettable that no date survives to contribute something to the vexed chronology of this year. The two dates available from papyri of the reign are equivalent to 13 June (XLIII **3107** 12–15) and 20 June (P. Yale inv. 156, in *AJP* 51 (1930) 62–6). This letter must have antedated the first of these, probably not by very long. See *ZPE* 9 (1972) 1–19 for the papyrological aspects of the chronology of the year, and for the latest bibliography of the whole question see H. Temporini, W. Haase, *ANRW* ii 2. 720–2.

. . . . .

```
                                                    ]...[
                                       ]ν..ντ.καὶ[.]..ϲνν[
                                       ]        (vac.)        [
                                       ]..[.]...........[
```

5 ±? Μάρκου Ἀντωνίου Γορδιανοῦ Ῥωμανοῦ Cεμπρ]ωνιανοῦ Ἀφρικαν[οῦ
```
                                       ].        (vac.)
                           δια]δεχομενο. τὴν ϲτρ(ατηγίαν)
                           -οτ]άτου ἡγεμό[ν]οϲ περὶ τῆ[ϲ
                           ]οϲ Μάρκου Ἀντωνίου Γορ-
```
10 διανοῦ (Ῥωμανοῦ Cεμπρωνιανοῦ Ἀφρικανοῦ?) ±?]του υἱοῦ τοῦ κυρίου ἡμῶ[ν
    ±? Μάρκου Ἀντωνίου Γορδιανοῦ Ῥωμανοῦ C]εμπρωνιανοῦ Ἀφρι-
κανοῦ   δε]δειγμένου διατάγμα-
τοϲ   πρ]οτίθεται ἵνα
```
                                       ] τῶν γεννᾳι[ο-
```
15 τάτων ϲτρατιωτῶν   ]λεια καὶ εὐχομ[ε-
                                        Μάρκ]ου Ἀντωνίου
Γορδιανοῦ (Ῥωμανοῦ Cεμπρωνιανοῦ Ἀφρικανοῦ?) ±? Μάρκου Ἀντω]νίου Γορδιανοῦ
                                                              Ῥωμα-
νοῦ Cεμπρωνιανοῦ Ἀφρικανοῦ   ] ἀϊδ[ίο]ν διαμονῆϲ
                                  ]ν προειρημέ-

. . . . . .

7 ϲτρϟ

It would be impossible to give a continuous translation without extensive restoration and no reliable restoration can be given where so much is lost. The completion of the titles in 16–17 requires forty-seven letters without bridging the gap between the lines, if, as is probable, there was yet another repetition of *Romanus Sempronianus Africanus*. Certainly at least thirty-one letters are needed in 11.

However, it is possible from comparison with several other documents to envisage a skeleton outline of 8–19:

[τοῦ πεμφθέντος μοι (e.g. SB V 8444 i 1–2) ὑπὸ τοῦ . . .] . . . ἡγεμό[ν]οϲ περὶ τῆ[ϲ κρατήϲεωϲ (P. Amst. inv. 22. 2 and n., in *ZPE* 8 (1971) 190, 192) . . .] . . . Μάρκου Ἀντωνίου Γορ[διανοῦ . . . καὶ (?)] τοῦ υἱοῦ . . . [. . . Μάρκου Ἀντωνίου Γορδιανοῦ . . .] . . . διατάγμα[τοϲ . . . ἀντίγραφον . . . πρ]οτίθεται ἵνα [. . . ἀκολούθωϲ τοῖϲ τῆϲ ἱερᾶϲ ϲυγκλήτου δόγμαϲι καὶ τῇ] τῶν γεννᾳι[οτάτων ϲτρατιωτῶν χειροτονίᾳ (SB VI 9528. 2–5 with X 10295. 6–7) . . . ἑορτάζοντεϲ ἐπὶ τῇ εὐτυχεϲτάτῃ αὐτῶν(?) βαϲι]λείᾳ (W. *Chr.* 490. 11–12) καὶ εὐχόμ[ενοι ὑπὲρ τῆϲ . . . Γορδιανοῦ . . . καὶ(?) . . . Γορδιανοῦ . . . νίκηϲ καὶ] ἀϊδ[ίο]ν διαμονῆϲ (XLIII **3116** 8 and n., cf. W. *Chr.* 490. 21–2) . . . ϲτεφανηφορήϲωμεν ἡμέραϲ (ποϲάϲ: W. *Chr.* 490. 23–4) . . . , 'A copy of the edict sent to me by the . . . prefect . . . about the accession . . . of Gordian I and (?) his son . . . Gordian II . . . is posted in public, so that . . . in conformity with the decrees of the sacred senate and the vote of the most valiant soldiers . . . we, celebrating their(?) most auspicious reign and praying for the victory and eternal continuance of . . . Gordian I and(?) . . . Gordian II . . . may wear garlands for (so many) days . . .'

Most of the parallels cited in the reconstruction were found with the help of the list of documents relating to accessions given by O. Montevecchi, 'L'ascesa al trono di Nerone', in M. Sordi (ed.), *I canali della propaganda nel mondo antico* 200–1. The details are open to question and variation, but there seems no doubt of the central hypothesis that this is a letter accompanying the publication of an edict of accession.

One of the possible variations might be important. The reconstruction supposes that both Gordians were proclaimed as co-emperors in Egypt at the same time, but it would be possible to restore the letter as proclaiming the accession of Gordian II only, i.e. περὶ τῆς κρατήϲεωϲ . . . Γορδιανοῦ . . . e.g. Ϲεβαϲ]τοῦ (instead of καὶ] τοῦ), υἱοῦ . . . Γορδιανοῦ, or, with the same sense, περὶ τῆς κρατήϲεωϲ τοῦ τοῦ Γορδιανοῦ Ϲεβαϲτοῦ υἱοῦ . . . Γορδιανοῦ. The best parallel would then be SB I 421, on the accession of Maximus Caesar, son of Maximinus Augustus.

Herodian tells us that Gordian I was forcibly proclaimed Augustus in Thysdrus by the rebels (vii 5, 7), whereas it was the senate which proclaimed Gordian II Augustus at the same time as it confirmed the accession of his father (vii 7, 2). We might reasonably expect the administrators of Egypt to follow instructions from Rome in these matters, but that they did not always do so is easily shown by the cases of Vespasian and Avidius Cassius. At the moment, however, it seems best to prefer the first reconstruction and assume that Egypt followed Rome in this case, unless any unambiguous evidence to the contrary emerges.

1–2 The blank in 3 suggests that 1–2 were at the end of a previous item, followed, perhaps, by a regnal-year date-clause in 4–6.

2 The traces suggest]ν πέντε and traces and space may permit πεντεκαί[δε]κᾳ, which could be relevant to the celebration of fifteen days prescribed in W. *Chr.* 490. 23–4.

4–6 The blanks in 3 and 6 suggest that 4–6 contained some sort of separate unit and the titles in 5 suggest that it may have been a date-clause, cf. 1–2 n. On the other hand, the two date-clauses from the joint reign which survive differ only slightly and in spite of the abrasion of 4, where no letter can now be identified for certain, I should have expected to be able to recognize elements of the formula if it were there. Possibly 4 contained something different and the date-clause, if any, was confined to 5–6. If it was a date-clause, the last trace in 6 should be part of the figure for the day, i.e. between 1 and 30 inclusive. This trace suits]η best, though it is a far from certain reading. If it were certain that this was the day-letter and that 4–6 or 5–6 contained a date, it might be worth speculating whether this was Payni 18 (ι]η), or 8 (η), or Pachon 28 (κ]η), etc., but in these circumstances it would be useless.

7 δια]δεχομενο . . The minute trace of the last letter is indeterminate. SB V 8444 i 1 suggests that the title stood in the nominative, but the genitive preceded by παρά might not be impossible.

The deputy strategus cannot be identified. A strategus called Flavius Harpocration was serving by some time in Phaophi (28 September–27 October) 238, see XII **1433** 33–4 with introd., and possibly also at some time in the preceding month of Thoth (29 August–27 September), cf. ibid. 2–3 (restored with the same name). The preceding strategus, Aurelius Leonides, was still serving sometime in 236/7 (XII **1405** 14, PSI X **1121**).

The deputy strategus would usually be the royal scribe, therefore βαϲιλικὸϲ γραμματεύϲ, *vel sim.*, may have filled part of the initial lacuna.

8 -οτ]άτου: i.e. διαϲημοτ]άτου or λαμπροτ]άτου.

ἡγεμό[ν]οϲ. The prefect of 238 is not yet known, but this informs us that there was a prefect in office in mid-year.

12]δειγμένου. Presumably restore ἀποδε]δειγμένου, but we cannot be sure either which Gordian is referred to, see the alternative reconstructions offered above, or to which office he was designated. From Gordian III till Carinus every emperor was consul in the January following his accession, so that ὑπάτου ἀποδε]δειγμένου is a possibility. If the word refers to Gordian II, Αὐτοκράτοροϲ ἀποδε]δειγμένου might be a possibility, like ἀποδεδειγμένοϲ Αὐτοκράτωρ in some titles of Caracalla as Caesar, cf. P. Bureth, *Les Titulatures* 95–6.

19]ν προειρημέ-. Restore presumably τὴ]ν προειρημέ|[νην, τὸ]ν προειρημέ|[νον, or τῶ]ν προειρημέ|[νων, but it is not clear which of the 'aforesaid' matters is meant.

3608–3610

Of these papyri the first two contain date-clauses by Decius and Herennius without Hostilianus, while the third appears to have a date-clause by Trebonianus Gallus only, without either Hostilianus or Volusianus. Both types were unknown before. The study of them offers an opportunity to set out what chronological information the papyri have to give for the period from the deaths of the Philips to the accession of Volusianus, roughly from the second half of 249 to the second half of 251.

We may begin from a table of significant dates:

Item no.	Regnal year	Date	Reference
1	7 Philippi	Thoth 25 = 22 September 249	P. Harris 80. 39–41
2	1 Decius	Choeac 1 = 27 November 249	XIV **1636** 39–41
3	2 Decius	no date = after 29 August 250	SB I 4651. 1–3
4	2 Decius and Herennius	Thoth 19 = 16 September 250	**3608** 1–7
5	2 Decius and Herennius	Phaophi 3 = 30 September 250	**3609** 11–15
6	2 Decius, Herennius, and Hostilianus	Phaophi 14 = 11 October 250	XXXVI **2795** 30–8
7	2 Decius, Herennius, and Hostilianus	Epeiph 6 = 30 June 251	O. Bodl. II 1633. 1
8	1 Trebonianus Gallus and Hostilianus	Mesore 20 = 13 August 251	SB VI 9235. 1
9	1 Trebonianus Gallus alone?	no date = before 30 August 251	**3610** 6, 8
10	2 Trebonianus Gallus and Volusianus	Choeac 7 = 4 December 251	XIV **1554** 11–16

From the numeration of his Egyptian years it is clear that the *dies imperii* of Decius fell after 28 August 249, the last day of the Egyptian year 248/9. The conclusion of M. Loriot in *ANRW* ii. 2. 788–97, where the papyrological evidence is also used, is that the death of Philip I cannot have fallen later than 11 September (p. 796). In Oxyrhynchus both Philips were still considered as living and ruling on 22 September, see item 1, but about thirty days is the conventional average allowance for news to reach Oxyrhynchus from Rome.

Contrary to what is imagined in *Chiron* 6 (1976) 428 there is no trace in the papyri of a sole rule of Philip II after his father's death. The fragmentary titulature of P. Lond. III 950 (description) is that of years 1–4 of the joint reign, when Philip II was still Caesar and not yet Augustus, as comparison of it with P. Bureth, *Les Titulatures* 114–15, clearly shows. See now also H. A. Pohlsander, *Historia* 31 (1982) 214–22. However, the reading ascribed to J. W. Shumaker on p. 217 is impossible. For his

1 [ετος .] του ευ[cεβ]ουc αυτο[κρατ]οροc κε[cαροc μαρκου
2 ιουλιου φιλιππου γεννεοτατου[

    read

1 ἔτους δ[ευτέρ]ου Αὐτο[κρά]τορος Κέ[σαρος (= Καίσαρος) Μάρκου Ἰουλίου Φιλίππου
   Εὐσεβοῦς Εὐτυχοῦς καὶ Μάρκου
2 Ἰουλίου Φιλίππου γεννεοτάτου (= γενναιοτάτου) [(καὶ ἐπιφανεστάτου?) Καίσαρος
   Cεβαστῶν μηνὸς month by two calendars, cf. SPP XX 71, day, ἐν
3 Ἑρμοῦ πόλι (= πόλει) τῇ μεγάλῃ, ἀρχαίᾳ [κ]αὶ [λαμπρᾷ κτλ.

I am indebted to Dr R. A. Coles for identifying the remains of the delta of δ[ευτέρ]ου. The year, therefore, is 244/5. The reading ἑ[βδόμ]ου, implied in P. Lond. III, has recently been reaffirmed by P. J. Sijpesteijn, *ZPE* 49 (1982) 102, no. 16, but is impossible, because the younger Philip was Augustus, not Caesar, in that year. The honorific titles of Philip junior are not fixed. If the day number was written out in full and was something long, e.g. τεσσαρεσκαιδεκάτῃ, the titulature may not have included καὶ ἐπιφανεστάτου, see Bureth, loc. cit.

Phaophi (September/October) of 1 Decius is attested retrospectively in SB I 4651 (with BL V 93), but the earliest surviving contemporary date-clause by Decius is item 2 above of 27 November 249. If M. Loriot is right, we may expect in the future to find earlier examples to fill the interval now existing between Decius and the Philips.

There follows a series of normal date-clauses by the first year of Decius alone which it has not seemed necessary to list. The next change is the accession of Herennius, which is specifically recorded by two of the new papyri, items 4 and 5 above, of 16 and 30 September 250. These fall in year 2 of Decius and Herennius. It may be, however, that there are traces of the arrival of the news of the accession of Herennius in year 1, that is, before 29 August 250. The evidence consists of two retrospective references to 249/50 as α (ἔτος) Δεκίων in documents of some twenty years later (XL **2913** ii 8–9; PSI V 457. 15). This form may be authentic, but it cannot be relied on, because it is possible that it has been affected by later formulae. The one clause from the second year of the sole rule of Decius, item 3 above, comes from Cysis in the Theban Oasis, one of the last spots in Egypt to which the news of an accession would penetrate. No day survives; it must have been after 28 August, the last day of year 1. The last example of dating by year 1 of Decius from Oxyrhynchus is of 4 August 250 (XLIV **3180** 1–2), the last from Thebes is of 18 August (WO 1471).

If the date-clause of *Cod. Just.* v 12. 9 is reliable, Herennius was Caesar already on 8 June 250, and the news was slow to penetrate to Egypt, possibly coming to

Oxyrhynchus between 4 and 29 August, certainly not getting to the Theban Oasis until after 28 August. However it cannot be assumed to be reliable.

The next change was the accession of Hostilianus, first known in the papyri from item 6 above, of 11 October 250. By this date it was known at Oxyrhynchus, where it had not been known on 30 September (item 5). Allowing the conventional month for travel to Oxyrhynchus, we would set his accession roughly between 30 August and 11 September, with the usual reservation that news is more likely to be delayed than accelerated, see the case of Herennius. The best evidence from other sources is a *terminus ante quem* of 22 September offered by a coin of Anazarbus and dated by its era, see *Bull. soc. franç. num.* 21 (1971) 128–9.

On the deaths of Decius and Herennius, Trebonianus Gallus became Augustus alongside the young Hostilianus, who remained Caesar, though one theory suggests that he returned to that rank after having been Augustus, see *ANRW* ii 2. 799. The news of the deaths reached Rome between 9 June and 24 June 251 (*CIL* VI 31120—*domini nostri*; 3743 = 31130 = 36760—*divi*). In the Egyptian texts the joint reign of Gallus and Hostilianus is known only from item 8 above, of 13 August. This ostracon is from Thebes. Again, since Decius and Herennius were dead by 24 June, we may well hope for earlier evidence of the accession of Gallus.

The third new papyrus from Oxyrhynchus, item 9 above, appears to attest a state of affairs not known before, namely a sole rule of Trebonianus Gallus. See **3610** 6 n. for the slight doubt occasioned by the damage to the papyrus. If, however, the clause is rightly interpreted here, Gallus did reign alone for a very short period. Our document is dated by year 1, that is, before 30 August 251. Volusianus has the same Egyptian regnal-year numbers as Gallus and therefore acceded before 30 August 251. The short space between the deaths of Decius and Herennius (May/June) and 30 August covers two reigns and part of a third, one of Gallus and Hostilianus, another of Gallus alone, the third of Gallus and Volusianus. It is conceivable that Gallus reigned first alone and only then took Hostilianus as a colleague, but it is more likely that he began by associating himself with Hostilianus to give his reign an air of continuity and ruled alone only after the death of Hostilianus. This theory suits the only possibility that has been thought of for restoring **3610** 6–7 without emendation, namely a date in the intercalary days of 251, 24–9 August, see note there.

This same papyrus shows that the death of Hostilianus was known in Oxyrhynchus before 30 August and therefore that it probably occurred before 30 July. *CIL* XI 4086, an inscription from Otricoli, Umbria, dated 15 July by the formula *ter et semel consulibus*, which reflects the *damnatio memoriae* of Decius and Herennius, may imply that Hostilianus was likewise dead, see *Studi Calderini-Paribeni* i 305–11, esp. 310–11.

3608. Fragment of a Date-clause

A B.3.5/8(e)   5.5 × 7 cm   16 September 250

The back is blank.

· · · · ·

  (ἔτους) β' Αὐτοκρ]άτορος Καί[c]αρ[ος
  Γαΐου Μεccίο]υ Κυΐντου Τραϊανοῦ
  Δεκίου Εὐceβ]οῦc Εὐτυχοῦc
  Ceβαcτοῦ καὶ Κ]υΐντου Ἐρεννίου
5 Ἐτρούcκου Μεc]cίου Δεκίου
  τοῦ ceβαcμιω]τάτου Καίcαρος
  Ceβαcτῶν.] (vac.) Θὼθ ιθ‾.

· · · · ·

2 τραϊανου

'Year 2 of Imperator Caesar Gaius Messius Quintus Traianus Decius Pius Felix Augustus and Quintus Herennius Etruscus Messius Decius, the most august Caesar, Augusti, Thoth 19.'

1–7 For the restorations and commentary see **3609** 11–15 and nn.

7 The foot is damaged. It is not possible to say whether or not this was the last line of the complete text.

3609. Receipt for Inheritance Tax

35 4B.101/J(3–4)a   14 × 16 cm   30 September 250

For the significance of the date-clause see the general introduction to **3608–10**.

The document was a contract for the payment of tax on an inheritance, incorporating a declaration on oath that the tax had been paid on the full value liable. No exact parallel has been discovered, but declarations of the values of inheritances, which do survive, are probably related, e.g. XLVI **3103**, P. Ryl. II 109, P. Amh. II 72.

There is little evidence on inheritance taxes in Egypt, see S. L. Wallace, *Taxation* 234. The *vicesima hereditatium* is the only one we know, and the information on this is poor from all sources, see *RE* VIII A. 2 (1958) 2471–7. If this receipt does refer to the *vicesima*, it is our latest evidence for it, superseding references dating from the reign of Severus Alexander, see *RE* VIII A. 2. 2474. 46–60; 2477. 34–8.

Dio Cassius tells us that it affected all except τῶν πάνυ cυγγενῶν καὶ πενήτων (55. 25), from which it has been deduced that beneficiaries who were closely related to the deceased were exempt and that small estates or inheritances were also exempt, but the details still remain uncertain. Here the deceased was brother of the legatee, though the wording in 9, τοῦ δηλουμένου μου ἀδελ(φοῦ), allows the possibility that he was a half-brother who had been more specifically described earlier in the text as a ὁμοπάτριος or ὁμομήτριος ἀδελφός.

Again providing that the tax here was the *vicesima*, we may calculate by multiplying the amount of the tax, 47 dr., by twenty, that the valuation of the inheritance was 940 dr. The wording, κατα[λε]λεῖφθαί μοι (8–9), perhaps implies that there was a will, and there may well have been other legacies, but we do not know for certain whether the limit on the amount implied by Dio (πλὴν τῶν . . . πενήτων) was fixed by reference to the full estate or to each legacy, see *RE* VIII A. 2. 2472. 52–2473. 31. However, it is probable that the fiscus would have placed its limit on the full estate, rather than allow tax to be avoided by dividing the estate. We cannot deduce, therefore, that the limit was below 940 dr., which is probably only part of the estate, though it has been convincingly argued that the limit was a comparatively low one, see J. F. Gilliam, *AJP* 73 (1952) 397–405.

The fragment was part of a cυγκολλήcιμον—a roll-file made by gluing individual items side by side. A small piece of the item adjacent on the right remains. It is mostly blank, but has the beginning of one line, διε.[, which looks like part of διέγραψα in the subscription formula, cf. 16. The back of the roll file was used subsequently for a register of names accompanied by amounts of land in aruras. The remains of it are very much damaged.

.   .   .   .   .

```
  c. 12      ]. ιτη[. ].. [
  c. 12      ]. καὶ χρημ( ) το...[...]...[
  c. 8   δρ]αχ(μ- ) τεccαράκοντα ἑπτά, (γίνονται) (δραχμαὶ) μζ [..
  c. 6  cύ]μβολον ἔcχον.     (vac.)
5   καὶ ὀμνύ]ω τὴν Γαΐου Μεccίου Κυΐντου Τραϊανοῦ
    Δεκίου] Εὐcεβοῦc Εὐτυχοῦc Cεβαcτοῦ καὶ Κυΐντο[υ
    Ἐρε]ν[νίο]ν Ἐτρούcκου Μεccίου Δεκίου τοῦ cεβαcμιωτ[άτου
    Κα]ίcαρος Cεβαcτῶν τύχην μηδὲν ἕτερον κατα-
    λε]λεῖφθαί μοι ὑπὸ τοῦ δηλουμένου μου ἀδελ(φοῦ) ἀνῆκον
10  τ]ῷ τέλει ἢ ἔνοχος εἴην τῷ ὅρκῳ καὶ ἐπερ[ω]τηθ(εὶс)
    ὡμολόγηcα.     (ἔτουc)] β' Αὐτοκράτορος Καίc[αρ]ος
    Γαΐου Μεccίου Κυ]ΐντου Τραϊανοῦ Δεκίο[υ] Εὐcεβοῦc
    Εὐτυχοῦc Cε]βα[cτ]οῦ καὶ ⟦Γα⟧ Κυΐντου Ἑρεννίου
    Ἐτρούcκο]υ Μεccίου Δεκίου τοῦ cεβαcμιωτάτου
```

2 χρημ⟨ς   3 δρ]αχ; /⟨ς   9 αδελ   10 επερ[ω]τηθ

15   Καίcαροc] Cεβαcτῶν, Φαῶφι γ̄. (m. 2) Μᾶρκοc Οὐαλέριοc

       c. 8   ]. . . διέγραψα καὶ ἔcχον τὸ cύμβολον καὶ ὤμα-

       cα τὸν ὅρ]κον ὡc πρόκιτε καὶ ἐπερωτηθεὶc ὡμο-

       λόγηc]α̣.   (vac.)

       ]   (vac.)

(m. 3?)   . . . .]. .[. . . . .]. . . . ( ) αϛ κολ(λημ-) λζ [

(m. 4?)   *c.* 20   ]μαρκιῶχρ[

21   *c.* 20   ]ζ (vac.) [

                     ]   (vac.) [

            .   .   .   .   .

16–17 l. ὠμο[cα]   17 l. πρόκειται

'. . . forty-seven drachmas, total 47 dr., . . . I received the receipt. And I swear by the fortune of Gaius Messius Quintus Traianus Decius Pius Felix Augustus and Quintus Herennius Etruscus Messius Decius the most august Caesar, Augusti, that nothing else has been bequeathed to me by my said brother which is subject to the tax, or may I be liable to the penalty of the oath, and in answer to the formal question I gave my assent. Year 2 of Imperator Caesar Gaius Messius Quintus Traianus Decius Pius Felix Augustus and Quintus Herennius Etruscus Messius Decius the most august Caesar, Augusti, Phaophi 3.

'I, Marcus Valerius . . ., paid and received the receipt and swore the oath as aforesaid and in answer to the formal question I gave my assent.'

2]. . . [. The second of these traces descends to the left in a way which suggests that it may have been a mark of abbreviation such as is used earlier in the line in χρημϛ.

3–4 The end of 3 may well have been blank or held no more than an oblique stroke to mark out the numeral. We expect something like ὧν τὸ cύ]μβολον ἔcχον or καὶ τὸ cύ]μβολον ἔcχον.

8–9 The words κατα[λε]λεῖφθαί μοι may suggest that there was a will, see introd.

11 The damaged year-number is guaranteed by the month-name and the presence of Herennius, since there is a good series of dates showing that Decius ruled alone till the end, or almost the end, of his first Egyptian year, see **3608–10** introd.

14 cεβαcμιωτάτου, cf. 7. This title appears only in connection with Herennius and Hostilianus, see P. Bureth, *Les Titulatures* 129. Latin inscriptions apparently have only the usual *nobilissimus* (*ILS* III. 1, pp. 297–8), for which the Greek equivalent is ἐπιφανέcτατοc. A Greek inscription calls Hostilianus ὁ θεοφιλέcτατοc Καῖcαρ, see *ILS* I 520n.

16 The last of the unread traces at the beginning is a horizontal which extends over the initial of διέγραψα. It might possibly be part of Μαρκί]ω⁻ = Μαρκίω(ν), see 20 and n., but the traces are not entirely satisfactory. ὤμαcα = ὤμοcα. Cf. F. T. Gignac, *Grammar* i 287–8.

19 It seems very likely that there is a reference here to roll and column of some public record, i.e. τομ(-) αϛ κολ(λημ-) λζ, 'roll 1, column 37'. However, the first superscript letter looks like the lambda of αδελ (9), and the second looks more like mu than lambda. I suspect that the clerk got the superscripts the wrong way round and wrote τολ( ) αϛ κομ( ) λζ. The trace immediately preceding this is also at a high level and may be part of yet another abbreviation.

20 Read probably the name Μαρκίω(ν); perhaps χρ[ηματίζων follows, but cf. 16n.

21 The zeta might be part of μζ—the number of drachmas paid in tax (3)—or, less likely, of λζ, the presumed column number of l. 19.

3610. APPLICATION FOR AN ORDER TO POSSESS

35 4B.71/J(9-11)b   10 × 7 cm   Before 30 August 251

For the significance of the date clause, see the general introduction to **3608–10**. See 6 n. for a problem about the form of it.

This fragment is the top right-hand corner of an application from a creditor to an acting strategus for the transmission to the debtor of an order to possess property pledged on mortgage. For the process see R. Taubenschlag, *Law²* 535, E. Seidl, *Rechtsgeschichte Ägyptens als römischer Provinz* 205.

The back is blank.

```
                    ]ωι διαδεχομένωι στρατηγίαν Ὀξυρυγχ(ίτου)
[παρὰ . . .          ]απίωνος Θέωνος τοῦ Διογένους μητρὸς Cαραποῦ-
[τος . . .           π]όλεως. οὗ ἐπόριςα ἐ῾κ῾τοῦ καταλογείου χρηματιςμοῦ ἐμ-
[βαδείας . . .        ] Αὐρήλιος Ἀπολλώνιος ὁ καὶ Διονύςιος ὁ ἱερεὺς καὶ ἀρχι-
[δικαςτὴς . . . Ὀξυρυγ]χείτου χαίρειν. τῆς τετελει⟨ω⟩μένης ἐμβαδείας ἀν-
[τίγραφον . . .        ἔρρ]ωςο.  (ἔτους) α Τρ[εβωνι]ανοῦ Γάλλου τοῦ κυρίου . [. .]. των
                             ]. [ςε]ςημ(είωμαι). (ἔτους) α῾Αὐτοκρ[άτορο]ς Καίςαρος
                             ].
```

· · · · ·

    1 οξυρυγχ   6 ∟α   7 [ςε]ςημᵘ ∟α´

'To . . . administering the strategiate of the Oxyrhynchite nome from . . .apion son of Theon grandson of Diogenes, mother Sarapus, from the city of the Oxyrhynchi. Here is a copy of the registration of the order to possess which I obtained from the office of the archidicastes:

'Aurelius Apollonius alias Dionysius priest and archidicastes, to the strategus of the Oxyrhynchite nome, greetings. A copy of the completed order to possess is to be delivered as it stands below. Farewell. Year 1 of Trebonianus Gallus the lord . . . I, . . ., have signed. Year 1 of Imperator Caesar . . .'

1 This acting strategus is not known, unless he is to be identified with the Syrus of I **62** = W. *Chr.* 278, who may date from about this time, see *ZPE* 29 (1978) 180, No. 87, and especially *CÉ* 62 (1956) 352.

1–6 Following in the main III **485** = M. *Chr.* 246 we see that the beginnings of the lines must have contained something like:

> 1. *Αὐρηλίωι Cύρ]ωι* (or another name), which makes *c.* 11 letters,
> 2. *παρὰ Αὐρηλίου] Ἀπίωνος* (or more likely *Cαρ]απίωνος*), *c.* 12–15.
> 3. *τος ἀπ' Ὀξυρύγχων π]όλεως, c.* 15,
> 4. *βαδείας ἐςτιν ἀντίγρ(αφον), c.* 19,
> 5. *δικαςτὴς ςτρ(ατηγῶ) Ὀξυρυγ]χείτου, c.* 18
> 6. *τίγρ(αφον) μεταδοθήτω ὡς ὑπ(όκειται). ἔρρ]ωςο, c.* 24.

4 The archidicastes is new, i.e. not in the list of P. J. Sijpesteijn, *The Family of the Tiberii Iulii Theones* 129–49, or among the additions collected by L. C. Youtie, *ZPE* 46 (1982) 224. There is a homonymous late third-century prytanis of Oxyrhynchus, who also held office in Alexandria, see A. K. Bowman, *Town Councils* 136 and n. 24, cf. 133 (three entries). There is just a possibility that the archidicastes is the same man, but the names are common and the Oxyrhynchite was prytanis as late as AD 291/2, so that his career would have been extraordinarily long. Cf. **3606** introd. (penult. para.) for a remark on the career of the prytanis.

6 Other papyri would lead us to expect here a date-clause by Gallus and Hostilianus or Gallus and Volusianus, though year 1 is not attested for the second coupling, see P. Bureth *Les Titulatures* 116–17. After *τοῦ κυρίου*, which itself looks like the end of the titulature, there is a trace of ink fairly low with blank papyrus above

it; κ[αί can hardly be accepted as a reading, so that a titulature of Gallus with both Hostilianus and Volusianus is not a likely interpretation.

If this is a date-clause by Gallus alone ending at τοῦ κυρίου, as seems most likely, the next thing ought to be the month and day. The date must be before 30 August 251, because year 2 began on that day. It should probably be not much if at all earlier than 13 August 251, when a Theban ostracon, SB VI 9235, was dated by Gallus and Hostilianus, see **3608-10** introd. Therefore it should fall in Mesore or in the intercalary days, of which there were six in this year. However, we certainly cannot read Μεσορή or Ἐπαγομένων here. Perhaps we might envisage something like τ[ρίτ]ῃ τῶν |⁷ [Ἐπαγομένων, but this is contrary to practice, which requires the pattern Ἐπαγομένων ᾱ, and to which I have as yet found no exception. Alternatively the titulature might have been intended to end with τοῦ κυρίου Cεβαστοῦ, cf. III **485** 7, for which the clerk wrote τοῦ κυρίου ζ[εβα]ϲτῶν by mistake. In the circumstances a doubt must remain, but it still looks very much as if we have here a date-clause by Gallus alone.

7 The singular Αὐτοκρ[άτορο]ϲ Καίϲαροϲ shows at least that we are not yet into the joint reign of Gallus and Volusianus, who were both Augusti and whose titulature begins Αὐτοκρατόρων Καιϲάρων, see P. Bureth, *Les Titulatures* 117. This beginning still allows us to envisage a titulature of Gallus as Augustus and Hostilianus as Caesar; compare the titulatures of Philip Augustus and Philip Caesar, or of Decius Augustus with one or two Caesars (Bureth 114, 116; **3608, 3609**).

It may be objected to this line of reasoning that in L **3567** 10-11 an otherwise normal titulature of 2 Gallus and Volusianus begins (ἔτουϲ) β″ Αὐτοκράτοροϲ Καίϲαροϲ, by mistake for Αὐτοκρατόρων Καιϲάρων, but this aberration is not likely to have occurred here as well.

3611. RESCRIPT OF VALERIAN AND GALLIENUS

66 6B.2/M(3-6)d   15 × 22.5 cm   *c*.253-7?

The rescript instructed the ἱερονῖκαι of Antinoopolis to apply to Magnius Felix, prefect of Egypt, for judgement of their claim to recover from the imperial treasury allowances which had been interrupted for a period of fifteen months and seven days. This period is described as being one of two which the Alexandrians called ἀφαιρέϲειϲ, an expression which is potentially of historical interest but of which no good explanation has yet been offered, see 7-10 n.

An endorsement in a second hand describes the text as 'a copy of a rescript of Caesar' (22), though it is clearly headed by the titles of both Valerian and Gallienus. The rescript system was the subject of a famous article by U. Wilcken, *Hermes* 55 (1920) 1-42 and has been much studied recently, see, for example, W. Williams, *JRS* 64 (1974) 86-103, *ZPE* 17 (1975) 37-78; 40 (1980) 283-94, T. Honoré, *Emperors and Lawyers* (1981), esp. 24-53, *JRS* 69 (1979) 51-64, D. Nörr, *Proceedings of the XVI International Congress of Papyrology* (1981) 575-604, *ZSS* (Roman. Abt.) 98 (1981) 1-46. Wilcken divided rescripts into two categories, *subscriptio* and *epistula*. The first was an answer to a petition (*libellus*), given in the form of a subscription at the foot of the petition itself. The second was a formal letter sent in reply to a letter submitted by a city, or a corporate body, or some prominent individual. Subsequent researchers have added that the word *subscriptio* was no longer used of imperial rescripts after the early third century and that the private rescript attained an independent form with a heading made up of the imperial titles, as in our example, Honoré, *Emperors and Lawyers* 47, Nörr, *Proc. XVI ICP*

576, 598-9. What distinguishes the *epistula* from the private rescript is the presence of a greeting formula at the end of the prescript and of a farewell formula at the end of the letter, cf. Williams, *JRS* 64 (1974) 87, Nörr, *ZSS* (Roman Abt.) 98 (1981) 9-10. Both are absent here. The absence of the farewell in a copy of an *epistula* is attested in IV **705** iii (= W. *Chr.* 407) 63, cf. probably i (= W. *Chr.* 153) 14, but in those two cases χαίρειν is retained in the prescripts (7, 58). The diplomatic forms indicate, therefore, that this rescript is not an *epistula* but a private rescript of the type developed from the *subscriptio*, although we might have thought it possible that the ἱερονῖκαι οἱ ἐν Ἀντινόου πόλει constituted a 'corporate body', which could have approached the emperors with an *epistula*, cf. Nörr, *ZSS* (Roman. Abt.) 98 (1981) 10.

This item raises again, but does not answer, the vexed question of the use of Greek in rescripts. The department of the *a libellis*, from which the private rescripts came, is not known to have dealt in Greek, although an *epistula* might be drafted by either the *ab epistulis Latinis* or the *ab epistulis Graecis*. It has never been settled whether the few private rescripts that survive in Greek only are always translations from the Latin or not, see Williams, *JRS* 64 (1974) 101-3, Nörr, *Proc. XVI ICP* 600. Here we must assume that a Latin original, if it existed, would have been likely to contain a Greek word, some form of ἀφαίρεσις, in its version of δυοῖν ἀφαιρέσεων τῶν καλουμένων παρὰ Ἀλεξανδρεῦσι (7-9).

There is a statistical probability that this document falls in the term of office of an *a libellis* whose Latin style has been isolated and analysed by Honoré, *Emperors and Lawyers* 93-6, and recognized by him in documents running from 4 July 254 to 8 March 259. It would be very interesting if there were anything substantial in this Greek which could be said confidently to reflect the style of that group of rescripts. If there is, I have not found it. More generally it can be said that the Greek text agrees with Honoré's characterization of the Latin group in that it is rather long for a rescript and has a rhetorical tone, but for the present I am content to heed his warning that it is unsafe to reach conclusions from the Greek texts of rescripts, op. cit. 37-8.

The date of the rescript can be set for certain between September 253 and 15 May 257, simply by reference to the names of the emperors and the prefect, see 1-4 n., 15 n. A further possibility of narrowing the range is considered in 1-4 n. We may perhaps add that there is a likelihood that the petitioners approached the emperors, or more probably one of them, in the East, see P. Coll. Youtie II 66 introd. (pp. 416-19). This would not narrow the period available very substantially, because Valerian is thought to have departed for the Parthian frontier not long after the beginning of his reign in late summer 253, see *ANRW* ii 2. 814. This copy might well be contemporary, but such rescripts were often used as precedents, so that it might be later than 257. The main script is a practised official cursive, much influenced by the 'Chancery' style, and therefore rather difficult to date. It can be compared with P. Med. inv. 63, see *Aegyptus* 45 (1965), tav. 6 (between pp. 250 and 251). It might belong anywhere in the second half of the third century or even in the early part of the fourth. The less formal hand of the endorsement does not look so late as the fourth century.

Αὐτοκράτωρ Καῖσαρ Πούπλιος Λικίννιος
Οὐαλεριανὸς Εὐσεβὴς Εὐτυχὴς Cεβαστὸς καὶ
Αὐτοκράτωρ Καῖσαρ Πούπλιος Λικίννιος
Οὐ[α]λεριανὸς Γαλλιηνὸς Εὐ[c]ϵβ(ὴς) Ε̣[ὐτ]υχ(ὴς) Ϲ[εβαϲ]τ̣(ὸς)
5   ἱερονείκαις τοῖς ἐν Ἀντ[ινόου π]όλει δ[ι]ὰ
Cεπτιμίου Καλλικλέους. (v.) [   ] (vac.)
ἐπεὶ κατὰ τὸν ἔν̣[α μ]ὲν χρόνον δυοῖν
ἀφαιρέϲεων τῶν καλουμένων παρὰ
Ἀλεξανδρεῦϲι, τὸ[ν] τῶν πεντεκαίδεκά τε
10   μηνῶν καὶ ἡμερῶν ἑπτὰ γενόμενον,
τοὺς μὲν Ἀλε[ξ]ανδρέα̣ς ἱερο̣νε̣ίκας εἰληφέ-
ναι τὰς ἐπὶ τοῖς ἀγῶϲι ϲυντάξεις παρὰ τοῦ
ταμείου φατέ, τὸ δ[ὲ] κατ[ὰ] τοὺς Ἀντινοέας
ὑμᾶς ἐπεϲχῆ[ϲθαι, πρόϲ]ιτε τῷ φίλῳ ἡμῶν
15   καὶ ἐπάρχῳ τ[ῆϲ Αἰγύπ]του Μαγνίῳ Φήλικι
παρεχόμενοι ταῦτα, [ὅϲ,] ἐὰν μηδενὶ λόγῳ
τὸ καθ᾽ ὑμᾶς ἐπεϲχημένον εὑρίϲκῃ, προϲτάξει
τὰς τοῦ ῥηθέντος χρόνου ϲυντάξεις ἀποδο-
θῆναι καὶ ἰς τὸ λοιπὸν ὑμῖν δίδοϲθαι ὅϲα
20   καὶ διὰ παντὸς τοῦ πρόϲθεν χρόνου τετυχήκατε. (v.) [   ]   (vac.)

Back, downwards. (m. 2) ἀ(ντίγραφον) ἀντιγραφῆϲ Καίϲαρος.

4 ϵυ[c]ϵβ̣.̓ϵ̣[υτ]υχ[̓]ϲ[εβαϲ]τ̣? 5, 11 l. ἱερονικ- 19 l. εἰς 22 ᾀ

'Imperator Caesar Publius Licinius Valerianus Pius Felix Augustus and Imperator Caesar Publius Licinius Valerianus Gallienus Pius Felix Augustus to the winners in sacred games in Antinoopolis through Septimius Callicles.

'Since you claim that for one period of the two which are called among the Alexandrians 'deprivations', the one that lasted for fifteen months and seven days, the Alexandrian winners in sacred games have received from the treasury the allowances in respect of games, but that what pertains to you the Antinoites was stopped, apply presenting this (document) to our friend and prefect of Egypt Magnius Felix, who, if he finds that your share was stopped for no reason, will issue a command that the allowances for the specified period be delivered and that for the future you be given also all that you have got over the whole of the preceding period.'

Back. (2nd hand) 'Copy of a rescript of Caesar.'

1–4 A *terminus post quem* for the rescript is provided by the fact that the Egyptian dating formula was by the titulature of the emperor Aemilianus as late as Phaophi of 253, see X **1286** and P. Got. 4. No day is preserved in these cases, so that the *terminus post quem* is Phaophi 1, the equivalent of 28 September 253.

A firm *terminus ante quem* is provided by the dated appearance of the *corrector* Ulpius Pasion in XLIII **3111** of 15 May 257. He cannot have governed the country while Magnius Felix, see here l. 15, was still prefect of Egypt.

That document is dated by Valerian and Gallienus as *Augusti* and by Valerian Junior as Caesar. It may well be that if Valerian Junior had been Caesar by the date of this rescript his name would have been associated with those of his father and grandfather, see C. Zaccaria, 'I figli dell'imperatore Gallieno', *Quaderni di storia antica e di epigrafia* 2 (1978) 102–4. He first appears in the dating formulae of the fourth Egyptian regnal year, 256/7. He does not appear in XXXIV **2714** of year 4, Thoth 1 = 29 August 256, but he is in BGU III 945 of year 4, Phaophi (no day) = September/October 256. The last day of Phaophi is equivalent to 27 October, so that, if the Caesar's name is to be expected in contexts like this, the *terminus ante quem* is 27 October 256, rather than 15 May 257.

4 There is an extra dot of stray ink after the raised tau of Ϲ[εβαϲ]τ(óϲ), but there is no real doubt that the usual titles, the equivalent of *Pius Felix Augustus*, were written here in abbreviated form. The undamaged hypsilon chi are enough to prove it. There is so far no trace in the papyri of Gallienus' short period at Caesar, for which see *ANRW* ii. 2. 809–9.

5–6 ἱερονείκαιϲ (= -νίκαιϲ) τοῖϲ ἐν Ἀντ[ινόου π]όλει. This looks like the designation of a corporate body, see introd., but there is room for doubt, cf. M. San Nicolò, *Ägyptisches Vereinswesen*² ii 64–5. For a recent demonstration of the large part that Egyptians played in the games of the imperial period, particularly as heavyweight athletes (boxers, wrestlers, etc.) see L. Robert, *CRAI* 1982, 272–3.

6 Septimius Callicles has not been located in any other text. He might have been the ambassador of the Antinoite sacred victors, to deliver their request to the emperors and bring back the emperors' reply, cf. *ZPE* 40 (1980) 285, 'the epistles of cities or of other corporate bodies in the provinces were normally delivered by embassies, which also brought back the emperors' replies'. But private rescripts were also directed through intermediaries, e.g. *FIRA* i 106, 107.

After the name there is a short blank space, then a gap wide enough for three or four letters, then 3.5 cm of blank papyrus. Clearly there was no formula of greeting, see introd.

7 δυοῖν. The dual is almost entirely absent from the papyri, see H. C. Youtie, *Scriptiunculae* i 334 (= *TAPA* 91 (1960) 242), but δύο offers a few exceptions, see F. T. Gignac, *Grammar* ii 188, where δυοῖν is seen to be even rarer than δυεῖν. It is perhaps less surprising in an imperial rescript than it might be in a humbler text.

7–10 As far as can be discovered from the papyrological dictionaries the word ἀφαίρεϲιϲ is rare in the papyri and always means a theft of goods, see XLVI **3289** 13, 18 (AD 258/9), P. Lips. 43. 12, 16 (iv AD)—both of papers or books, Pap. Lugd. Bat. XIII 8. 8 (AD 421)—of hay, XVI **1938** 3, 4 (vi AD)—of wood. Several other meanings are listed in *LSJ*, so that the Alexandrians' metaphor need not have been taken from this one, but it seems the most likely. One possibility that springs to mind is that the Alexandrians used this term to refer to two reigns of usurpers, but there is no reign of the right length. There is plenty of vague evidence of troubles such as plague, persecution, and civil disturbance, in Alexandria in the mid third century, see H. Braunert, *Binnenwanderung* 210–12, S. I. Oost, *Class. Phil.* 56 (1961) 1–20, but I have found nothing that can plausibly be identified with this passage.

12–13 Sacred winners were winners in games designated sacred, usually by an emperor, cf. K. Rigsby, *CÉ* 52 (1977) 147–55. No particular games are specified here, because the same title might have been acquired at a number of different locations. In theory the prize in sacred games was a garland of leaves, but it is well known that more substantial advantages were gained, cf. P. Coll. Youtie II pp. 472–3. It is interesting to learn that in this case the payment came from the imperial treasury. Usually they come from the city fund (πολιτικὸϲ λόγοϲ) of the winner's home town, cf. loc. cit. 473, *CÉ* 52 (1977) 152. Perhaps it is relevant that in P. Mich. XI 623 (to be read in conjunction with *ZPE* 29 (1978) 190) money paid in lieu of supplying bulls for games went to imperial funds (τῷ κυριακῷ λόγῳ, 17), though the city fund was mentioned in 20, in a passage that was cancelled in the draft.

15 For Magnius Felix see *ZPE* 17 (1975) 314. The Septimius who is listed as a possible prefect of Egypt in *ZPE* 38 (1980) 87 is far too uncertain to count as his predecessor.

16 ταῦτα. Unfortunately this does not help to define the rescript as *epistula* or *subscriptio*, cf. introd. It might be the equivalent of ταύτην τὴν ἐπιστολήν or ταύτην τὴν ὑπογραφήν, i.e. the text that we have before us, or it might refer to a *libellus* together with this, its *subscriptio*.

20–1 τετυχήκατε. The Attic form τετύχηκα is less familiar in the papyri than τέτευχα, see H. C. Youtie, *Scriptiunculae* i 534 and n. 69. Cf. B. G. Mandilaras, *The Verb* 206 (§434), 208 (§435. 8; the phrasing is misleading, '. . . stem τευχ-, e.g. τετύχηκα . . .', but the facts seem to be right), and F. T. Gignac, *Grammar* ii 298, where τετεύχηκα is wrongly ascribed to XXII **2343** 9 (τετύχηκα) and to P. Lond. II 412. 15 (p. 280; [τ]ετ[εύ]χηκα) = P. Abinn. 55. 15 (τετ[ύ]χηκα).

21 The bottom edge of the sheet is not preserved, but it seems probable that the text is complete. The lacuna is wide enough for only about nine letters, so that ἐρρῶϲθε would have to have been very unluckily placed to fall entirely in the gap. Probably there was no farewell formula. To the right of the lacuna and below the line on the left there is blank papyrus, which is about 2 cm deep at one point.

22 The abbreviation for ἀ(ντίγραφον) is badly damaged. Possibly it was an alpha with an oblique stroke passing through it from below on the left to above on the right, cf. W. Schubart, *Papyri Graecae Berolinenses*, no. 37b, *Aegyptus* 45 (1965), tav. 12 (lower item).

3612. Letter of a Prefect

38 3B.85/A(1-2)a   18 × 15 cm   29 May 271-5

A strip has been torn from the left-hand edge of this papyrus, but no letters are wholly lost from ll. 1-8. Unfortunately a bigger piece has come away at the bottom left corner, removing about five letters of l. 9 and among them the regnal-year number, which would have given us a fixed date in the term of the prefect of Egypt Statilius Ammianus, see 9n. The back is blank.

The prefect appoints the recipient of the letter embolarches of the Oxyrhynchite nome and orders him to see that all public transport animals work to load the grain ships without delay. This is the earliest appearance of the embolarches and the fact that the prefect makes the appointment of a liturgical official is noteworthy, see 4n.

      Ϲτατίλιοϲ (vac.) Ἀμμιανὸϲ (vac.) Ϲεπτιμίῳ Εὐδαίμονι
      κοϲμητεύϲαντι Ἀλεξανδρέων υἱῷ Ϲεπτιμίου
      Ϲερήνου (vac.) χαίρειν. (vac.)
      κατέϲτηϲά ϲε τοῦ Ὀξυρυγχίτου ἐνβολάρχην.
5   εἰδὼϲ τοίνυν τὸν τῆϲ ὑπηρεϲίαϲ κείνδυνον
      φρόντιϲον τὰ δημόϲια κτήνη ϲύνπαντα ποιῆϲαι
      τῇ ἐνβολῇ ὑπηρετῆϲαι ὡϲ ἂν μὴ τὰ πεμπόμενα
      πλοῖα εἰϲ τῆϲ ϲιτοπομπίαν ἐπειϲχεθείη. (m. 1?) ἐρρω[.].....[
(m. 1?) (ἔτουϲ) . τοῦ] κυρίου ἡμῶν Αὐρηλιανοῦ Ϲεβαϲτοῦ, Παῦνι δ.

2 ϋἱω   4 οξυρυγ'χιτου; l. ἐμβολάρχην   5 l. κίνδυνον   6 l. ϲύμπαντα   7 l. ἐμβολῇ;
ὑπηρετηϲαι   8 l. ἐπιϲχεθείη   9 l. Παῦνι

'Statilius Ammianus to Septimius Eudaemon, ex-cosmetes of the Alexandrians, son of Septimius Serenus, greetings. I have appointed you superintendent of lading for the Oxyrhynchite nome. So then, as you know the risk entailed in the service, take care to make all the public transport animals serve the lading, so that the boats which are sent for the grain transport shall not be delayed. (1st hand?) I pray for your health (?).

(1st hand?) 'Year . . . of our lord Aurelianus Augustus, Payni 4.'

1 There are traces in the first space. It looks as if the cognomen was originally written or at least begun there and was afterwards imperfectly washed out.

1-3 On Septimius Eudaemon son of Septimius Serenus see *JRS* 71 (1981) 92, L **3596** 1 n., and **3597** 1.

4 κατέϲτηϲα. The verb has no special implications for the manner or circumstances of the appointment, see *CÉ* 44 (1969) 339–40. The fact that it is the prefect who makes the appointment to what is known from elsewhere as a curial liturgy, see below, indicates that the circumstances were not normal. Perhaps Eudaemon petitioned the prefect to annul the appointment made by the council and the prefect rejected the petition and reinforced his decision by this threatening letter.

ἐνβολάρχην, l. ἐμβ-. The word is known only from papyri of the fifth century (P. Vindob. G. 21078. 8 in *Aegyptus* 61 (1981) 89) and eighth century (P. Lond. IV 1441. 60, 64; 1457. 117). The name of the office, ἐμβολαρχία, occurs only once, in P. Mert. II 90. 11. The date of that document is probably 310 or 311, see XXXIII, p. 95. Mention is made in it of two persons elected by the Oxyrhynchite council εἰϲ τὴν ἐμβολαρχίαν. The general nature of the post is evident from the name. The officials were in charge of loading the boats which were to take the grain received by the state as taxes and convey it to Alexandria. For the ἐμβολή see E. Börner, *Der staatliche Korntransport*. From the terms of this letter we gather that their duties chiefly concerned the organization of animals to convey the grain from the granaries of the district to the embarkation points. This, together with the date of this document, excludes the suggestion of the editors of P. Mert. 90 that the ἐμβολαρχία was the successor to the δεκαπρωτεία. From N. Lewis, *The Compulsory Public Services of Roman Egypt* 21, it appears that the decaproti continued to act until 302, see also *ZPE* 19 (1975) 111 and especially *BASP* 11 (1974) 60–8.

The rarity of the references to this office is probably accidental. If not, and if an embolarch was appointed only in exceptional circumstances, there is no obvious indication of the nature of those circumstances. It has been pointed out already that the prefect's concern with the appointment indicates that there were unusual circumstances in this case. That the supply of transport animals did run into difficulties from time to time is well illustrated by XVIII **2182**. In that document of 166 the matter is dealt with by strategi. Of course, the embolarchy as a curial liturgy cannot have existed before the creation of the local town councils about 200 and this document of about 272 is our earliest evidence of it.

5 For the personal and financial responsibility assumed by liturgists see U. Wollentin, Ὁ κίνδυνοϲ *in den Papyri* (Diss. Köln 1961) 77–9, cf. *Atti dell' XI Congresso internazionale di papirologia* 532–7, which is however more particularly concerned with the *periculum nominatoris*.

6 δημόϲια κτήνη. See F. Oertel, *Liturgie* 116–21.

7-8 ὡϲ ἂν μή . . . ἐπειϲχεθείη (l. ἐπιϲχ-). For this literary flourish see W. Schmid, *Atticismus* iii 86–7, iv 88.

8 The form of the farewell is uncertain, partly because of damage and partly because of an attempt to write small at the end of the line. The traces may best suit ἐρρῶϲ[c]θ(αί) ϲε εὔ[χ(ομαι). A similar phrase with βούλομαι would also suit the common usage, cf. VIII **1100** 5 n., XII **1408** 20 n. If the papyrus were an original, which is unlikely, the farewell would be in the hand of the prefect himself. It is not at all clear that it is written in a second hand, though it might possibly be.

9 The last line is written on a slightly smaller scale than the body of the document, but it may well be by the same hand.

The lost regnal-year number would have given us a fixed date in the term of the prefect Statilius Ammianus, on which see G. Bastianini, *ZPE* 32 (1978) 81–4. Ammianus took up office in 271, in the course of the Graeco-Egyptian year 270/1, which was referred to contemporaneously as 1 Aurelian and (4) Vaballathus and was only subsequently known as 2 Aurelian, see P. Oxy. XL pp. 15–26, esp. 20, 25. The date-clause here mentioning Aurelian alone appears to show that **3612** cannot belong to that year, but if the farewell formula is in the same hand as the rest, as I think, see 8 n., the copyist may have been writing in or after summer 272 and so may have used the corrected date-clause by Aurelian alone. In that case the letter would date from 29 May 271.

The next Graeco-Egyptian year, 271/2, was known as 2 Aurelian 5 Vaballathus as late as Pharmuthi 22 (= 17 April 272) and began to be called 3 Aurelian some time before Payni 30 (= 24 June 272), see P. Oxy. XL, p. 25. If **3612** were found to date from this year, the *terminus ante quem* for the change of the date-formula, which resulted from Aurelian's recovery of Egypt from Palmyrene control, would be placed nearly a month earlier, 29 May instead of 24 June, 272. Again this applies only if the date-clause in the copy is the same as the one used in the original. Of the possible dates for this document 29 May 272 is the nearest to the best defined date for Ammianus, some time in Mesore (July/August) 272.

Year 4 = 272/3 is also a possibility. In that case the date of **3612** would be 29 May 273, which, if certain, would be the latest known date for Ammianus.

By the same day in the next year the chief authority in Egypt would very likely have been the *corrector Aegypti* C. Claudius Firmus, whose only certain date is 8 February 274, but who may have been in office as early as 14 July 273, though the year-number is uncertain, see *ZPE* 17 (1975) 317. This probably indicates that Ammianus was already out of office. Two earlier *correctores* were in the country at the same time as L. Mussius Aemilianus, but so far as is yet known Aemilianus remained acting prefect under them and was probably only promoted to full prefect after their periods of office were ended. See the discussion in XLIII **3111** introd.

If, however, Ammianus remained in Egypt alongside Firmus, the next two years are also possible, that is, he might have been prefect still on 29 May 274 or 29 May 275. By the same day in 276 the date-clause in use referred to the emperor Tacitus.

Παριϊ (l. *Παῦνι*) δ̄. For the spelling cf. F. T. Gignac, *Grammar* i 198(2). After the delta, which seems certain, there is some more ink which is not expected. It could possibly be an offset. If not, it is presumably accidental.

Liturgies most often began on the first day of the Graeco-Egyptian year, Thoth 1, but other dates were possible, see *Proc. IX Int. Congr. of Papyrology* (1958) 232, 239–42; *TAPA* 100 (1969) 255–60. In P. Mert. II 90 the appointment of two persons to the embolarchy took place in the council on 25 May, which agrees very well with the 29 May of this document.

This time of year was appropriate because of the nature of the duty. The great bulk of the grain was shipped not long after the harvest and during the period of the high Nile. Justinian, in Edict xiii ch. 24, gives some interesting dates in his instructions for the shipment of grain from the Thebaid. It was to be embarked on the river boats by 9 August and delivered in Alexandria by 10 September. The end of May would be a good time to begin organizing the land transport.

3613. EDICT OF A PREFECT

36 4B.99/F(5–7)b　　　　　　　　13.5 × 25 cm　　　　　　30 August–28 September 279

The sheet bearing this edict has been badly damaged, having lost the middles of ll. 8–17 and the beginnings and ends of 18–25, besides other less extensive losses and abrasions. The wording cannot be reconstructed in detail, but the content is clear enough in outline.

Orders had been issued that each person who had served in the council of Alexandria since the second year of Aurelian, 270/1, should contribute one talent towards the repair of certain Thermae in the city. The prefect Hadrianius Sallustius, whose appearance here is the earliest yet known for him, see 1 n., had played his part in trying to communicate that message to councillors not in residence at Alexandria. The response had been unsatisfactory and he now orders them to declare themselves within thirty days or suffer the penalty.

At the foot there are six lines of shorthand, a script which has not yet found its decipherer, cf. O. Montevecchi, *Papirologia* 60–1. The back is blank.

Ἀδριάνιος Cαλλούcτιος ὁ διαcημότατ[οc ἔπαρχοc
Αἰγύπτου λέγει. προcταχθὲν ὑπὸ . [. .] . . . . . [. . . .
τῶν βεβουλευκότων ἔκαστον ἐν τῇ λαμπροτάτῃ
Ἀλεξανδρέων πόλι ἀπὸ τοῦ δευτέρου ἔτους τῆς

5   Αὐρηλι⟨αν⟩οῦ τοῦ ἐν θεοῖc βαcιλείαc, διατρειβόντων
τε οὐκ ἐπὶ τῆc πόλεωc μόνηc, ἀλλὰ καὶ ἐν ἅπα-
cιν τοῖc τῆc Αἰγύπτου νομοῖc, τάλαντον εἰcκομίcαι
πρὸc τὴν τῶ[ν   *c*. 15 letters   ] . ων θερμῶν ἐπι-
cκευήν, π[*c*. 17 letters   ἐπ][.] ἳ' τῶν ὄντων

10   ἑκαcταχοῦ [*c*. 16 letters   ]c διὰ γραμμ[άτων
δεδήλωκα, [*c*. 15 letters   ]ηcει τιναc γεγ[ο-
νόταc κατὰ τὴ[ν   *c*. 9 letters   δια]τρείβιν, ἀναγκα[ί-
ωc διὰ τούτου μ[ου τοῦ διατάγμ]ατος προαγορεῦ-
cαι τούτοιc ἔκρειν[α φανεροὺ]c ἑαυτοὺc ὡc ἐν-

15   ταῦθα, εἰ ἀναπόγ[ραφοί εἰcιν, κ]αταcτῆcαι καὶ τὴν
. . . . θεῖcαν τοῦ α[*c*. 8 letters κ]ατὰ τοὺc δημοcίου[c
τῆc πόλεωc λό[γουc] . . . . [. .] . αι, εἰδότεc ὅτι εἰ μ[ὴ
δι]ά τε τῆc ἀπογραφῆc καὶ τῆc κα[*c*. 15 letters
. .] . ηcεωc φανεροὺc ἑαυτοὺc [*c*. 15 letters

20   . .] . ν εἴcω τριάκοντα ἡμερῶν [*c*. 14 letters
. . . .]cον τῆc βουλευτικῆc ἀξίαc . [*c*. 14 letters
. . .] . αν ἑαυτοῖc λογιοῦνται προc[*c*. 14 letters
προ]cηκόντωc ὡc τοῦ τε κοινοῦ . [*c*. 12 letters
. . .]τοc καὶ τῆc ἡγεμονικῆc κελεύcε[ωc   *c*. 8 letters

25   . .] πεπληρωκότεc. πρόθεc. [
(m. 2)   (ἔτουc) ε″ Πρόβου Cεβαcτοῦ, Θώθ.   (vac.)

27–33: shorthand.

4 l. πόλει   5 l. διατριβόντων   12 l. διατρίβειν; αναγ'κα[14 l. ἔκρινα

'Hadrianius Sallustius, *vir perfectissimus, praefectus Aegypti*, says:

'Whereas it was commanded by . . . that each of those persons who have served as councillors in the most glorious city of the Alexandrians from the second year of the reign of Aurelian, now among the gods, and not those who live in the city alone but in all the districts of Egypt as well, should contribute a talent to the repair of the . . . Thermae . . .' (See 9 n. for a translation of the later lines as restored by conjecture.)

1 Ἀδριάνιος Cαλλούcτιος. The order of the prefect's names, the only ones known for him, is frequently reversed, as in the latest list of prefects (*ZPE* 17 (1975) 317–18), contrary to the unanimous evidence of the

documents. I must therefore withdraw the doubtful reading of P. Ryl. II 114. 1 as Cαλλουcτίῳ Ἀδρ]ειανίῳ, which I put forward in *BASP* 5 (1968) 40.

A Πό(πλιοc) Ἀδριάν(ιοc) Cαλλούcτι[οc] ἀρχιερεὺc δι' ὅπλων dedicated a statue in Philippopolis (Plovdiv) to an ex-governor of Thrace, Q. Sicinius Clarus, who held office in 202, see *AÉ* 1972, no. 554. If that man is his ancestor, our prefect is a recruit to the scantily attested 'Illyrian' group of officials, which is presumed to have been promoted by the 'Illyrian' emperors and to have exercised influence in the second half of the century, cf. G. Barbieri, *L'Albo senatorio* 459, H.-G. Pflaum, *Procurateurs* 194, L. de Blois, *The Policy of the Emperor Gallienus* 55-7.

The date of this document leaves no doubt that he was the patron of the *beneficiarius praefecti Aegypti* in PSI VII 807, cf. *ZPE* 17 (1975) 317; *PLRE* i 798.

2 . [. .] . . . . . [. . . . This is a puzzle. It can hardly be ὑπὸ τοῦ βαcιλέωc *vel sim.*, because that would be too curt a way to make a first reference to the emperor. Perhaps τῶν (or τοῦ) πρὸ ἐμοῦ might suit, though that too seems curt without at least ἡγεμονευcάντων (or -τοc). It might be τ[ῆc] κρϛ (= κρατίcτηc) βο[υλῆc, leaving it to emerge in 2-4 that it was the Alexandrian council. This would suit the traces, but is far from certain.

4-5 The second year of Aurelian, for those writing after Aurelian's recovery of Egypt in the period April–June, AD 272, was AD 270/1, cf. XL Introd., pp. 23-4. This was the year in which Egypt came under Palmyrene control. It may possibly be that the repairs to the Thermae were intended to make good dilapidations caused during the fighting to recover Alexandria in 272, though this is not a necessary conclusion.

5 For the correction Αὐρηλι⟨αν⟩οῦ cf. XLIII 3111 6, Οὐαλερι⟨αν⟩ῶν.

8 For baths in Alexandria see A. Calderini, *Dizionario dei nomi geografici* i 1. 97. No Alexandrian Thermae are known by name, but the lacuna is likely to have held a name, perhaps preceded by ἐνταῦθα. There is a strange story in Malalas (*SHB*, p. 293) that Septimius Severus confiscated the estate of a man named Θερμόc, who had built a public bath called Θέρμα after himself. Malalas also mentions a Cεβήριον λουτρόν, but the context is too fictional to lend support to a guess such as τῶ[ν ἐνταῦθα Cεουηρια]νῶν θερμῶν.

9 From this point the text is too badly damaged to be restored in any reliable fashion. The following version is conjectural:

> π[ρότερον μὲν τοῖc ἐπ][ ][ἵ τῶν ὄντων
> 10 ἑκαcταχοῦ [τόπων καταγινομένοι]c διὰ γραμμ[άτων
> δεδήλωκα, [νῦν δέ, ὁρῶν ἐν ἀναχωρ]ήcει τινὰc γεγ[ο-
> νότας κατὰ τὴ[ν χώραν ἔτι δια]τρείβιν, ἀναγκα[ί-
> ωc διὰ τούτου μ[ου τοῦ διατάγμ]ατοc προαγορεύ-
> cαι τούτοιc ἔκρειν[α φανεροὺ]c ἑαυτοὺc ὡc ἐν-
> 15 ταῦθα, εἰ ἀναπόγ[ραφοί εἰcιν, κ]αταcτῆcαι καὶ τὴν
> ὁριcθεῖcαν τοῦ α['(ταλάντου) καταβολὴν κ]ατὰ τοὺc δημοcίου[c
> τῆc πόλεωc λό[γουc π[ο]ιήc[αc]θαι, εἰδότεc ὅτι εἰ μ[ὴ
> δι]ά τε τῆc ἀπογραφῆc καὶ τῆc κα[ταβολῆc ἐξ ἀνα-
> χω]ρήcεωc φανεροὺc ἑαυτοὺc [καταcτήcουcιν εἰc τὴν
> 20 ἰδί]αν εἴcω τριάκοντα ἡμερῶν, [cτερηθήcονται
> οὐχ ὅ]cον τῆc βουλευτικῆc ἀξίαc, μ[ᾶλλον δὲ τὴν ἐπι-
> τιμ]ίαν ἑαυτοῖc λογιοῦνται πρόc[τιμον, καὶ ταῦτα
> προ]cηκόντωc ὡc τοῦ τε κοινοῦ π[ᾶcιν cυμφέ-
> ρον]τοc καὶ τῆc ἡγεμονικῆc κελεύcε[ωc τὸ δίκαιον
> 25 μὴ] πεπληρωκότεc.

'. . . I earlier informed by letter those who were in temporary residence in localities everywhere, and now, seeing that some persons have taken to flight and are still living in the country, of necessity I have decided to command them by this edict of mine to declare themselves here, if they are unregistered, and to make the prescribed payment of the one talent in accordance with the public accounts of the city, in the knowledge that if they do not declare themselves returned from flight in their usual place of residence by registration and payment within thirty days, not so much will they be deprived of their councillor status, but rather they will prescribe for themselves a penalty of their citizen rights, and that fittingly, as persons who have not satisfied the just claim of the prefectural order and of the common good of all.'

11 The restoration of ἐν ἀναχωρ]ήcει here and of ἐξ ἀναχω]ρήcεωc in 18-19 suits what is known of the bad

period through which Alexandria passed *c.*250-75, see H. Braunert, *Binnenwanderung* 210-13, but it is conjectural and does not therefore actually contribute to the evidence.

16 .... θεῖcαν. The first four letters or so have been heavily overwritten.

20-2 The restoration, see 9 n., is particularly hazardous here. Another line of thought might be that offenders were to be deprived of councillor status and also fined; e.g. ζημ]ίαν at the beginning of 22. For ἐπιτιμ]ίαν cf. XLIII **3105** 7-8.

21 βουλευτικῆc ἀξίαc, cf. e.g. SEG XII 95. 43-4. In the papyri the phrase is known only from its restoration, βουλευτι]κὴν ἀξίαν, in another damaged context in SB IV 7261. 2; cf. A. K. Bowman, *Town Councils* 30 n. 28. See also βουλευτικοῦ ἀξιώματοc, in the same sense, in P. Beatty Panop. 1. 372, 400.

26 A fleck of ink on the right-hand edge may be part of the day-number, but the distance from the month-name is so great that it seems more likely that the day was never written and that the trace is stray ink.

3614. JUDGEMENT OF SEVERUS

A a³/11(e)1   14 × 9.5 cm   Third century

The papyrus presents two extracts from a judgement delivered by Septimius Severus in Alexandria in the early part of 200, during the famous visit which has left so many traces of his legal activity in the papyri, see the lists in P. Col. VI pp. 27-30, add XLII **3018, 3019**, XLIII **3105**, P. Mich. IX 529. 39-53, and *BASP* 6 (1969) 17-19 = SB X 10537; cf. F. G. B. Millar, *The Emperor in the Roman World* 244-5. Only XLII **3019** and **3614** have a framework which identifies them as coming from proceedings before the emperor, the others being in the main *responsa* or edicts.

The introductory formula is most unusual in telling us that on this occasion the emperor delivered his judgement in Latin, see 3 n.

The first extract states that procurators shall be required to lease tax concessions at prices which are fair for the current conditions and not by reference to the sums for which the concessions had been leased in past years. The second extract relates to the appointment of ἐπιτηρηταί, but the damage to the papyrus, which is broken at the foot and to the left, makes it uncertain what point is at issue.

For this type of text in general see R. A. Coles, *Reports of Proceedings in Papyri* (Pap. Brux. 4; 1966), and for an account of our knowledge of imperial hearings see F. G. B. Millar, op. cit. 228-40.

The handwriting, a good rounded cursive, looks as if it belongs still to the third century. The back is blank.

Cεουήρῳ κ]αὶ Οὐϊκτωρείνῳ ὑπάτοις πρὸ μιᾶς νωνῶν

7-8] ἐν Ἀλεξανδρείᾳ. μετ' ἄλλα. Καῖcαρ cκεψάμε-

νοc μετὰ] τῶν φίλων τῇ πατρίῳ φωνῇ ἀπεφήνατο,

ἀναγ]νοὺc ἐκ βιβλίου, "οἱ μὲν ἐπίτροποι ἡμῶν ἔξου-

5　cιν δι]ὰ φροντίδοc μιcθοῦ[ν] τὰ τέλη μετὰ πίcτεωc οὐ πρὸc

. . . .]. [. .] κεφάλαιον οὗ ἐμεμίcθωτο τοῖc πα[ρ]ελθοῦ-

cιν ἐνια]ντοῖc, ἀλλὰ πρὸc ἐκείνην τὴν ποcότητα τῆc

6-7]ϛεωc". μεθ' ἕτερα. "τοὺc ἐπιτηρητὰc ἀρκο'ύ'ντωc

7-8]c τριϛτι[. .] καθίcταcθαι αὕτη ἡμῶν ἡ ἀπό-

10　φαcιc　c. 18 letters　　　　　　]. [. .]ϛι", κα[ὶ] τὰ ἐξῆc.

· · · · · ·

1 ουϊκτωρεινωϋπατοιc　　6 At the end a horizontal filler sign　　10 Cap of final sigma prolonged to act as a filler sign

'In the consulship of Severus and Victorinus, first day before the Nones of . . . in Alexandria. After other matters: Caesar, after deliberation with his friends, delivered judgement in his native tongue, reading from a paper, "Our procurators shall take care to lease taxes in good faith, by reference not to (some other?) sum at which they had been leased in past years, but to the specific amount of the (valuation?)." After yet more matters: "This (judgement?) of ours (gives the order?) to appoint for a three-year period superintendants who are sufficiently (wealthy?) . . . ", and so on.'

1-2 For the heading cf. XLII **3019** 2-5. At the beginning of 2 space is too short for Ἰανουαρίων or Φεβρουαρίων; therefore either Μαρτίων (= 6 March 200) or Ἀπριλίων (= 4 April 200) is possible. See P. Col. VI pp. 27, 30, for the duration of Severus' visit to Alexandria. Caracalla, who accompanied his father to Egypt, reached his twelfth birthday on 4 April 200, cf. *PIR*² iv 313-14 (I 663: Iulia Domna). Undoubtedly there would be celebrations in the imperial household, compare the festivities for the birthday of Severus Alexander in the remote region of Syene (W. *Chr.* 41 iii 8-16) and the Christians condemned to the beasts for Geta's birthday in the martyrdom of Perpetua and Felicitas (H. Musurillo, *Acts of the Christian Martyrs*, 8. 7. 9), but we cannot say for certain that Severus would not have transacted judicial business on that day. Professor Millar draws my attention to a passage of Dio, who says that in peace time it was the daily habit of Severus to hold hearings unless there were some great festival (Dio 76. 17. 1 εἶτ'ἐδίκαζε, χωρὶc εἰ μή τιc ἑορτὴ μεγάλη εἴη).

2 μετ' ἄλλα. Cf. μεθ' ἕτερα (8). Both are well-known formulae indicating where the original record has been cut, see R. A. Coles, *Proceedings* 48 and n. 3.

2-3 cκεψάμε[νοc μετὰ] τῶν φίλων. This is a well-known formula, see Coles, *Proceedings* 51; *JEA* 21 (1935) 225-6; 240-1. On the *amici* see F. G. B. Millar, op. cit. 110-22, esp. 119-22, for their legal functions.

3 τῇ πατρίῳ φωνῇ. Severus was competent or better in Greek as well as Latin and is supposed to have spoken fluent Punic, see A. J. Birley, *Septimius Severus* 60-1, add Dio 76. 17. 2. The only parallel discovered so far is a phrase introducing a proconsul's judgement in the martyrdom of Pionius (20. 7): καὶ ἀπὸ πινακίδοc ἀνεγνώcθη Ῥωμαϊcτί, see H. Musurillo, *Acts of the Christian Martyrs* 162. The proceedings are set in Smyrna, where they would probably have been conducted largely in Greek. Delivery of judgement in Latin after proceedings in Greek would be part of the effort to achieve an authoritative text to serve as a precedent, like the drafting of a written text of the judgement before delivery, see 4 n. It seems to me likely that this was so much a matter of course as usually to be passed over in silence, but it might be argued that these two cases were exceptional.

4 ἀναγ]νοὺc ἐκ βιβλίου. I have not found this wording elsewhere, but a similar procedure is implied by the cases cited in Coles, *Proceedings* 51 and n. 4. Of these the closest is Bruns, *Fontes*⁷ no. 186. 11-12 *Rufus leg(atus) c(um) c(onsilio) c(ollocutus) decretum ex tilia recitavit*. In another case the presiding judge wrote the judgement on a tablet and ordered it to be read out (SB VI 9016 i 12-14, μετὰ τὰ λεχθέντα Λυcίμαχοc ἐν πινακίδι διαγράψαc

ἀπόφασιν ἐκέλευσεν ἀναγνωσθῆναι κατὰ λέξιν οὕτως ἔχουσαν). In four other cases the judge, after consultation, dictated the judgement, which was then read out. These are P. Tebt. II 286. 15–18, CPR I 18(= M. *Chr.* 84). 23–5, VIII **1102** 5–6, BGU II 592 ii 4–5. The wording is very similar in all four, but the fullest is P. Tebt. II 286. 15–18, as restored in VIII **1102** 5 n., ἀνας[τὰ]ς εἰς cυμ[βούλιον (or -ίαν?) κ]αὶ cκεψάμ[ενος με]τὰ [τ]ῶν [π]α[ρό]ν[τω]ν [ὑπηγόρ]ευςεν ἀπόφα[cιν ἦ κ]αὶ ἀνεγνώcθ[η κα]τὰ λέξ[ιν] ού[τ]ως ἔχουςα. All this is guaranteed by the parallels except for ἀνας[τὰ]ς εἰς cυμ[βούλιον (or -ίαν), and this phrase looks as if it states something which is merely implied by the rest, that is, that the judge retired with his advisers to consider the case and prepare a written version, rather than consulting them in the public court.

Professor Millar has pointed out that there are many parallels in H. Musurillo, *Acts of the Christian Martyrs*. The phrase *decretum ex tabella recitavit* occurs three times (M. 6. 14; 11. 4. 3; 17. 3. 1), which suggests to Professor Millar that *tilia* in Bruns, *Fontes*[7] no. 186. 12, see above, is a misreading of *tabella*. Other comparable passages are: καὶ ἀπὸ πινακίδος ἀνεγνώcθη Ῥωμαϊcτί (M. 10. 20. 7), cf. 3 n. above; καὶ τὴν ἀπόφαcιν ἐκ χάρτου ἀνέγνω (M. 22. 4. 4); καὶ αἰτήcας χάρτην, πρὸς αὐτὴν ἀπόφαcιν ἔγραψεν (M. 22. 6. 3); *sententiam de libello legit* (M. 24. 4. 1); *intra velum interius ingrediens sententiam dictavit. et foras egressus, afferens tabellam, legit* (M. 25B. 3. 1).

The last passage is reminiscent of the four papyri with ὑπηγόρευσεν ἀπόφασιν, see above. *De libello* in M. 24. 4. 1 is virtually equivalent to ἐκ βιβλίου here.

ἡμῶν, cf. 9. Severus probably intends to include Caracalla, who in spite of his youth, see 1–2 n., was already his father's colleague. Caracalla's name is normally attached to imperial pronouncements of this period, see P. Col. VI pp. 4, 6, 28.

4–8 In spite of uncertainties at the beginnings of ll. 6 and 8, see nn., the principle enunciated is clear. The prices of tax contracts farmed out to lessees are to be set fairly by reference to current conditions, not on the basis of any sum paid in previous years. Equally clear is the implication that this is an answer to a complaint against compulsory appointment to the position of tax-farmer. This was a perennial problem in Roman provincial administration, see e.g. G. Chalon, *L'Édit de Ti. Julius Alexander* 101–9. Especially revealing are the legal rulings cited in n. 36, pp. 108–9. Most prohibit compulsion, to which the notable exception is *D*. 39. 4. 11. 5, yet it is evident that compulsion continued to be applied from time to time.

4–5 ἕξου[cιν δι]ὰ φροντίδος, 'shall take care to', cf. LSJ s.v. διά, A.IV. Marcus and Verus had already formulated the same principle, though it is applied to sales by the fiscus, not to leases of tax contracts. Their rescript is worth quoting for the help it may afford to the restoration of this text: *D*. 49. 14. 35, *Divi fratres rescripserunt in venditionibus fiscalibus fidem et diligentiam a procuratore exigendam et iusta pretia non ex praeterita emptione, sed ex praesenti aestimatione constitui. sicut enim diligenti cultura pretia praediorum ampliantur, ita, si negligentius habita sint, minui ea necesse est.* Even earlier the same principle was applied by Hadrian to leases of state land: Ἁδριανοῦ . . . cτήcαντος τὴν βαcιλικὴν γῆν καὶ δημοcίαν καὶ οὐcιακὴν γῆν κατ' ἀξίαν ἑκάcτης καὶ οὐκ ἐκ τοῦ παλαιοῦ προcτάγματος γεωργεῖcθαι, see P. Giss. 4. 6–10, cf. P. Lips. inv. 266 (*APF* 5 (1913) 245).

6 The translation is based on the conjectural restoration ἄλλ]ο [τι], which is a stopgap.

8 The translation uses the conjectural restoration cυντιμής]εως, based on the phrase *ex praesenti aestimatione* in the Digest passage quoted in 4–5 n. Unsold state land, which could be leased out, was valued by liturgical officials, see W. *Chr.* 398, M. Rostowzew, *Röm. Kolonat* 150. A similar procedure may have been adopted for tax contracts. Other possibilities are αἱρέc]εως, ὑποcχέc]εως (both meaning 'bid at auction'), and μιcθώc]εως; many more might be thought of.

8–10 In spite of their title ἐπιτηρηταί are found issuing receipts and acting as collectors rather than as supervisors, see S. L. Wallace, *Taxation* 288, but the office was a compulsory service, see N. Lewis, *The Compulsory Public Services* 29–31 s.v. The juxtaposition in this judgement of Severus of sections on compulsion in tax-farming and on appointment of ἐπιτηρηταί suggests the guess that, when it became difficult to find bidders for taxes customarily farmed, procurators had ἐπιτηρηταί appointed to collect the tax at the previous rate precisely because liturgists were compulsorily appointed and had to make up deficiencies out of their own pockets.

The translation adopts the following text, restored partially and by conjecture: τοὺς ἐπιτηρητὰς ἀρκούντως [εὐπόρους εἰ]c τριετί[αν] καθίcταcθαι αὕτη ἡμῶν ἡ ἀπό[φαcις κελεύει. Mr Parsons suggested [εὐπόρους εἰ]c τριετί[αν]. The adjective is a regular technical term for the financial capability of liturgists.

A three-year ἐπιτήρηcις is clearly mentioned in PSI XII 1245. 21 (τὸν ὡριcμένον τριετῆ χρόνον), and it ran in that case over the Egyptian years 203/4, 204/5, and 205/6. A document of 139 seems to envisage the same length of time, P. Amh. II 77 (= W. *Chr.* 277). 7–9 Πολυδεύκους τετραετεῖ ἤδη χρόνῳ παρὰ τὰ ἀπειρημένα ἐπιτηροῦντος τὴν προκειμένην πύλην, but it is not certain that the illegality began only in the fourth year.

A one-year ἐπιτήρηϲιϲ for 236/7 is concerned in BGU IV 1062 = W. *Chr.* 276. These references are given in Lewis, loc. cit.

αὐτή may be possible instead of αὕτη, and ἀπό[φαϲιϲ likewise is not certain, though attractive.

10]. [. .]ϵι. The trace is a high riser which would suit iota, kappa, phi, and possibly psi, though it is not like the psi in 2. This may be the verb conjecturally represented by κελεύει in the last note.

The manner of writing the last letter, see app. crit., and the sense of the last phrase show that this is the end of a section, but there is no means of guessing what or how much may have followed.

3615. OFFICIAL LETTER

5 1B.44/D(a)   10.5 × 9.5 cm   Third century

The title of an official, wrongly read and restored in its only other appearance, can be recovered from this document as ἐπιτηρητὴϲ ἡγεμονικῶν ἐπιϲτολῶν καὶ ἄλλων. In XVII **2116** 2, read now ἐ]πιϲτο[λ]ῶν for] πλοίων, see 2–3n. Little more than the prescript survives here, but the body of the letter begins in much the same way as that of **2116**—there οὓϲ ἐπέμψατε . . . λόγουϲ, here ἃ ἔπεμψ[α]ϲ . . . βιβλία, from which we may probably conclude that this too was an acknowledgement of the receipt of records sent to Alexandria to be filed.

The sender in this case was a royal scribe of the Hermopolite nome, Aurelius Hierax alias Sarapion, unknown to the lists of H. Henne, *Liste des stratèges*, and G. Mussies, *Supplément* (in P. Lugd. Bat. XIV 13–46). Possibly he was an Oxyrhynchite who brought home some official papers from his stay in Hermopolis. A man with the same combination of common names, a councillor, ex-gymnasiarch, and ex-prytanis of Oxyrhynchus, is mentioned in PSI XII 1249. 14–16, as the father of one of the parties to a contract of 265.

The date of this papyrus must be after the end of 214, when the use of the name Aurelius began to be common in Egypt as a result of the *constitutio Antoniniana*, see *JEA* XLVIII (1962) 128–9. If, as recent researches suggest, see *ZPE* 19 (1975) 119 n. 41, the office of royal scribe disappeared during the reforms of Philip the Arabian, the *terminus ante quem* would be 249.

The back is blank. A join is visible running parallel to and about 1.5 cm away from the right-hand edge of the front.

> Αὐρήλιοϲ Κλαύδιοϲ Λυκαρίων ὁ καὶ
> Ϲαραπάμμων ἐπιτηρητὴϲ ἡγεμο-
> νικῶν ἐπιϲτολῶν καὶ ἄλλων
> Αὐρηλίῳ Ἱέρακι τῷ καὶ Ϲαραπί-
> 5   ωνι βαϲιλ(ικῷ) γρ(αμματεῖ) Ἑρμοπολ(ίτου) τῶι φιλ-
> τάτωι   (vac.)   χαίρειν.
> ἃ ἔπεμψ[α]ϲ . . . . . ιᾳ βιβλία κα-
> ταχ[ωριϲ]θηϲό[μενα

> .   .   .   .   .

4 ϊερακι   5 βαϲ� γρϲ ερμοπο̣λ

'Aurelius Claudius Lycarion alias Sarapammon, overseer of prefectural letters and other matters, to Aurelius Hierax alias Sarapion royal scribe of the Hermopolite nome, his dearest colleague, greeting.'

'The . . . records which you sent to be filed . . .'

2–3 The rare title leaves much obscure. In both instances, cf. introd., the official is apparently concerned with the registration of records reaching Alexandria from the districts, rather than with what we might expect from the title, the correspondence of the prefect. In P. Strasb. inv. 31 + 32 recto iv 18 (= *Archiv* 4 (1908) 123) there is mention of records registered in Alexandria ὑπὸ τοῦ ἐπιτηρητοῦ τῶν ἐπιστολῶν, who seems very likely to have held the same office. The form of this reference perhaps implies that there was a single official with the title and not a board, cf. N. Lewis, *Inventory of Compulsory Services* s.v. ἐπιτηρητής. Wilcken suggested in *Archiv* 4 (1908) 127 n. 6 that the same official is also meant in the repeated entry ἐπιτηρητῇ ὑπὲρ καταπομπῆς μηνιαίου in BGU II 362 (= W. Chr. 96). In all these cases the records in question are intimately connected with the revenues of the province, not at all what we should have expected from the title. The contrast of name and function recalls the Byzantine *cura epistolarum*, who handled financial correspondence, though these appear to belong, not to provincial administrations, but only to the *officia* of vicars and prefects, see A. H. M. Jones, *LRE* i 565–6, cf. 450, 587–8, 590.

7 . . . . . ιą. The two or three letters before ιą, though written fast, are comparatively well preserved, so that a good suggestion could be verified. Not δημόσια or μηνιαῖα.

3616. Wanted Notice for a Runaway Slave

23 3B.1/M(4–7)a   16 × 9.5 cm   Third century?

The notice requires anyone finding the slave whose description is given to deliver him to the army in exchange for a reward. For runaway slaves in the papyri see I. Bieżuńska-Małowist, *L'Esclavage* ii 140–3, ead. *Studi E. Volterra* vi 75–90; for the Roman period in general see H. Bellen, *Studien zur Sklavenflucht.*

It is unfortunate that several of the details here and in **3617** are obscured by damage, since the only other such notice surviving is UPZ I 121 of 156 BC. However, the procedure by way of a πρόγραμμα or *libellus propositus* is already well documented, cf. SB VI 9532. 10–12; BGU VIII 1774. 12–15; P. Harr. I 62. 6; Bieżuńska-Małowist, *L'Esclavage* ii. 141, *Studi Volterra* vi 86–8; Bellen, op. cit. 7–8, and there are parallels for most of the discernible details, see commentary. Worth comparing is P. Lond. VII 2052, of the middle of the third century BC, which contains descriptions of four missing slaves but is not a public document and promises no reward. Other recent documents relating to runaway slaves are P. Beatty Panop. 1. 149–52 and P. Turner 41.

It seems not unlikely that **3616** is actually the notice posted in public, rather than a formula. It resembles other papyri with texts of public notices in being written in a good clear documentary hand without any pretension to calligraphy. Palaeographically it is close to XXXIII **2664** (pl. viii), of *c*.245–8, but it may be somewhat later, probably in the second half of the third century, and possibly in the early part of the fourth. In format, however, it more resembles XL **2924** (pl. iii), which measures 19 × 9.5 cm. This may be illusory to some extent, since the bottom of **2924** is broken off, but its text seems to be drawing to a close. Here a lower margin of *c*. 3 cm survives, though the foot is much worn. The back is blank.

The text strongly resembles a passage in Lucian, *Fugitivi* §27, spoken by Hermes in the character of a herald: εἴ τις ⟨εἶδεν⟩ ἀνδράποδον Παφλαγονικὸν τῶν ἀπὸ Ϲινώπης βαρβάρων, ὄνομα τοιοῦτον οἷον ἀπὸ κτημάτων—a joke, cf. §26, προσκαλῶν Κτήςωνας ἢ Κτηςίππους κτλ.—ὕπωχρον, ἐν χρῷ κουρίαν, ἐν γενείῳ βαθεῖ, πήραν ἐξημμένον καὶ τριβώνιον ἀμπεχόμενον, ὀργίλον, ἄμουσον, τραχύφωνον, λοίδορον, μηνύειν ἐπὶ ῥητῷ αὐτονόμῳ. OCT (M. D. Macleod, vol. iii, 1980) supplies εἶδεν (Fritzsche). Our text begins εἴ [τι]ς [ἐ]ῦρεν. It is likely that this was a formula, which Lucian also used.

εἴ [τι]ς [ἐ]ῦρεν δοῦλον ὀνόματι Φίλιππον, ... ν,
ὡς ἐτῶν ιδ⁻, λευκόχροον, ψελλόν, πλατύρυγχον,
μ . [.] . [.] . . αε . . ν, ἐνδεδυμένον ςτιχάριον
ἐρεο[ῦ]ν παχὺ{ν} καὶ βάλτιον ἀπὸ χρήςεως
5   . . . . ε]νεγκάτω ἐν τοῖς ςίγνοις λαμβάνων
      . . . . .]   (vac.?)

1 φιλιππον   2 πλατυρυχ.’χον; l. πλατύρρυγχον   4 βαλτιον   5 -ε]νεγ’κατω

'If any person has found a slave called Philippus, . . ., about fourteen years old, pale-skinned, speaking badly, broad-nosed, having(?) . . ., wearing a thick(?) woollen tunic and a used shoulder-belt, he should (report?, deliver him?) at army headquarters and receive . . .'

1 . . . . . . ν. Here we might expect the nationality of the slave, cf. 2 n., **3617** 1, or possibly his trade, if he had one. For nationalities see *CÉ* 46 (1971) 363–6; for trades *Historia* 26 (1977) 74–88.

2 λευκόχροον. For the spelling cf. Mayser, *Grammatik²* i 2. 57–8. This description may suggest that the boy was of non-Egyptian origin, cf. A. Caldara, 'I connotati personali', *Studi della Scuola Papirologica* (Milan, 1926) iv. 2. 55. See also 1 n. and below on ψελλόν. However, it may be used chiefly because it is unflattering, see A. W. Gomme–F. H. Sandbach, *Menander: A Commentary* 654 (on *Sicyonius* 200), and cf. **3617** introd.

ψελλόν. As examples of the mispronunciations implied by this word *LSJ* gives πιττεύω for πιστεύω and ἄρτον for ἄρκτον. Spellings indicating such mispronunciations can be found in fair numbers in the papyri, see F. T. Gignac, *Grammar* i 130, 65. In this case, however, they amounted to a distinguishing feature, which may again indicate non-Egyptian origin, cf. 1 n. and above on λευκόχροον.

In *Acme* 27 (1974) 314 M. Vandoni pointed out that although the papyrological dictionaries do not list the word, it has been wrongly treated as a name in two, perhaps three places. We should read Ϲωϲιβίῳ τῷ ψελ[λ]ῶι in P. Ryl. IV 588. 6 and Ϲαβῖνον τὸν ψελλόν in P. Fay. 119. 8; Ψέλλον in a fragmentary context in P. Fay. 110. 21 is doubtful. We should also be doubly suspicious of the doubtful readings of SB V 7966 (τὸ προςκύνημα Ψέλλου Ἀπολιναρίου) and P. Cair. Masp. III 67303. 23 (Ψέλλως Ἰϲακίου).

πλατύρυγχον. Cf. Timocl. 14. 7 ('broad-snouted', of a fish, the ϲαπέρδης), Arist. *PA* 662b12 ('broad-billed', of water birds). For the simplification of ρρ to ρ see Mayser–Schmoll i. 1, 187–8, F. T. Gignac, *Grammar* i 156.

3 μ. [.] . [.] . . αε . . ν. The end looks as if ἔχων was written originally and then written over, possibly to correct it to ἔχοντα. If so, this might still be part of the physical description, cf. **3617** 5, 7, on the lines of μῆλα μεγάλα (or μείζονα) ἔχοντα, cf. P. Petrie I 14. 45 (= III 6a), III 1. 24 (= I 21), or it might possibly concern property stolen by the slave, cf. UPZ I 121. 9–10 ἔχων χρυςίου ἐπιςήμου μναῖα γ, κτλ. Neither of these possibilities has suggested any wholly satisfactory reading and restoration.

4 παχύ{ν}. The fact that the only certain letter is put between braces shows how doubtful this reading is. However, pi and chi are almost unavoidable, though badly damaged; alpha is more suitable than any other vowel, and hypsilon, the most doubtful, seems to suit the other examples of the letter well enough. Intrusive nasals are very common, see F. T. Gignac, *Grammar* i 112–14, cf. *Akten d. XIII. Papyrologenkongresses* 141–3, but the only close parallel I have found—from Mayser–Schmoll i. 1, 172 (d)—is P. Amh. II 59. 7, ἥμιϲυ{ν}.

ἀπὸ χρήςεως. Cf. Diocl., *Edictum de pretiis* vii 55, 57, 59, 61, 63, with ἀπὸ χρήςεως answering to *ab usu*; P. Fouad I 74. 6 ςτιχάριον . . . ἀπὸ ὀλίγης χρήςεως.

5 . . . . ε]νεγκάτω. The meaning might be either that the finder is to produce the slave (παραφέρειν *vel sim.*) or simply to lay information (ἀναφέρειν *vel sim.*, cf. Lucian, *Fugitivi* §27, μηνύειν), see UPZ I 121 introd., p. 569.

The space suggests that about four letters, possibly five, are lost before -ε]νεγκάτω. Possibly the verb was a double compound.

ἐν τοῖϲ ϲίγνοιϲ. For references to ϲίγνον = *signum* see S. Daris, *Lessico latino* s.v. See especially P. Lond. VI 1914. 18 n. on the associations of the word and its passage into Coptic and even Arabic in the sense of 'prison'.

For the role of the army in the pursuit of runaway slaves see H. Bellen, op. cit. 11–13.

If the verb means 'deliver' rather than 'report', ἐν indicates 'motion towards', cf. Mayser, *Grammatik* ii. 2. 372–3 (§111.3 b). It has that sense in the same phrase in P. Lond. VI 1914. 18.

6 This line specified the sum of money offered as a reward, cf. UPZ I 121.13–14, 24–5; H. Bellen, op. cit. 7–8. There are some traces of ink on the papyrus which survives after the broken left edge. They are so slight that they are probably offsets, but it may be that the amount of money was written out here in words, instead of being written, as I have supposed, in symbols and numeral letters as in UPZ I 121.

3617. Wanted Notice for a Runaway Slave?

62 6B.76/F(5–6)b   9 × 13.5 cm   Third century

The unflattering description links this papyrus with the previous one, though it must be admitted that descriptions of slaves can be unflattering even when they are not runaways, cf. e.g. XLII **3054** 15–17. The fact that an ethnic is given suggests that the person described was a slave and this may have been stated in the small area of damage in l. 1 or at the foot, which is lost. See **3616** introd. for notices of the type envisaged.

The handwriting is a good round official cursive of the third century. Neither it nor the format specially suggests that the sheet was intended to be posted in public, but it may have been, cf. **3616** introd. The back is blank.

```
.......... ροϲ Αἰγύπτιοϲ ἀπ[ὸ
Χενρῆϲ τοῦ Ἀθρειβίτου νομοῦ τ.[
Ἑλληνιϲτὶ μὴ εἰδώϲ, μακρόϲ, λεπτ[
ψειλόκουροϲ, ἐπὶ τοῦ ἀριϲτεροῦ [μέ-
5      ρουϲ τῆϲ κεφαλῆϲ ἔχων τραῦ[μα
ρον, μελίχρουϲ, ὑπόχλωροϲ, ϲπ[ανοπώ-
γων—τὸ καθ' ὅλον τρίχαϲ μὴ ἔχ[ων
ἐπὶ τοῦ πώγωνοϲ, λεῖοϲ, ϲτε[νὸϲ
ἐκ τῶν γνάθων, ἐπίριν (v.) [
10    τέχνην γέρδιοϲ, περιπα.[
ωϲ ϲαλακᾶτοϲ ὀξείᾳ φωνῇ [
λαλῶν. ἔϲτιν δὲ ὡϲ (ἐτῶν) λβ. [τριβω-
νάρια δὲ φορεῖ ἰδιόχρωμα ῥ.[
ἔχει [.]. ἐπὶ τω[
.......... ].. [
```

2 l. Ἀθριβίτου   4 l. ψιλόκουροϲ   9 l. ἐπίρριν   12 ⌐λβ   13 ἰδιοχρωμα

'. . .rus, an Egyptian, from (the village of?) Chenres in the Athribite nome, utterly (?) ignorant of Greek, tall, lean (?), smooth-shorn, with a slight (?) wound on the left side of the head, honey-complexioned, somewhat pale, with a scanty beard—(or rather) with no hair at all to his beard, smooth-skinned, narrow in the jaws, long-nosed. By trade a weaver, he walks around as if he were somebody important, chattering in a shrill voice. He is about 32 years old. He wears undyed (and ragged?) clothes. He has on the . . .'

1 Part of the blank top margin is preserved above the end of the line. UPZ I 121. 2–3 has παῖς ἀνακεχώρηκεν ᾧ ὄνομα κτλ., but even this is too long if the text began in this column. If this were one of a series of such notices, perhaps the verb could have been omitted, to give something like παῖς ᾧ ὄνομα Ὧρος. The traces, which are tiny and scattered over twisted and broken fibres, do not permit verification.

At the end of the line restore ἀπ[ὸ κώμης or simply ἀπ[ό followed by the beginning of a longish village name.

2 Χευρῆς. Unknown. Also possible is (-)χευρῆς, part of a longer village name, see previous note. None suitable is to be found in F. Dornseiff–B. Hansen, Rückläufiges Wörterbuch der griechischen Eigennamen.

At the end of the line restore perhaps τὸ [καθ' ὅλον, cf. 7–8.

3 (Αἰγύπτιος) Ἑλληνιστὶ μὴ εἰδώς. He was probably not unusual in this respect, see W. Peremans, 'Über die Zweisprachigkeit', in Festschrift Oertel 49–60, R. Taubenschlag, 'The Interpreters in the Papyri', Op. Min. ii 167–70.

Restore λεπτ[ός, or a compound of this word.

5–6 Perhaps restore μικ]ρόν, 'a slight wound', but there must be many more possibilities.

8–9 For στε[νὸς] ἐκ τῶν γνάθων, 'narrow in the jaws', cf. LSJ s.v. ἐκ I, 6 ad fin., and πλατὺς ἀπὸ τῶν ὤμων, 'broad in the shoulders', UPZ I 121. 19.

9 At the end of the line a short blank space before the edge may indicate strong punctuation. If so, something on the lines of [ὢν δὲ] τέχνην γέρδιος περιπατ[εῖ may be preferable to [τὴν] τέχνην γέρδιος, περιπατ[ῶν.

On ἐπίριν = ἐπίρριν cf. 3616 2 n. on πλατύρυγχον. The word is not in the papyrological dictionaries at all. The nominative ending in nu is not in LSJ or Suppl., but takes its place with other compounds based on ῥίς, cf. E. Mayser, Grammatik i, p. 213, ² i. 2, p. 44 and n. 1, p. 56, ² i. 3, p. 188, Mayser-Schmoll i. 1, p. 188, F. T. Gignac, Grammar ii 141.

11 σαλακᾶτος. Add. lexx. This is evidently connected with σαλάκων, 'pretentious person', glossed in the Suda s.v. with προσποιούμενος πλούσιος εἶναι, πένης ὤν, cf. H. Stephanus, Thesaurus s.v. Mr Parsons draws my attention to its use by Cicero, ad Fam. vii 24 (ed. D. R. Shackleton Bailey, vol. ii, no. 260). 2. The form here looks like a genitive, since the ending -ᾶς gave rise to many new coinages in the Greek of the post-Ptolemaic period, see L. R. Palmer, Grammar of the Post-Ptolemaic Papyri 49–50, but I find the text hard to restore on that basis. Perhaps we should emend to ὡς σαλακᾶς, as assumed for the translation. If not, ως might be the end of an adverb such as σκαιῶς, with a vowel before the omega, and σαλακᾶτος might go with what follows, 'he walks awkwardly, chattering in the shrill voice of a boaster'.

11–12 The end of the line may have been blank or we may need a compound of λαλεῖν, e.g. καταλαλῶν, περιλαλῶν, see P. Kretschmer–E. Locker, Rückläufiges Wb., 570, for these and other possibilities. Mr Parsons suggests [ἀεί, or another adverb, as an alternative way of filling the space.

12–13 [τριβω]νάρια seems the best possibility, cf. Kretschmer-Locker, op. cit. 164. The word has not yet appeared in the papyrological dictionaries, but see LSJ and Suppl., s.v. τριβυνάριον, which is probably a bad variant spelling.

13–14 Restore perhaps ῥά[κινα vel sim., since the next line looks as if it begins ἔχει [δ]ὲ ἐπὶ κτλ.

3618. OFFICIAL LETTER

5 1B.44/C(d)   7.5 × 13 cm   305–10

The recipient of this fragmentary letter is asked, probably, to report in writing the names of persons liable to a levy of a commodity which was to be used by the imperial mint at Alexandria. The name of the commodity is new and its nature not certain, see 12 n. The senders of the letter were probably two syndics and a prytanis, see 1–4 n. The orders for the levy rested on the imperial authority of Galerius Augustus and Maximinus Caesar and were transmitted by the *magister privatae* Neratius Apollonides, whose known tenure of office is perhaps extended, see 6–7 n.

The back is blank.

$Aὐρ]ήλιος Διος. [$ c. 20 letters

$βου]λευτὴς ἔναρχο[ς πρύτανις$ c. 10 letters

$καὶ Μάξιμος . . [$ c. 20 letters

$καὶ λαμ(προτάτης) Ὀξυ[ρ]υγχ[ιτῶν πόλεως$ c. 10 letters

5 $Cιλβανῷ γραμμα[τεῖ$ c. 17 letters

$ὁ διαςημότατος μ[άγιςτρος τῆς πριουάτης$

$Νεράτιος Ἀπολ[λωνίδης$ c. 13 letters

$προςέτ[α]ξ[εν .].ιτο..[$ c. 15 letters?

$τῶν δεςπο[τ]ῶν ἡμῶ[ν Μαξιμιανοῦ Cεβαςτοῦ$

10 $καὶ Μαξιμίν[ου] Καίςαρο[ς$ c. 15 letters?

$τοῦ ἐτη[ςίως] ἐπιβλη[θέντος τῷ νομῷ$

$ξυλοςαγχ[άθου] κεντηνα[ρίων (-?)χιλίων$

$τὴν cυνάθρ[οι]ςιν καὶ κα[τακομιδὴν(?) ποιεῖ-$

$cθαι προχωρ[οῦν]τος εἰς [$ c. 15 letters?

15 $ἱερᾶς μονήτης. διὸ ἐδ[ηλώςαμεν καὶ$

$ςοὶ ὅπως ἐγγράφως δηλ[ώςῃς ἡμῖν τοὺς$

$ὑπευθύνους τῇ εἰςφο[ρᾷ τοῦ ἐπιβληθέντος$

$τῷ νομῷ ξυλοςαγγάθου κ[εντηναρίων$ c. 5 letters?

$χειλίων μετὰ τὰ εἰςφερ[$

20 $ἀπὸ τῆς πόλεως [.].. [$

.   .   .   .   .

4 l. Ὀξυρυγχιτῶν   12 ξυλοςαγ'χ[αθου   15 ἵερας   16 εγ'γραφως   17 ὕπευθυνους
18 ξυλοςαγ'γαθου

'Aurelius Dios ... councillor, (prytanis) in office, (and So-and-so?) and Maximus ... (syndics?) of the glorious and most glorious city of the Oxyrhynchites, to (Aurelius?) Silvanus secretary ...

The most perfect *magister privatae* Neratius Apollonides, (in conformity with the orders given by?) the ... of our masters Galerius Augustus and Maximinus Caesar, (has ordered us?) to make collection and dispatch of the *xylosangathum*, to the amount of ... thousand hundredweight, annually imposed upon the nome to go to (the service of the) imperial mint. Therefore we have (also?) informed you so that you may inform us, in writing, of those who are liable to the contribution of the *xylosangathum*, to the amount of ... thousand hundredweight, imposed upon the nome, after the ... from the city ...'

1–4 Comparison with the other two documents mentioning the *magister privatae* Neratius Apollonides (XXXIII **2665, 2673**) suggests that the senders of this letter were the prytanis in office and the syndics. See also M. *Chr.* 196, where the orders come from a *procurator privatae*, and PSI IV 310, as revised in *CÉ* 49 (1974) 170, where a receipt relating to the *ratio privatae* was issued to the prytanis and syndics of Heracleopolis. Cf. A. K. Bowman, *Town Councils* 49.

The name of the prytanis of 306/7 would fit well into 1–2, i.e. Αὐρ]ήλιος Διόςκ[ορος ὁ καὶ Ἑλλάδιος γυμ(νασιαρχ-)]|²[βου]λευτὴς ἔναρχο[ς πρύτανις, cf. XLIV **3192**, though see below for some major doubts. After ἔναρχο[ς πρύτανις in 2 there is room for about ten letters, not enough for καὶ Αὐρήλιοι plus a name. Probably Αὐρ]ήλιος in 1 should have been Αὐρήλιοι, in which case the end of 2 had simply καί and a name of about seven letters. Line 3 could have ended with cύνδικοι τῆς λαμ(πρᾶς), preceded by other titles abbreviated, e.g. γυ[μ$βοῦ, or we could restore ςύ[νδικοι βουλ(ευταὶ) τῆς λαμ(πρᾶς). These would give twenty-two or nineteen letters, which agree well enough with the virtually certain restoration of twenty letters in 6 and with the twenty letters proposed for 1.

The name of Maximus in 3 recalls the syndic in **2665** 5 (. . .]μῳ ed. pr.; perhaps Διδύ]μῳ BL VI 111). If they are the same, the possibility arises that the syndic here in 2 might have been the Sarapion of **2665** 5, but in that case the order of names and the layout of the titles would be different.

The consideration of the date of the papyrus is complicated. Limits are provided by the mention of Maximinus Caesar in 10. He was appointed on the abdication of Diocletian and Maximian on 1 May 305 and became Augustus some time in 310. Like Constantine he was given the title of *filius Augustorum* at the conference of Carnuntum in November 308, but that title could possibly have been lost at the end of 10 here, cf. XLVI **3270** 28, and therefore no conclusion can be based on its presumed absence.

The name of the prytanis of 306/7 fits well here, cf. XLIV **3192**, and this is perhaps the most likely date. On the other hand the absence of the mention of any western ruler may indicate rather a date in 308, see 9–10 n. It may be, therefore, that Aurelius Dioscorus alias Helladius served as prytanis also in 307/8, cf. **3606** introd., or it may be that the remains here represent a different name, such as Δῖος or Διοσκουρίδης, or, if it was a Dioscorus, that this Dioscorus had a different alias, such as Hermias, or Serenus, to mention two possibilities which might be significant, see below.

If we go so far in admitting doubt, we must also allow that the document might date from the end of 304/5, for which no prytanis is yet attested. The next year, 305/6, is seemingly excluded by the term of another prytanis (VIII **1104**, XXXIII **2665**, cf. P. Cornell 45), but evidence is accumulating for the occasional appearance of two prytaneis in one regnal year, see **3606** introd. 307/8 is free, because the Hermias mentioned in XLIV **3193**, which is undated, though tentatively assigned to this year, might have served in any year during the term as logistes of Valerius Heron alias Sarapion, whose successor is first known on 16 March 313 (XLVI **3305**), i.e. for our purposes 307/8, 308/9 (if he was called Hermias alias Serenus, see below), 309/10, 310/11. 308/9 is occupied by a prytanis with the alias Serenus, see M. *Chr.* 196, P. Mert. II 90, but the traces here could suit, e.g. Dioscorus alias Serenus. No prytanis is known for 309/10 or 310/11. See the list for this period in A. K. Bowman, *Town Councils* 133–4, 137.

4 At the end of the line restore probably Αὐρηλίῳ.

5 γραμμα[τεῖ. This word seems certain, but it is not certain what the post was. A γραμματεὺς τῆς πόλεως still existed at this period, see XXXIII **2667** 10 (309); contrast P. Mertens, L'État civil 2–7. There was also a γραμματεὺς πολιτικῶν (XII **1413**, XLIV **3185**), on whom see A. K. Bowman, *Town Councils* 38. The title γραμματεὺς τῆς βουλῆς does not appear to have existed at Oxyrhynchus, see ibid. 39. This line, which is the end of the prescript, may have been shorter than usual.

6–7 Neratius Apollonides, *magister privatae*, has appeared before in XXXIII **2673** (5 February 304) and **2665** (305/6). This text may carry his term of office forward into 306/7 or 307/8, see 1–4 n., 9–10 n., and so lend force to the suggestion that he is the unnamed *magister* of 9 May 307 mentioned in XLIV **3192** 12–13, see n. He might also be the unnamed *magister* mentiond in PSI IV 310 of 11 August 306; see *CÉ* 49 (1974) 173 for the date.

A very convenient summary of the literature and evidence on the *ratio privata* is to be found in F. G. B. Millar, *The Emperor in the Roman World* 625, 627–30. Note also his doubts of the authenticity of the form *res privata*, which is found only in the codes of Theodosius and Justinian, as applied to this period.

8 The remains in the middle of the line,]. ιτο. . [, are intractable. The translation rests on the following partially restored version, ὁ . . . μ[άγιστρος . . .] . . . [. . ., ἀκολούθως οἶς]|⁸ προσέτ[α]ξ[εν κ]αὶ τὸ . . [c. 20]|⁹ τῶν δεσπο[τ]ῶν ἡμῶ[ν Μαξιμιανοῦ Cεβαστοῦ]|¹⁰ καὶ Μαξιμίν[ου] Καίσαρο[ς, ἐκέλευσεν ἡμᾶς. Something on the lines of τὸ θεῖον πρόσταγμα would provide a subject, though πρόσταγμα . . . προστάξει is clumsy. Without these traces ἡ θεία διάταξις or ἡ θεία τύχη would have seemed quite suitable, and a neuter abstract such as τὸ μεγαλεῖον (used of high officials) is possible, though no satisfactory one has been found. After τό the remains suggest hypsilon. Also possible is the pattern ὁ . . . μάγιστρος . . . προσέταξεν . . . κατὰ κέλευσιν . . . τῶν δεσποτῶν.

9–10 Only Galerius and Maximinus are mentioned here. Maximian eliminated Severus in spring 307, but Constantine was recognized as Caesar in Egypt long before this. The news reached Caranis between 17 November and 25 December 306, see P. Cair. Isid. 115. 10; 116. 12–16, and reached Oxyrhynchus between 13 October and 30 November, see I **102** 21, XIV **1750**. Since these places, about sixty miles apart, must have received the news within a period of a few days, we can reasonably say that the news reached Middle Egypt between 17 November and 30 November. He continued to be recognized throughout 306/7, see e.g. P. Grenf. II 78 (= M. *Chr.* 63). 29–32, SB I 5679. 21–4 (both February/March 307); P. Thead. 10. 16–18 (3 April); XLIV **3192** 25–8 (9 May); XII **1542** 12 (27 May); P. Cair. Isid. 8. 1–2 (14 June); 45. 1 (June/July); 47. 48–50 (26 August); 46. 9 (3 September—already into the Egyptian year 307/8). Therefore, if 306/7 is the year of this papyrus, see 1–4n., we must conclude that the absence of mention of a western ruler had no political implications, but showed only that this transaction was regarded as a purely eastern affair.

On the other hand the omission of western rulers may give some reason to be suspicious of the date based on the restoration of the name of the prytanis. Galerius recognized Constantine as Caesar only, and that some time after 29 August 306, as his Egyptian regnal years tell us, cf. above, although Constantine's troops had proclaimed him Augustus at the death of his father Constantius I on 25 July 306. Subsequently, about September 307, Constantine was invested as Augustus by Maximian, but this was not accepted by Galerius and Maximinus, within whose spheres of influence Constantine's name is then omitted for some time, e.g. ILS I 658 (Aquincum; undated); P. Cair. Isid. 87 (29 April 308), 88 (7 May 308), 125 (6 August 308; all from Caranis in Egypt), and for the whole of the Egyptian year 308/9, even while his name appears in consular dates of 309 with the title *filius Augustorum*, his name and regnal-year number are omitted from the regnal-year date-clauses, e.g. XII **1499** 7 (5 June 309), P. Cair. Isid. 47. 8, 22 (both 18 June); 48. 7 (14 August). These papyri are dated by regnal years of Galerius and Maximinus only. Note that the dates for this year with three or four numbers, to include Constantine and Licinius, see A. Chastagnol, *La Datation par années régnales égyptiennes à l'époque constantinienne*, in *Caesarodunum* x *bis*, p. 234, are all retrospective. The consulship of 309, held with Licinius, was attributed to Constantine in the East, but Constantine himself never counted it, see T. D. Barnes, *The New Empire* 25.

If, then, the omission of any western ruler has a political connotation here, we would expect the date to be some time in 308 or 309. To accept this, however, we have to reject the simplest view of the restoration of 1–2. In addition, we begin to get further away from the last known date for the *magister privatae*, cf. 6–7n.

11 Cf. 17–18 for the restoration of the end of the line.

12 ξυλοσαγγ[άθου]. For the restoration see 18. The form with ξυλο- is new, but confirms that caγγαθ- is the name of a plant, as suggested in P. Turner 47. 2n., cf. ἄνηθον, ξυλάνηθον; βάλcαμον, ξυλοβάλcαμον. If τοῦ is recognized correctly in 11, it shows that the gender is either masculine or neuter, excluding the possibility of its being feminine, as envisaged in *LSJ* s.v. cάγγαθον. The other references to caγγαθ- or caγκαθ- are O. Bodl. (Petrie) 262. 5, SPP XX 96. 7 (as corrected in *BASP* 13 (1967) 37) and P. Turner 47. 2, 7. All these documents are in the form of lists which give little clue to the nature of this particular substance. However, in modern Greek caγκαθιά is a sort of berberis, see P. Turner 47. 2n., and this seems to be our best evidence. The use to which this substance might be put in a mint can only be guessed. It might perhaps have been one of the special plants from which charcoal was made, cf. R. J. Forbes, *Metallurgy in Antiquity*, 312. For a short account of ancient minting practices and a bibliography see D. Sellwood, 'Minting', in D. Strong and D. Brown (eds.), *Roman Crafts* (1976) 63–74.

For the number, (-?)χιλίων, cf. 18–19n.

13 κα[τακομιδήν(?). Or, e.g., καταγωγήν, καταπομπήν.

14 Supply e.g. ⟨τὴν⟩ ὑπηρεcίαν τῆc or τὰc χρείαc τῆc.

15 μονήτηc. *LSJ* and *Suppl.* contain no reference to this word, for the nominative of which I have found no evidence. See E. A. Sophocles, *Lexicon*, s.v. μονῆτα, G. W. H. Lampe, *PGL*, s.v. μόνητα, citing Malalas p. 608, and *AÉ* 1913, no. 143, *a* 11, ibid. 1924, no. 81, 8–9, both of the reign of Trajan and referring to the same man as ἐπίτροπον ... μονήτηc, i.e. *procurator monetae*. The lemma is given as μονήτη in H. J. Mason, *Greek Terms for Roman Institutions* 68, with a reference to E. M. Smallwood, *Documents Illustrating the Principates of Nerva, Trajan, and Hadrian*, no. 286, which is the same as *AÉ* 1924, no. 81.

On the Alexandrian mint and the coinage of this period see *RIC* vi 65–73, 645–86.

18–19 By itself κ[εντηναρίων, cf. 11, is too short to fill the space, so that χειλίων in 19 is virtually certain to be incomplete at the beginning. Numbers from 2,000 to 9,000 are available.

19–20 Restore possibly something like μετὰ τὰ εἰϲφερ[όμενα καὶ ὑπὸ τῶν]|²⁰ ἀπὸ τῆϲ πόλεωϲ, sc. κεντηνάριά ποϲα, 'in addition to the (so many hundredweight) contributed also by the inhabitants of the city'. Some levies were divided between the city and the nome in the proportion 1:2, see P. Beatty Panop. 1. 379 and n., cf. XLIII **3121** 10–11 and n. The same may well have been the case here.

3619. Proceedings before a *Praeses Iouiae*

| 75/89a | fr. 1 *c*. 15 × 24 cm | *c*.314–324/5 |
| | fr. 2 *c*. 19 × 23 cm | |

A single phrase, repeated fourteen times, contains most of the interest of this item. It is, '*Isidorus, u(ir) p(erfectissimus), praes(es) Aeg(ypti) Iouiae, . . .*' Here we have the first contemporary evidence of the existence of the short-lived province of *Aegyptus Iouia*, known otherwise only from the famous list of the provinces contained in a seventh-century manuscript preserved in Verona, the 'Verona List', see T. D. Barnes, *The New Empire of Diocletian and Constantine* 201–8, 211. We learn for the first time the name of one of its governors, see Barnes, op. cit. 150, and we also learn the interesting fact that his title was *praeses Aegypti Iouiae* and not *praefectus Aegypti*.

It seems an obvious conclusion that *Iouia*, named after the dynasty of Diocletian, was 'the twin of *Herculia*', named after the dynasty of Maximian, and therefore founded at the same time, 'after January 314 (P. Cair. Isid. 73) but before 27 December 315 (P. Cair. Isid. 74)', see Barnes, op. cit. 211. If it is right to believe that *Herculia* contained, as well as Middle Egypt, also a large portion of the Eastern Delta, see L **3574** introd., all that is left for *Iouia* is Alexandria and the Western Delta. Now that we see that *Iouia* too was governed by a *praeses*, we are forced to conclude that there was no prefect of Egypt during the period of the existence of *Iouia* and *Herculia*. A recently published Florentine papyrus, PL III 484 (*ZPE* 46 (1982) 261–3), again attests the prefect Julius Julianus, this time with an undoubted date clause of 314. He was probably the last prefect before the division. These provinces were reunited into a province of *Aegyptus*, governed once again by a *praefectus*, at some time after the abdication of Licinius in September 324. We know that Sabinianus, *praeses Herculiae*, was still in office at some time within the year 324 (XLV **3261**). The next firmly dated *praefectus Aegypti* is now Tiberius Flavius Laetus, known on 2 February 326 (**3620**), by which date *Iouia* and *Herculia* must no longer have existed.

The text is a record of proceedings before the *praeses* in which the formal framework is given in Latin while the words of the participants are given mostly in Greek. The judge in these cases usually speaks Greek, but he may address his staff in Latin (e.g. P. Lips. 40 ii 7) and give judgement in Latin (e.g. P. Ryl. IV 653). For a short discussion of the type of text see R. A. Coles, *Reports of Proceedings* (Pap. Brux. 4) 36–8. Dr Coles refers to a few early examples in which some Latin appears (add now P. Wisc. II 48. 42–3; ii AD), but the fully developed form is an innovation of the reign of Diocletian, whose policy of encouraging the use of Latin is well known, cf. J. Kaimio, 'Latin in Roman Egypt', *Actes du XVe Congrès International de Papyrologie*, 3e partie (Pap. Brux. 18), 28 and n. 2. The instances known to me are:

1. P. Cair. Cat. Gén. 10268 (298–300; edition by R. A. Coles in *Bull. du Centre d'Études de Papyrologie* 1 (Ain Shams, forthcoming)
2. CPR VII 21 (*c*.301; cf. J. R. Rea, *ZPE* 41 (1981) 282)
3. XVIII **2187** 24–32 (before 304; Latin represented only by the word Ῥωμαϊκά)
4. P. Cair. Cat. Gén. 10723 (iii/iv; edition by R. A. Coles forthcoming, as in item 1 above)
5. SPP XIV No. X (= C. Wessely, *Schrifttafeln*, No. 14; III/IV)
6. XLI **2952** (*c*.315?)
7. LI **3619** (314–24/5)
8. P. Sakaon 33 (= P. Ryl. IV 653 = ChLA IV 254; 320)
9. P. Sakaon 34 (= P. Thead. 13; 321)
10. ChLA XII 522 (327 or 331?; cf. D. Hagedorn, *ZPE* 34 (1979) 104–7; for *Febrar(ias)* ˙ ...... *in seç[retario* read possibly *Febr(uarias) Arṣịnọịṭ(um ciuitate) ịṇ seç[retario*, cf. P. Ryl. IV, Pl. iv = ChLA IV 254)
11. P. Ryl. IV 654 (= ChLA IV 255; 300–350)
12. P. Ryl. IV 702 (= ChLA IV 257; 300–350)
13. P. Berl. Zilliacus 4 (= ChLA X 463; *c*.350; in 16, 23, 26 for *comes pres(es)* read *com(es) et pres(es)*, or possibly *pṛạes(es)*: restore the same in 10 and 13)
14. P. Bouriant 20 (= M. *Chr.* 96 = P. Abinn. 63 = ChLA X 407; *c*.350)
15. P. Lond. V 1825 (= ChLA III 210; 352)?
16. ChLA V 292 (352–4?; in 5 for *pṛạe[s(es) Ae]g(ypti)* . [.] . . . read probably *pṛạe[s(es) A]uguṣṭamṇ(icae)*
17. P. Lips. 33 (= M. *Chr.* 55 = ChLA XII 525; 368)
18. P. Lond. V 1650 (the only trace of Latin is *r(espondit)* in 3, but see below **3619** 9 n.; *c*.372)
19. P. Lips. 38 (= M. *Chr.* 97 = ChLA XII 520; 390)
20. P. Lips. 44 (= ChLA XII 526; iv)
21. XXII **2352** (= ChLA IV 263, cf. D. Hagedorn, *ZPE* 34 (1979) 111; iv)
22. P. Lond. III 971 (pp. 128–9, Facsimiles iii, no. 64. The only trace of Latin is *r(espondit)* in 9, 10, 11, but see below **3619** 9 n.; iv)
23. ChLA V 287 (iv)
24. P. Lips. 40 (= ChLA XII 518, where we are told that the original is lost and no photograph exists; iv/v)
25. XVI **1879** (434)
26. SPP XIV No. XII (= C. Wessely, *Schrifttafeln*, no. 26; *c*.434)
27. ChLA XI 470 (458)

28. XVI **1878** (461; in 1 for *hemol*( ) read *heracl*ʃ, i.e. *Heracl(eopoli)*, the location of the court)
29. XVI **1876** (480)
30. ChLA III 217 (483?)
31. XVI **1877** (*c*.488)
32. P. Mich. VII 463 (= ChLA V 293; v)
33. SB I 5357 (= ChLA X 407; v)
34. ChLA XI 471 (v?)
35. PSI XIII 1309 (v–vi; cf. M. Norsa, *Papiri greci delle collezioni italiane* (Scritture documentarie), pp. 41–2, tav. XXVI)
36. P. Cair. Masp. III 67329 (524/5, cf. P. Ross.-Georg. III 34 introd.)
37. P. Cair. Masp. II 67131 (vi)
38. P. Mich. XIII 660–1 (vi)
39. ChLA V 291? (vi; 'Lettre officielle' ed., but at the beginning of 5 his chrism should be read as *fl*ʃ, i.e. *Fl(auius)*, and the name *Fl(auius) Anastasius Anatoliu̱[s*, occurring in the nominative after four lines of Greek, looks like that of an official presiding over proceedings in court, cf. ChLA V 293).

Apart from some debris containing nothing that can be transcribed unambiguously, only two fragments have survived. Both have damaged remains of an account in talents and drachmas upside down on the back, indicating that they are parts of the same roll at any rate, but all attempts to join the fragments have failed. Some of the entries concern fruit and nuts, ἰςχάδω[ν, φυνικίων (twice, l. φοιν-), ϲτροβίλων (twice), καροίω[ν (l. καρύ-), two at least begin with names (Τύραννος, Ϲαραπίων), and one is for χόρτου (hardly χάρτου).

On the front fr. 1 has the beginnings of seventeen lines, mostly introducing speeches of the *praeses* with his name and titles in Latin, followed by *d(ixit)*. Lines not of this nature are indented by *c.* 2.5 cm. The fragment is broken on all sides, although a small area of blank papyrus may preserve about 1 cm of the lower edge of the roll. At the top left there are meagre remains in Greek from a preceding column and between the columns there is a sheet join. The writer used the common convention that each pronouncement by the presiding official should begin a new line, cf. Coles, *Reports of Proceedings* 54 n. 3, in conjunction with a format of very long lines, which is also usual in this type of text. The exchanges were short, probably mostly short questions from the *praeses* and short answers from another party, see 9 n. on *r(espondit)*, with the result that fourteen of the seventeen line-beginnings in fr. 1 col. ii mention the *praeses*, cf. especially XLI **2952** (Pl. V), which is quite similar to fr. 1 here, and P. Herm. Rees 18, the interrogation of a slave in Greek, which is well enough preserved to give an idea of the original complete shape.

Fr. 2 is also badly damaged, but shows substantial remains of a top margin of *c.* 3 cm. It too has a sheet join, which is about 7 cm from the left edge. The writing here is mostly in Greek, giving the words of the parties. The longer lines are broken at both sides, but several others come to an end and are followed by various widths of blank papyrus. Here too we have bilingual proceedings and it is very possible that these lines are part of fr. 1 col. ii. No connection has been made, but this may be explained by the extent of the damage. The fibres on the right of fr. 1 and on the left of fr. 2 are badly twisted, and the pattern of creases and worm damage show that the papyrus was not rolled up or folded regularly when the worms began to eat it. This is clearest from the bottom right of fr. 2, where two creases cross in the shape of an X and there are matching holes in each of the four compartments, showing that this area was folded first from bottom right to top left and then again from bottom left to top right. Other creases run at various odd angles.

The headings of these texts give a date-clause and the location of the proceedings. Since there is no heading at the top of fr. 2, those lines must be part of a text running to two columns or more. If they do not belong to fr. 1 col. ii, they may be from fr. 1 col. i, or even from a more distant part of the roll. The subject here is dimly seen to be the sale of grain, with which some local councillors were concerned. The price seems to have been unsuitable (29). No reason emerges for the presence of this copy of the proceedings at Oxyrhynchus, which lay in the province of *Herculia*. The case may have concerned transactions between Oxyrhynchus and the Delta, but it is also possible that the papyrus was simply brought in to Oxyrhynchus by a visitor.

Fr. 1

  i   ii

 . . .   .

].δε   5 *I̦[s]i̦d̦[orus*

] (vac.)   *Isidor[u]ș [u(ir)] p(erfectissimus)* [

]οςεκ.ι̣   *Isidorus u(ir) p(erfectissimus) p̦r̦a̦e̦ș(es) A̦e̦[g(ypti)*

].[..].   (vac.) . . .α. cυνε. . . . [

            (vac.) ματ[.]ς. *r(espondit)*. τρ. [

        10 *Isidorus u(ir) p(erfectissimus) praes(es) Aeg(ypti) Ioui̦[a]e̦* [. . .]. [

           I̦și̦[dor]u̦s u(ir) p(erfectissimus) praes(es) Aeg(ypti) Iouia̦e̦ d̦(ixit). . .[

           Isidoru̦s u(ir) p(erfectissimus) praes(es) Aeg(ypti) Iouiae d(ixit). . . .ν̦[

           Isidorus u(ir) p(erfectissimus) praes(es) A̦eg(ypti) I̦ouiae ad off(icium) d(ixit). . .[

           Isidorus u(ir) p(erfectissimus) praes(es) Ae̦g(ypti) I̦ouiae d(ixit). . . .[

        15 *Isidorus u(ir) p(erfectissimus) praes(es) Aeg(ypti) Iouiae d(ixit)*. [.].. [

          (vac.) *i̦n̦d̦u̦c̦ți̦s Hieracapol[line*

           Isidorus u(ir) p(erfectissimus) praes(es) [A]e̦g(ypti) I[o]uiae. [

           I̦[sidoru]ș u(ir) p(erfectissimus) praes(es) Aeg(ypti) Ioui̦[ae

           Isidorus u(ir) p(erfectissimus) pra]e̦ș(es) Aeg(ypti) Iouiae̦ [

        20 *Isidorus u(ir) p(erfectissimus) pra]e̦ș(es) A̦eg(ypti) I̦ou[iae*

           Isidorus u(ir) p(erfectissimus) pra]e̦ș(es) A̦e̦[g(ypti)

                ] (vac.) [

                Foot?

---

7 *uppraesaeg*: and so throughout   9 *f*   11 *d̦*: and so throughout   13 *off*

7–8 The space between these lines is a little wider than expected, *c.* 1.5 cm rather than *c.* 1 cm, but there seems not to be room for an extra line.

9 *r(espondit)*. Cf. 25, 26. The abbreviation is a Latin *R* cut by an oblique stroke rising from below on the left to above on the right, see ChLA XII 522. 9 (l. 11 in the revised numbering by D. Hagedorn, *ZPE* 34 (1979) 106). The reading and resolution of the symbol are offered without comment in ChLA, but the Latin *R* resembles a Greek pi very closely and has been read as such in P. Lond. III 971 (pp. 128–9 = M. *Chr.* 95). 9, 10, 11 (Facsimiles III Pl. 64), V 1650. 3, and SPP XIV Taf. X (= C. Wessely, *Schrifttafeln*, no. 14—transcript p. 14). 5. Only the last of these texts is a normal bilingual record of proceedings like **3619**. The writer of P. Lond. 971 seems to have been copying a bilingual original without knowing Latin. He left large gaps for most of the Latin framework, but transcribed this abbreviation. He may not have understood it, but he faithfully copied the chief feature which distinguishes *R* from pi, namely the extension of the first upright well below the base line. Wilcken, *Gdz.* 86 n. 2, pointed out that the gaps implied a Latin original and realized that the abbreviation must be a Latin letter, though he was inclined to recognize it as *S*. In P. Lond. 1650 the

Fr. 2

```
]              (vac.)               . . [ . . . . . . . . . ]        (vac.)
] . ζ . . . . . . αι ὑμῖc οἱ βουλευταὶ πῶc ἐπράθη ὁ cῖτοc. Ạpoḷḷọṇịus ex[
] . um.   (vac.)   quọ ụẹxato                      (vac.)
```
25
```
] . κων ἐξετάζω. ἐγχωρεῖ γὰρ το[ὺc] β[ο]υλευτὰc ψεύδεcθαι. ṛ(espondit). τριάκοντạ [
] . . .  r(espondit).  ναί.  (vac.)  [ c. 10 letters ]   (vac.)
```
```
] . . . . . . . [ . . . ] . . . . . . . . . . κατη[ . . ] . . ṿ . [ . . . ]αζωτη[
] . . . . . . . . πολλάκιc . [ . . ]παρην . . . κạ[
] . η . ạ . . [ . . . . ]ịạc ἐλάττονοc πράcαντεc πλε̣ί[ο]ṿοc [
```
30
```
]                    (vac.)
] . . . . . [ . ] . . . . εc . . . .     (vac.)
] . . . . . [     c. 10         ] . . . . [ . ]νην.    (vac.)
] . . . . . ̣[     c. 10         ] . .   (vac.)
] . . . . . [     c. 10         ]        (vac.)
```
35
```
] . . [       c. 20              ] . [ . . . . ]τωṇ ἀγροίκωṇ [
]   (vac.)    [
] . ạị[
```
.   .   .   .   .

23 l. ὑμεῖc   25 l. ἐγχωρεῖ; †   26 ⟊

introductions to the speeches of the *praes es* are given in Greek, but the other speakers' words are prefaced by *r(espondit)*. Strangely enough, although ἀπεκρίνατο is very frequent in Greek proceedings, see R. A. Coles, *Reports of Proceedings* 43–4, *respondit* is almost entirely absent from Latin ones, ibid. 45–6 (45 n. 6). The use of it in Bruns, *Fontes*⁷ no. 188. 11 is not perhaps quite comparable.

16 The least we need to restore is a conjunction and the name of another person, meaning, 'When Hieracapollon and . . . had been brought into court, . . .'. Cf. CPR VII 21. 6, P. Lips. 38 i 12, 40 ii 8, *Cod. Just.* 48 (47). 2.

17 The last trace seems not to be from a tall letter such as would suit *d(ixit)*; ạ[*d off(icium)*, cf. 13, is possible.

22 . . [. These traces in the top margin are very faint, but look deliberate. If so, they probably come from a column number. The absence of a heading shows that this was not the first column of the record of proceedings, see introd. There are not necessarily two figures. The second trace might be from a stroke marking the numeral, e.g. β′.

23 The remains would suit ἐπ]ιζητεῖcθαι, 'You councillors (must?) be investigated on the manner of the sale of the grain'. I have allowed cῖτοc its older generic sense of 'grain', but by this date it may already mean specifically 'wheat', see H. Cadell, *Akten des XIII. Internationalen Papyrologenkongresses* (1974), 61–8, esp. 64–5.

At the end of the line *ex*[may introduce the speaker's origin, i.e. *ex ciuitate* . . ., cf. P. Lond. V 1825. 2, P. Mich. XIII 661. 11, or give his title such as *exactor*, *exceptor*, or *ex protectoribus*, *vel sim.*

24 I take it that the *praes es* spoke here to his staff in Latin, saying something like *uexa] ẹum*, and that '*quo*

uexato' means 'when he had been beaten', which was followed in 25 by the formula to introduce another speech by the *praeses*. Compare P. Lips. 40 iii 20–22, and, for Latin to the staff, ii 7. For *uexo* = 'beat' see P. G. W. Glare, *Oxford Latin Dictionary* s.v., and *CGL* iv 401. 6, where it is glossed '*mulcare, uerberare, exagitare*'. See now also *JRS* 72 (1982) 105 (l. 75), where in a scene of judicial torture there occurs the sentence *ei pectus uexatur*. The corrupt Greek has εατω το cτηθοc †cτρεβετε = αὐτῷ τὸ cτῆθοc cτρέφεται? cτρεβλοῦται? (ed.). This shows that the word does not refer to flogging, but to some form of torture inflicted on the chest.

25 Perhaps there was another reference here to ἀγρο]ίκων, cf. 35. Understand, perhaps, 'I am enquiring (from the country folk?), for it is possible that the councillors are lying'.

26 *r(espondit)*. ναί. This is exactly the wording of ChLA X 522. 9, see 9 n. above.

27–9 If fr. 2 does represent the same column as fr. 1, see introd., it seems likely that either 27–8 or 28–9 correspond with 7–8, because 7–8 must have been lines that occupied the full width of the column and it is only at this point in fr. 2 that we have groups of two successive long lines. We might argue further that, because 16 is indented, 15 was a long line and that it must correspond with 35. This would pin down 7–8 as corresponding with 27–8. We could envisage the *praeses* saying in 35 something like καλείcθωcαν (cf. P. Lips. 38 i 12) or εἰcαγέcθωcαν (cf. P. Lips. 40 ii 8) οἱ ἐκ τῶν ἀγροίκων, 'Let the representatives of the country folk be called', or '. . . brought into court', followed in 16 = 36 by 'When Hieracapollon and . . . had been brought into court'. This looks attractive and fairly convincing, but it has not be possible to confirm it from the physical state of the papyrus and it has led to no further understanding of the text.

27 Perhaps κατη[γο]ρῶν, or κατη[γό]ρων, ἐ[ξετ]άζω, cf. 25.

28 Perhaps κ[αὶ?] παρήγγελκα[(*vel sim.*)?

35 Cf. 27–9 n.

3620. PETITION TO NYCTOSTRATEGI

66 6B.26/F(1–3)a   15.5 × 25.5 cm   2 February 326
66 6B.26/G(1–3)c

Two fragments have been put together to form a document which is substantially complete, but lacks a strip from the upper left and has suffered severe damage further down on the same side. Line 17 is shared between the fragments. There is a sheet join running vertically less than 1 cm from the right edge, showing that the piece was cut from a roll in the normal way, see E. G. Turner, *Greek Papyri* 4. The back is blank.

The chief point of interest is the name and date of a new prefect of Egypt, Tiberius Flavius Laetus. A person with the same *tria nomina*, who may well be the same, appears in an inscription of 337–40, see 24 n.

The petition is from a man whose wife had been physically assaulted and probably robbed of some gold by another woman and a slave girl. He asked for a midwife to be sent to inspect his wife and certify her state of health in writing, so that he might have documentary evidence to submit if there should be proceedings in the prefect's court. This is only the third mention of a midwife in the papyri, see 17–18 n.

ὑπατείας τῶν δ]εςποτῶν ἡμῶν Κωνσταντίνου

Αὐγούςτο]υ τὸ ζ″ καὶ Κωνσταντίου τοῦ ἐπιφανεστάτου

(vac.) Κ]αίσαρος τὸ αϛ″, Μεχεὶρ η″.   (vac.)

Αὐρηλί]οις Ἀφθονίῳ καὶ Τιμοθέου ἀμφοτέροι⟨ς⟩ νυκτο-

5   στρατήγ]οις τῆς λαμ(πρᾶς) καὶ λαμ(προτάτης) Ὀξ(υρυγχιτῶν) πόλεως

παρὰ Α]ὐρηλίου Θωνίου Ὀννώφριος ἀπὸ τῆς αὐτῆς

. . . . . .] π[ό]λεως. κατὰ τὴν χθὲς ἡμέραν, τῆς ἡμε-

τέρας cυ]μβίου κατ' ὕκων τυγχανούςης, Ταπῆςίς τις,

ἅ[μα τῇ ἑα]υτῆς οἰκέτιδει Οὐϊκτωρᾷ, ἑςπεριναῖς

10   ὥραις ἐν τοῖς πολὺ ἄπωθεν τῆς ἡμετέρας οἰκίας

οἰκοῦσα, ἐπιστᾶςα{ι} ὕβρις προςετρίψατο τῇ⟦ν⟧ cυμβί-

ῳ μο]υ ἀρήτους, ὥςτε μὴ μόνον τὴν ἐςθῆτα ⟨α⟩ὐτῆς

διαραγῆναι ἀλλὰ καὶ cῶ[μα], προςενεγκτιςῶν

. . . .]. . .νπλω[. .]. ν αὐτὴν cυμβίῳ μου

15   . . . .]. [.]. . .κ. [. . . .]. ης χρυςίου. ἐπὶ τοίνυν

c. 22 letters   ] τὴν βιβλιδίων

ἐπίδοςιν ποιοῦμαι ἀξι[ῶν . . . .]. μέαν ἐπιςτα-

λῖςαν ὑφ' ἡμῶν ἀπαντῆςαι καὶ ςημιώςαςθαι τὴν

διάθεςιν αὐτῆς καὶ ἐνγράφως προςφωνῆςαι ⟦την⟧ ⟨καὶ⟩

20   τῆς προςφωνήςεως γεγενημένης καὶ γνωςθέντος

τοῦ ἀτοπήματος ἐγγύας αὐτὰς παραςχέςθαι ἵν' εἰ cυμβέ-

η τι τῇ{ς} cυμβίῳ μου ἡ δέουςα{ν} ἐκδικία γένηται παρὰ

τῷ ἀχράντῳ δικαστηρίῳ τοῦ κυρίῳ μου διαςημοτάτου

ἐπάρχου τῆς Αἰγύπτου Τιβερίου Φλαυΐου Λαίτου.

4 l. *Τιμοθέῳ*	5 λαμϛ″, λαμϛ″οξ′	8 l. κατ' οἶκον	9 l. οἰκέτιδι; οὐϊκτωρα
11 ὕβρις, l. ὕβρεις	12 l. ἀρρήτους	13 l. διαρραγῆναι, προςενεχθειςῶν	15 l. ἐπεί
17 l. μαῖαν	17–18 l. ἐπιςταλεῖςαν	18 l. ὑφ' ὑμῶν, ςημειώςαςθαι	19 l. ἐγγράφως
21 εγ′γυας, ἵν	21–2 l. cυμβαίη	23 l. κυρίου	24 φλαυΐου

'In the consulship of our masters Constantine Augustus for the 7th time and Constantius the most noble Caesar for the 1st time, Mecheir 8.

'To Aurelius Aphthonius and Aurelius Timotheus, both *nyctostrategi* of the glorious and most glorious city of the Oxyrhynchites, from Aurelius Thonius son of Onnophris from the same city. In the course of yesterday while my wife was at home a certain Tapesis, who lives in the regions far distant from our house (?), during the evening hours made an attack together with her slave-girl Victoria (?) and inflicted unspeakable acts of violence on my wife, so that not only was her clothing torn, but her person . . . my said wife . . . gold. Since, therefore, . . . , I make submission of this petition requesting that . . . midwife should be officially instructed by you to come and take note of her condition and report in writing (and that) when the report has been made and the outrage investigated, they should provide guarantees, so that, if anything should befall my wife, the appropriate action for retribution may take place in the immaculate court of my lord the most perfect prefect of Egypt Tiberius Flavius Laetus.'

1–3 Cf. R. S. Bagnall and K. A. Worp, *Chronological Systems* 109 (AD 326).

2 Αὐγούϲτο]υ. This, rather than Ϲεβαϲτοῦ, seems to be the formula in the Oxyrhynchite nome, see XLV **3249** 1. In P. Princ. II 79. 1, where the edition has Κ]ωνϲταντίνου τοῦ Ϲ[εβ(αϲτοῦ) τὸ ζ], a better reading is Κ]ωνϲταντίνου Ἀγούϲ[του τὸ ζ], as Professor Ann E. Hanson has kindly confirmed from the original.

4–5 νυκτο|⁵[ϲτρατήγ]οιϲ. See the material collected by P. J. Sijpesteijn for Pap. Lugd. Bat. XVII (= *Antidoron Martino David*), No. 17, the text of which has appeared again as SB X 10287. Sijpesteijn's conclusions have been modified in *CÉ* 44 (1969) 347-52 by J. D. Thomas, who has shown that nyctostrategi did not appear in the nome capitals till the municipalization of Egypt. The earliest Oxyrhynchite example is now L **3571** (286); see too P. Oxy. Hels. 26 (296).

Especially to be compared with this document is P. Lips. 42, which is a doctor's report to a nyctostrategus, like the one requested in 17–19.

6–7 It is more usual to have simply ἀπὸ τῆϲ αὐτῆϲ πόλεωϲ. Before κατά the sigma has a long straight cap which suggests that we should punctuate strongly after it, and the very meagre traces suit π[ό]λεωϲ. Probably the name was repeated in an abbreviated form, cf. I **55** 6 ἀπ[ὸ] τῆ[ϲ] αὐτῆ[ϲ] λαμπρᾶϲ Ὀξ(υρυγχιτῶν) πόλεωϲ (283), XIV **1643** 4-5 ἀπὸ τῆϲ αὐτῆϲ Ὀξυρυγ[χιτῶν πόλε]ωϲ.

9 Οὐϊκτωρᾷ. Cf. XVII **2151** 13, where the text gives Οὐϊκτωρία but the note says, 'The second ι of Οὐϊκτωρία is very uncertain, and perhaps -τωρα was written'. Neither Οὐϊκτωρία nor Οὐϊκτωρᾶ appears in F. Preisigke, *NB* or D. Foraboschi, *Onomasticon*. I have assumed that the form here is another example of the loss of accented iota before a back vowel, see F. T. Gignac, *Grammar* i 302-3, and have accented it according to the rule given there.

9–10 It seems likely that ἑϲπεριναῖϲ ὥραιϲ should be read, since the nyctostrategi are involved and the meagre traces at the beginning cover less space than νυκτ- ought to. If it is correct its placing is odd. Where it stands it ought to modify οἰκοῦϲα, which would give a strange sense. It is far more probable that it refers only to the time of the assault, cf. R. Taubenschlag, *Law²* 441. A similar difficulty attaches to the placing of ἅ[μα τῇ ἑα]υτῆϲ οἰκετίδει (= -ιδι). This almost certainly refers to the slave-girl's complicity in the crime, cf. Taubenschlag, loc. cit., the ungrammatical but suggestive plural ἐπιϲτᾶϲα{ι} in 11, and αὐτάϲ in 21, but in its present place seems to say only that she shared her mistress's residence. For the purposes of the translation it is assumed that the order should have been something like Ταπῆϲίϲ τιϲ, ἐν τοῖϲ πολὺ ἄπωθεν τῆϲ ἡμετέραϲ οἰκίαϲ οἰκοῦϲα, ἑϲπεριναῖϲ ὥραιϲ ἅμα τῇ ἑαυτῆϲ οἰκετίδι ἐπιϲτᾶϲα κτλ.

10–11 ἐν τοῖϲ πολὺ ἄπωθεν τῆϲ ἡμετέραϲ οἰκίαϲ οἰκοῦϲα, 'who lives in the regions far distant from our house'. An alternative translation might be, 'who lives in the far distant parts of our house', taking ἄπωθεν as an adverb rather than as a preposition. The two occurrences of the word in the papyri, P. Masp. I 67005. 14 (adv.?), II 67151. 206 (prep.), both of the sixth century AD, do not help, still less does the suggestion that it appeared in P. Harr. I 158. 2, cf. BL III 83, H. C. Youtie, *Scriptiunculae* ii 813-14.

11 ἐπιϲτᾶϲα{ι}. This is the simplest correction. Evidently the writer was thinking of mistress and slave rushing to attack together, cf. 9–10 n.

ὕβριϲ (= ὕβρειϲ) προϲετρίψατο. Cf. XVII **2133** 23.

12 ἀρήτουϲ = ἀρρήτουϲ. For simplification of ρρ to ρ see F. T. Gignac, *Grammar* i 156. Add especially SB VI 9421. 10-11 ἐξύβριϲεν ἡμᾶϲ ῥητοῖϲ τε καὶ ἀρήτοιϲ. Cf. διαραγῆναι (13).

13 διαραγῆναι = διαρραγῆναι. Cf. 12 n. and P. Lips. 37. 19 ἐ]ϲθῆτα διαρ[ή]ξαντεϲ.

προϲενεγκτιϲῶν = προϲενεχθειϲῶν. The gamma was probably added on the analogy of ἐνεγκεῖν, and it implies προϲενεγχθειϲῶν as the 'correct' form. This type of formation is said to be found almost only in the third century BC, see Mayser-Schmoll, *Grammatik* i 1. 167.

14 It seems likely that we should envisage restoring τ]ὴν αὐτὴν ϲυμβίῳ, which must be corrected either to τῇ{ν} αὐτῇ{ν} ϲυμβίῳ or to τὴν αὐτὴν ϲύμβιω⟨ν⟩ = ϲύμβιον, both of which would suit the prevailing phonetic uncertainty about nasals. Before that the succession of letters -νπλω- is very intractable.

15 The gold was perhaps stolen by the assailant.

17–18 It is clear from ἐπιϲταλῖϲαν (= -λεῖϲαν) that the preceding letters are to be articulated as μέαν = μαῖαν, cf. e.g. I **52** 6, VI **896** 26 in which δημόϲιοι ἰατροί use this term to refer to their instructions to perform a medical inspection. Cf. also P. Lips. 42, a medical report which had been requested by a petitioner and was submitted by a δημόϲιοϲ ἰατρόϲ to a νυκτοϲτράτηγοϲ. All this suggests the possibility that we should here restore τὴν δημοϲία]ν μέαν, but a mere possibility is what it remains at the moment. The latest study of this subject is D. W. Amundsen and G. B. Ferngren, 'The Forensic Role of Physicians in Ptolemaic and Roman Egypt', in the Johns Hopkins Hospital's *Bulletin of the History of Medicine* 52 (1978) 336–53.

The only other reference to a μαῖα in the papyri is in a complicated and damaged document republished and elucidated by Wilcken in *Archiv* 3 (1906) 369–79, cf *ZPE* 47 (1982) 255–8. This part of the papyrus (ii 1–9) refers to an *inspectio ventris*, a medical examination to confirm the pregnancy of a woman recently widowed, see ibid. 371, 373–5. In this case too the wife may have been pregnant. A midwife would not necessarily have been sent just because the patient was a woman, as we can see from extant reports by male doctors on a slave girl (P. Osl. III 95) and on the daughter of a free man (I **52**). If the wife was pregnant, the fact may well have been specified in one of the places now damaged, cf. P. Ryl. II 68. 13–14, SB X 10239. 14–15.

Another term meaning midwife has turned up once in a private letter, XII **1586** 12, ἡ ἰατρίνη ϲε ἀϲπάζεται, and it is possible that **3642** 16 also refers to a midwife, see n.

19 ⟨καί⟩. Obviously something has been left out. Other stopgaps could be thought of, e.g. ὥϲτε or πρὸϲ τό.

21–2 On εἰ with the optative see B. Mandilaras, *The Verb* 283–5, esp. §649. (6).

24 In *AÉ* 1927, no. 165, an inscription of 337–40, a Ti. Flavius Laetus, *vir clarissimus* and *comes*, cf. *PLRE* i 492 (Laetus 1), is recorded as having restored the circus at Emerita in Lusitania. Also mentioned on the stone is the *praeses* of Lusitania, a *vir perfectissimus*, from which we may probably deduce that Laetus was a prominent native of the town or province. Our prefect of Egypt was a *vir perfectissimus* in 326 and it is perfectly conceivable that he could have acquired the clarissimate and the title of *comes* by 337–40. If it could be proved that the two documents relate to the same man it would be interesting to have another undisputed Westerner as prefect of Egypt. Unfortunately the individual elements of the name are common, so the most that can be claimed is that there is a strong likelihood of identity.

3621. Nomination of Village Liturgists

50 4B.23/K(2)a   14.5 × 24.5 cm   10 May 329

Addressed to the *praepositus* of the third *pagus* by the *tesserarius* and comarchs of the village of Seneceleu, this document nominates collectors for taxes in kind, two each for grain (sitologi), meat, chaff, and clothing, cf. J. Lallemand, *L'Administration civile* 207–10, with 134–7 for village administration in general. It confirms the early start of the indiction in this period as recently established by R. S. Bagnall and K. A. Worp, *The Chronological Systems of Byzantine Egypt* 9–16, see 9n.

The back is blank.

       ὑπατείας τῶν δεσποτῶν ἡμῶν Κωνσταντίνου
         Αὐγούστου τὸ η⁻ καὶ Κωνσταντίνου
           τοῦ ἐπιφανε[σ]τάτου Καίσαρος τὸ δ.
         Αὐρηλίῳ Πλουτίωνι πραι(ποσίτῳ) γ⁻ πάγου
5   παρὰ Αὐρηλίων Πε'τ'τίριος Παελαίνους τεσσα-
       λαρίου καὶ Παυςᾶ Βηςᾶτος καὶ Πανεχώτου
       Ἡρακλέου κωμαρχ(ῶν) κώμης Cενεκελεῦ γ⁻ πάγο[υ.
       δίδομεν τῷ ἰδίῳ ἡμῶν κι⟨ν⟩δύνῳ εἰς τὰς παρακι-
       μένας χρίας τῆς εὐτυχούςης γ⁻ ἰνδικ(τίωνος)
10   τοὺς ὑπογεγραμμένου⟨ς⟩ ὄντας εὐπόρους καὶ
       ἐπιτηδίους πρὸς τὴν χρίαν. εἰςὶ δὲ
       Αὐρήλιοι   (vac.)
       σ]ιτολόγος   ἐπὶ ἀχύρου
       Παυςῖρις Παμμάχου   Ἀτρῆς Ἀμμωνίου
15   Κλᾶρος Πανεχώτου   Παυςᾶς Παταύριος
       ἐπὶ κρέως   ἐπὶ στιχ(αρίων) καὶ παλ(λίων)
       Παπνοῦθις Μοΰιτος   Παελένης Ἀμοϊτᾶ
       Ἀτρῆς Cιλβανοῦ   Ἀτρῆς Τάχιος
       οἱ πάντες ἀπὸ τῆς αὐτῆς κώμης.
20   ὑπατείας τῆς προκ(ειμένης), Παχὼν ιε.
(m. 2)   Αὐρ(ήλιοι) Πετσεῖρις τεσσαλάριος καὶ Παυςᾶς καὶ Πανεχώτης
       οἱ π]ρ[ογεγραμμένοι ἐπιδ]ε̣δώκαμεν. Αὐρ(ήλιος) Ἰςίων Ἡρᾶτος
       ἔγρ(αψα) ὑ(πὲρ) αὐτῶν μὴ [εἰ(δότων) γράμ(ματα).] (vac.)

4 *Πλουτίωνι*: final ι over οσ; πραι)   5 l. *Παελένους*   7 κωμαρχ   8 ϊδιω
8–9 l. *παρακειμένας χρείας*   9 ινδικ   11 l. *ἐπιτηδείους, χρείαν*   16 στιχ, παλ)
20 προκ   21 αυρ'πετ'ςειρις   22 αυρ'   23 εγρ∫υ)

'In the consulship of our masters Constantine Augustus for the 8th time and Constantine the most noble Caesar for the 4th time.

'To Aurelius Plution *praepositus* of the 3rd *pagus*, from Aurelius Pettiris son of Pahelenes, *tesserarius*, and from Aurelius Paysas son of Besas and Aurelius Panechotes son of Heracles, comarchs of the village of Seneceleu of the 3rd *pagus*. We present at our own personal risk for the specified services of the auspicious 3rd indiction the undermentioned persons, who are financially sound and fit for the service. Viz. Aurelii,

'Sitologus:

Paysiris son of Pammachus

Clarus son of Panechotes

'In charge of meat:

Papnuthis son of Muis

Hatres son of Silvanus

'In charge of chaff:

Hatres son of Ammonius

Paysas son of Patayris

'In charge of tunics and cloaks:

Pahelenes son of Amoitas

Hatres son of Tachis

—all from the same village.

'In the aforesaid consulship, Pachon 15.'

(2nd hand) 'We, Aurelius Petsiris, *tesserarius*, and Aurelius Paysas and Aurelius Panechotes, the aforesaid, have submitted (the document). I, Aurelius Ision son of Heras, wrote on their behalf because they do not know letters.'

4 Aurelius Plution has not been identified with any other bearer of that common name. On the position of *praepositus* see J. Lallemand, *L'Administration civile* 131-4.

5 *Πε᾽τ τίριος*. The amanuensis called him *Πετςεῖρις* (21). Both names existed, and it is uncertain which writer was mistaken.

5-6 *τεccαλαρίου = τεccεραρίου*. On the spelling see P. Got. 6. 7 n. On the office see R. P. Coleman-Norton, *Studies in Roman Economic and Social History* 322-35. N. Lewis, *The Compulsory Services of Roman Egypt* 49, s.v. *τεccεράριος*, gives the span of its known existence as 307/8-24, but PSI X 1106 and 1107 refer to one in 336. A variety of duties is attested and the basic sense is not clear. The Greek–Latin glossaries gloss *tesserarius* with *γραμματεύς* (*CGL* ii 264. 53; iii 28. 5; 298. 27; 352. 51; 395. 38; 420. 18; 512. 9). Two of these references are in alphabetical lists (ii 264. 53; iii 512. 9); the rest have a military context, cf. Plut. *Galb.* 24, *ὁ μὲν ὀπτίων, ὁ δὲ τεccεράριος. οὕτω γὰρ καλοῦνται οἱ διαγγέλων καὶ διοπτήρων ὑπηρεςίας τελοῦντες*. In Egyptian villages illiterates held the post, as here, but the *tesserarius* may have been the later equivalent of the village scribe. See P. Petaus introd. p. 21 and H. C. Youtie, *CÉ* 41 (1966) 127-43, esp. 137 for the minimal standards of the literacy which was legally required for that office.

7 *κωμαρχ(ῶν)*. See H. E. L. Missler, *Der Komarch*, with *ZPE* 19 (1975) 113-15.

Cενεκελεὺ γ¯ πάγο[υ. The *pagus* of Seneceleu was not previously known, see P. Pruneti, *I centri abitati* 164. It had been in the Western toparchy, see e.g. X 1265 80, XIV 1659 36. This agrees with what is known about the relation of the toparchies to the *pagi*, cf. XII 1425 4 n.

9 *γ¯ ἰνδικ(τίωνος)*. Indiction 3 = 329/30. At this period the indiction began early in Pachon, see R. S. Bagnall and K. A. Worp, *The Chronological Systems of Byzantine Egypt* 9-16. These liturgists are to begin work immediately, as is fairly evident for the collectors of chaff and wheat, since the harvest was imminent, if not begun. The early beginning of the indiction in connection with meat is proved already by XXXI 2571, see Bagnall–Worp, op. cit. 9.

3622. Contract of a Systates

42 5B.75/E(2–5)a   19 × 12 cm   29 August 356

This and the following item give us two more dates which extend to about thirty years the long career as systates of Aurelius Muses son of Theon, known previously from VIII **1116** (363/4), PSI X 1108 (381/2), and XXXIV **2715** (386/7). Together with the accumulating evidence for the collegiate activity of the systatae, see XLVI **3301**, XLIII **3137** introd., this suggests that the post was a permanent one, not involving reappointment at intervals as previously thought, see XXXIV **2715** introd.

By analogy with the third-century system, described in XLIII **3095–8** introd., we should expect to find at any one time a fixed number of tribes providing public servants in a fixed rotation. We should expect the systates to be busiest in the years his tribe was providing liturgists and to be employed in the intervening years with liturgical liabilities dragging on beyond the proper year and with matters of taxation and registration of persons. In **3622** the tribe is actually said to be 'now providing public servants' (5) in 356/7. All the other documents are nominations to liturgies and name the same tribe, implying that it was serving in the years mentioned. We ought, therefore, to be able to construct a table of the tribe's years of service. Unfortunately the intervals are incompatible with any simple rotatory system that I can discover. It is possible, however, that the number of tribes changed more than once over this period, as they did in the third century. No other systates is known over the thirty-year period of the activity of Muses.

After ten lines the text breaks off, leaving just enough to show the contract would have been a parallel to the badly damaged *W. Chr.* 405 (= P. Flor. I 39), re-edited in *CÉ* 46 (1971) 146–9. The systates would have acknowledged that satisfactory arrangements had been made to carry out the public duty allocated by him to the other party, see ibid.

The back of the sheet is blank, so far as it is preserved.

ὑπατείας [τῶν δεσποτ]ῶν ἡμῶν Κων[στα]ντίου αἰωνίου Αὐγούστου
τὸ η″ καὶ Ἰο[υλιανοῦ] τοῦ ἀνδριοτάτου καὶ ἐπιφανεστάτου Καίσαρος τὸ α,
     (vac.)   Θὼθ α.   (vac.)
Αὐρήλιος Μουσῆς Θέων[ο]ς ἀπὸ τῆς λαμ(πρᾶς) καὶ λαμ(προτάτης)
5   Ὀξυρυγχιτῶν πόλεως συστάτης τῆς νυνεὶ λιτουργούσης
    φυλῆς Δρόμ[ο]υ Γυμνασίου καὶ ἄλλων ἀμφόδων
    Αὐρηλίῳ Π. [. . .] . . [.] Σιλβανῷ ἀπὸ τῆς αὐτῆς πόλεως τῆς
    αὐτῆς φυλῆ[ς χ]αίρειν. ὁμολογῶ συνηλλαχέναι σοι
    τ[ὴ]ν ἐ[γχειρισθεῖcά]ν cο[ι ἐ]νιαύ[cιο]ν λιτουρ[γ]ίαν τῶν
10   c. 30 letters   ] . . . [. .] . . [c. 8

   ·   ·   ·   ·

1 ὑπατειας   2 ϊο[υλιανου]; l. ἀνδρειοτάτου   4 λαμ ς″, λαμ ς″   5 l. νυνὶ λειτουργούσης
7 l. Σιλβανοῦ?   9 l. λειτουργίαν

'In the consulship of our masters Constantius, eternal Augustus, for the 8th time, and Julian, the most valiant and noble Caesar, for the 1st time, Thoth 1.

'Aurelius Muses son of Theon from the glorious and most glorious city of the Oxyrhynchites, systates of the tribe of Gymnasium Street and other districts, now providing public servants, to Aurelius . . . son of Silvanus (?), greetings. I acknowledge that I have contracted with you for the year-long public service entrusted to you . . .'

1–2 The same unusual formula with both ἀνδρειότατος (= *fortissimus*) and ἐπιφανέστατος (= *nobilissimus*) appears in PSI IX 1078 of 25 November 356, which is the only other consular formula of this year quoted from the papyri in R. S. Bagnall and K. A. Worp, *Chronological Systems* 112.

7 The traces, though fairly scanty, do not favour τῷ καὶ Cιλβανῷ, and in this official context a patronymic is expected. Probably, therefore, Cιλβανοῦ was intended. The name Ptolemaeus son of Silvanus occurs in XLV 3249 9 (AD 326) and L 3578 3, 7, 10 (AD 342). Here Πτ[seems suitable, but the space is short for Πτολεμαίῳ and the later traces are also hard to reconcile with it.

9 Cf. W. *Chr.* 405. 6 τὴν ἐνχιρισςτιςάν cοι ὑπ' ἐμοῦ κ. [. . . . .] λιτουργίαν, PSI I 86. 10–11 τὴν ἐνι[α]ύσιον δημοτικὴν λειτουργίαν.

3623. NOMINATION TO A PUBLIC SERVICE

31 4B.13/A(2–4)a   11.5 × 9 cm   359

The addressee is a new logistes, see 2 n., and the nomination is submitted by the systates Aurelius Muses, whose long career is discussed in **3622** introd.

For the little that is known about the government packet-boats on the Nile, upon which the nominee was to serve, see P. Beatty Panop. 1. 60, 252; 2. 275 and notes, with XXXIII **2675**. Add J. Shelton, *BASP* 7 (1970) 9–19.

The document breaks off after nine lines and is blank on the back.

ὑπατείας Φλ(αουΐων) Εὐ]ϲεβίου καὶ Ὑπατίου τῶν λ[αμ(προτάτων)
. . . . . .]ῳ Ἀπ[ο]λλωνίῳ τῷ καὶ Θεοδούλῳ
(vac.)   λογιϲτῇ Ὀξυρυγχίτου   (vac.)
παρὰ Αὐρηλίου Μουϲῆ Θέωνοϲ ἀπὸ τῆϲ
5   αὐτῆϲ πόλεωϲ ϲυϲτάτηϲ φυλῆϲ Δρόμου
Γυμναϲίου καὶ ἄλλων ἀμφόδων. δίδωμι
καὶ εἰϲαγγέλλω ἰδίῳ μου κινδύνῳ
εἰϲ χώραν ἁλιαδίτην ἤτοι γραμ-
ματη]φ[όρο]ν τ[ο]ῦ ὀξέου δρόμου ἐφ' ἐνιαυτό(ν)

.   .   .   .   .

5 l. ϲυϲτάτου   7 ειϲαγ'γελλω, ΐδιω   8 l. ἁλιαδίτου   9 l. ὀξέοϲ; εφενιαυτο̄; l. ἐπ' ἐνιαυτόν

'In the consulship of Flavius Eusebius and Flavius Hypatius, *viri clarissimi*.

'To Flavius (?) Apollonius alias Theodulus logistes of the Oxyrhynchite nome, from Aurelius Muses son of Theon from the same city, systates of the tribe of Gymnasium Street and other districts. I present and introduce at my own personal risk to the position of sailor otherwise letter-carrier of the *cursus velox* for (one) year . . .'.

1 Lack of space forbids the restoration of μετὰ τὴν ὑπατείαν. It seems unlikely that there would have been room for month and day at the end of the line. Probably there was a line near the foot with ὑπατείας τῆς προκειμένης, vel sim., plus month and day, cf. the parallel nomination XXXIII **2675** 20. There the day is Tybi 20 = 15 January 318, which, as the note observes, is a late date for a liturgy supposed to run from 29 August 317 to 28 August 318 (ll. 11–13). The other nomination to the same liturgy, PSI X 1108, is dated Thoth 1 = 29 August 381, see BL VI 184. The divergence make it impossible to say for certain whether this document should be assigned to the Egyptian year 359/360 or to 358/9, but obviously the normal date would be close to Thoth 1 for the incoming year. In that case the ideal date would be 30 August 359, for the year 359/360.

2 Restore probably Φλαουΐ]ῳ, but cf. XLVI **3306** 1 n., **3308-11** introd., for the possibility of Αὐρηλί]ῳ. The logistes is new, i.e. not in the latest list in *BASP* 13 (1976) 38–40.

4 Μουσῆ. So also in VIII **1116** 4; Μουσέως in PSI X 1108. 4; XXXIV **2715** 4. The nominative Μουσῆς appears in **3622** 4. For the short genitive cf. XLIII **3102** 5 n., XLIV **3169** 181 n.

8 ἁλιαδίτην (l. ἁλιαδίτου). PSI X 1108. 8–9 has εἰς χώραν ἁλιαδί[τ]ου ἤτοι γραμματηφ[όρου]|⁹ τοῦ ὀξέου δρόμου; cf. W. *Chr.* 405. 6–7.

9 ὀξέου (l. ὀξέος). The same spelling occurs in PSI X 1108. 9, see previous note.

ἐφ'ἐνιαυτό(ν). For the false aspiration cf. F. T. Gignac, *Grammar* i 135. The next word was no doubt ἕνα, cf. e.g. VIII **1116** 12.

3624-3626. DECLARATIONS OF PRICES

40 5B.110/B(5-6)a   19 × 21 cm   25 January 359

Parallels to these sworn declarations of commodity prices by Oxyrhynchite guilds are contained in I **85** = Sel. Pap. II 332 (AD 338; revised by R. A. Coles, *ZPE* 39 (1980) 115–23), XXXI **3570** (329), PSI III 202 (s.d.), cf. *ZPE* 39 (1980) 124–5, and P. Harris I 73 (s.d.; revised by R. A. Coles, *ZPE* 37 (1980) 229–39). The format of all these varies only in minor matters of wording and layout. A similar declaration is made in P. Ant. I 38, but it is not surprising that its format is rather different, since it comes from Antinoopolis and is of an earlier date, 12 April 300, see SB X 10257.

The Oxyrhynchite declarations are dated on the last day of the month, wherever the day is verifiable. In P. Ant. 38 the day is Pharmuthi 17, which may be due to the early date or the different provenance.

In all the certain cases the substance is the raw material of the guild concerned, e.g. here silver for silversmiths (**3624**), wheat for bakers (**3625**), cf. R. A. Coles, *ZPE* 37 (1980) 229–30. A possible exception may be found in PSI 202 col. i, where the price of pork is probably declared by pork-butchers (χοιρομαχείρων, 3–4 ed. pr., χοιρομαγίρων R. A. Coles, *ZPE* 39 (1980) 125). Here, however, weavers of Tarsian linen (ταρσικάριοι) were apparently supposed to declare the prices of types of garment woven by themselves, see **3626** 17–30. The wording of the declaration, προσφωνοῦμεν . . . τὴν ἑξῆς ἐγγεγραμμένην τιμὴν ὧν χειρίζομεν ὠνίων εἶναι ἐπὶ τοῦδε τοῦ μηνός, 'we report that the price entered below for the saleable goods which we handle has been in force during this month', could apply whether the price was that of the raw material or the finished product of the guild. Diocletian's schedule of controlled prices covers both types of product, as well as some rates of pay and transport charges. However, in all the certain cases the representative of the guild declares under oath the price its members have paid for the raw material of their craft during the expiring month. Note that there is no allusion to the guilds' stocks of raw materials, as stated in I **85** introd., cf. T. Reil, *Beiträge zur Kenntnis des Gewerbes* 190, 194. In XXXI **2570** introd. it is correctly observed that it is a price which is reported, cf. P. Ant. I 38 introd., Sel. Pap. II 332, but the price is defined further as the price 'of the goods in stock', which is not stated in the texts. Very possibly some of the materials bought in the course of a month remained on hand at the end of it, but this is not mentioned in the declarations and does not appear to be relevant to them.

It may be that these documents are connected with the rapid inflation well attested for the fourth century, but it is not easy to envisage exactly what purpose they served. Since the prices are not entered in **3626**, cf. R. A. Coles, *ZPE* 39 (1980) 115, it appears that the declarations were supposed to be genuine reports of observed fact and not, for instance, statements of conformity with prices fixed in advance, though we are reduced to guessing whether the stated price is the average for the month or the highest price reached during it. Perhaps the government intended to use the information to control prices from time to time, see A. H. M. Jones, *LRE* ii 859, but a different hypothesis is suggested by the frequent references in the law-codes to market prices as the standard by which payments of *annona* to soldiers or officials were to be commuted into money (e.g. *C. Theod.* vii 4. 10), and also as the standard by which goods required by the government were to be bought from the provincials (*C. Theod.* xi 15. 2), cf. J. Karayannopulos, *Finanzwesen* 104, 219–20, A. H. M. Jones, *LRE* i 461, 630. These obviously imply an official mechanism for ascertaining the local market prices, and it seems very likely that the papyrus declarations of prices are part of that mechanism. So far this type of document is confined to the fourth century, but the lists of commodity prices in **3628–33**, of the fifth century, may have been compiled from similar reports.

The papyrus also reveals the *nomen* of the senior consul of 358, Censorius Datianus, see **3624** 19 n.

The declarations are written on a fragment of a roll badly worn along the top edge and broken on the other three sides. The right-hand edge has broken along the line of a join, and another join is visible *c.* 15 cm to the left running down the middle of col. ii (**3624**). These joins, which are beginning to come apart, show a new phenomenon which has been described in E. G. Turner, *Recto and Verso* (Pap. Brux. 16), 20, with reference to this papyrus. The right-hand edges of the sheets lack vertical fibres for a width of *c.* 2.5 cm, the whole width of the rather irregular joins being *c.* 2.75 cm. Evidently a deliberate effort was made to reduce the bulk of the joins, which at their right-hand edges consist of only three layers instead of four. Experiment might reveal that this was a normal practice, since this particular roll gives no special impression of fine workmanship. No experiments have yet been conducted to separate original sheet joins, but observations by me and by Dr Coles since the date of the remarks in E. G. Turner, loc. cit., have confirmed that manufacturers' joins are often of this type, and no instance of a manufacturers' join with four layers of fibres has been detected.

Except for the sole surviving subscription in **3624** 22–5 all the writing appears to be in a single hand. We may conclude that the roll of declarations was written by a clerk in the logistes' office and that the guild representatives attended there to subscribe or have subscriptions written on their behalf. Probably the roll was prepared in advance. The prices appear to be in the chief hand, but it seems likely that they were added at the same time as the corresponding subscription. Unfortunately the foot of **3626** is lost, so that we cannot see for certain that it lacked a subscription as well as prices. The name of the guild representative, though now illegible, did stand in **3626** 5. In other uncompleted declarations gaps were also left for the names, see *ZPE* 39 (1980) 115. Presumably in this case the clerk felt justified in guessing that the representative would be the same once again.

The remains of col. i are in no case more than a portion of the final letter of a line. On the back there are some scattered traces of ink, most of them clearly offsets, though some on the back of col. iv (**3626**) might just possibly belong to an endorsement.

3624

ii

```
        Φλ . . . . . . . . . [
        λογιϲτῇ Ὀξυρυγχείτου
        πα]ρὰ τοῦ κοινοῦ τῶν
        ἀργ]υροκόπων τῆϲ
  5     αὐ]τῆϲ πόλεωϲ
            δι(ὰ) Διοϲκόρου.
        προϲφωνοῦμε[ν]
        ἰδίῳ τιμήματι τ[ὴν]
        ἑξῆϲ ἐνγεγραμ[μέ-]
  10    νην τιμὴν ὧν χι-
        ρίζομεν ὠνίων
        εἶναι ἐπὶ τοῦδε τοῦ μη-
        νὸϲ καὶ ὀμν[ύομε]ν
        τὸν θεῖον ὅρκ[ον]
  15    μηδὲν διεψεῦϲθαι.
            ἔϲτι δέ.
            (vac.)
```

6 δι΄   9–11 l. ἐγγεγραμμένην . . . χειρίζομεν

ἀϲήμου λί(τραϲ) α (δην. μυρ.) ϛω.

   (vac.)

μετὰ τὴν ὑπατείαν

Κηνϲωρίου Δατιανοῦ

20   πατρικίου καὶ Νηρετίου

Κερ]εαλίου τ[ῶ]ν̣ λαμ(προτάτων) Τῦβι λ.

(m. 2)   Αὐρήλιοϲ Διόϲκοροϲ

προϲφω]νῶ ὡϲ πρόκειται.

Αὐρ(ήλιοϲ) Μ]έ̣λαϲ ἔγρ[α]ψ[α

. . . . . .]. γρα[. . . . . .

· · · · · · ·

17 λα×∩ ϛω   20 l. Νηρατίου   21 λαμϛ   23 l. πρόκειται

'To Flavius . . ., logistes of the Oxyrhynchite nome, from the guild of silversmiths of the same city, by agency of Dioscorus.

'We report at our own financial risk that the price entered below for the saleable goods which we handle has been in force during this month and we swear the divine oath that we have made no false statement.

'Viz: For one pound of silver, 68,000,000 denarii.'

'After the consulship of Censorius Datianus, *patricius*, and Neratius Cerealis, *viri clarissimi*, Tybi 30.'

(2nd hand) 'I, Aurelius Dioscorus, report as aforesaid. I, Aurelius Melas, wrote on his behalf because he does not know letters.'

1 The fibres along the top edge are very much frayed and distorted, but the level ends of many of the vertical fibres seem to show that the original edge is partly preserved. If so, the name of the logistes occupied only one short line and this is not sufficient to accommodate the name of the known logistes of later 359, Apollonius alias Theodulus, see **3623**, even though the *nomen* was probably abbreviated to Φλ( ). The latest list of logistae (*BASP* 13 (1976) 38–40) contains no names near enough to 359 to be candidates.

The *nomen* is likely to have been Flavius, see *ZPE* 11 (1973) 49, and the traces favour Φλ´ = Φλ(αουΐῳ). Aurelius is also theoretically possible, see XLVI **3306** 1 n., **3308–11** introd., but it is not likely in this case.

8 For the meaning of ἰδίῳ τιμήματι see XLIII **3105** 4 n.

17 The sign denoting thousands is here an oblique stroke running up to the figure from below on the left. Cf. P. Ryl. IV p. 162 n. 3.

The price is an addition to our meagre information about the price of silver bullion, viz:

Dioclet., *Edict. de pret.* 28. 9 (Giacchero)	6,000 den.	301
SB VI 9253	8,000 den.	s.d.
PSI IV 310	8,328 den.	11.8.306
3624	68,000,000 den.	25.1.359
3629	190,000,000 den.	fifth cent.
3629	192,500,000 den.	fifth cent.
3628, 3630, 3631, 3633	195,000,000 den.	fifth cent.
3628, 3632	200,000,000 den.	fifth cent.

19 Κηνϲωρίου Δατιανοῦ. Cf. *PLRE* i 243–4, O. Seeck, *Die Briefe des Libanius* 113–17. His *nomen*, also in **3625** 18, was not known.

20 πατρικίου. See T. D. Barnes, *Phoenix* 29 (Toronto, 1975) 169, 'Constantine converted the patriciate from an inheritable status to a rank bestowed upon an individual for his lifetime alone (Zosimus 2. 40. 2)'. According to the same author, ibid., Datianus was hitherto first attested as *patricius* on 18 January 360 (*C. Theod.* xi 1. 1), so that this document of 25 January 359 is now the earliest evidence.

25 Various versions of the clause certifying the illiteracy of the principal might be restored, e.g. υ) (= ὑπὲρ) αὐτο]ῦ γρά[μματα μὴ εἰδότος, or ὑπὲρ α].´ (= αὐτοῦ) γρ. μὴ εἰδ., or υ) (= ὑπὲρ) αὐτοῦ] ἀγρα[μμάτου ὄντος.

3625

iii

Φλ . . . . [. . . .] . . . . .
λογιϲτῇ ['Ο]ξ[υ]ρ[υ]γχείτ[ο]υ
παρὰ τοῦ κοινοῦ τῶν
ἀρτοκόπων τῆϲ αὐ-
5   τῆϲ πόλεωϲ
     δι(ὰ) Λεοντίου.
προϲφωνο[ῦ]μεν ἰδ[ί-]
ῳ τιμήματι τὴν ἑξῆϲ
ἐνγεγραμμένην τι-
10   μὴν ὧν χιρίζομεν
ὠνίων εἶναι ἐπὶ τοῦ-
δε τοῦ μηνὸϲ καὶ ὀμνύο-
μεν τὸν θεῖον ὅρκον
μηδὲν διεψεῦϲθαι.
15   ἔϲτι δέ.
ϲίτου (ἀρτάβηϲ) α (δην. μυρ.) ϲ . ϛ .
     (vac.)
μετὰ τὴν ὑπατείαν
Κηνϲωρίου Δατιανοῦ
πατρικίου καὶ Νηρετίου
20   Κερεαλίου τῶν λαμ(προτάτων)
     Τῦβι λ.

· · · · · ·

6 δι´   9 l. ἐγγεγραμμένην   10 l. χειρίζομεν   16 ⨪α⤬∩   19 l. Νηρατίου
20 λαμϛ

'To Flavius . . ., logistes of the Oxyrhynchite nome, from the guild of bakers of the same city, by agency of Leontius.

'We report at our own financial risk that the price entered below for the saleable goods which we handle has been in force during this month and we swear the divine oath that we have made no false statement.

'Viz.: For one artaba of wheat, 2,050,000 (?) denarii.

'After the consulship of Censorius Datianus, *patricius*, and Neratius Cerealis, *viri clarissimi*, Tybi 30.'

4 ἀρτοκόπων. Cf. I **85** introd. The document mentioned there is the equivalent declaration for 26 November 338, and has now been published by R. A. Coles, *ZPE* 39 (1980) 118.

16 ϲ. ϝ. The second figure is blotted and has probably been altered or even cancelled. The last is probably epsilon = 5, just possibly alpha = 1. In **3628–33**, of the fifth century, the prices of wheat range from 240 to 500 myriads of denarii at this period of the year in different areas of Middle Egypt. The Oxyrhynchite figure is den. myr. 316⅔ (12 art. per solidus of den. myr. 3,800), so that the figure here ought to be below that. We might possibly read ϲ⟦. ⟧ϝ (205), or, if the middle figure is corrected rather than cancelled, ϲιϝ (215), or ϲκϝ (225), or ϲλϝ (235). Higher numbers, μ, ν, ξ, ο, π, ϙ (40–90), seem not to be compatible with the remains in second place.

It is worth noting that the inflation of the official price of wheat in the interval between **3625** and **3628–33** is proportionately very much less than that of the price of silver bullion, see **3624** 17 n. One guess at the reason might be that the government controlled the price of wheat to avoid discontent, but the variations attested by **3628–33** speak rather against that idea, and we should probably look for economic causes.

A difference is also to be observed in the relations between the prices of wheat and barley. In 338 (I **85** introd., *ZPE* 39 (1980) 115–23) wheat cost 24 talents (36,000 den.) per artaba, barley 13⅓ talents (20,000 den.), while at the date of **3628–33** wheat cost 240–500 myriads of denarii, barley 225–400 myriads. The gap between wheat and barley diminished greatly. This case too might suggest that the price of wheat was controlled, but a diminution in the supply of barley, for example, might have produced the same effect in the figures.

3626

iv

Φλ . . . . [

λογιστῇ [Ὀξυρυγχίτου

παρὰ τοῦ κοινοῦ τῶν

ταρcικαρίων τῆc αὐτῆc

5   πόλεωc

        δι(ὰ) . . . . ·

προcφωνοῦμεν

ἰδίῳ τιμήματι τὴν

ἑξῆc. ἐνγεγραμμέ-

10 νην τιμὴν ὧν χι-

ρίζομεν ὠνίων εἶναι

ἐπὶ τοῦδε τοῦ μηνὸc καὶ

ὀμνύομεν τὸν θεῖον

ὅρκον μηδὲν διεψεῦ-

15 cθαι. ἔcτι δέ.

ὀθόνηc παντοί(αc) τοῦ τετρα-

λάccου. δαλμ⟨ατ⟩ικ(ῶν) γυναικ(είων) ταρcικ(ῶν)

μεγάλο(υ) μέτρ(ου) α΄ εἰδ(έαc) (δην. μυρ.) (vac.)

β εἰδέαc (δην. μυρ.) (vac.)

20 γ εἰδέαc (δην. μυρ.) (vac.)

ἀναβολ( ) ὁμοί(ωc) α εἰδ(έαc) (δην. μυρ.) (vac.)

β εἰδέαc (δην. μυρ.) (vac.)

γ εἰδέαc (δην. μυρ.) (vac.)

cτιχ( ) ὁμοί(ωc) α εἰδ(έαc) (δην. μυρ.) (vac.)

25 β εἰδέαc (δην. μυρ.) (vac.)

γ εἰδέαc (δην. μυρ.) (vac.)

φακιαλ(ίων) ὁμοί(ωc)

α΄ εἰδέαc (δην. μυρ.) (vac.)

β[΄ εἰ]δέαc (δην. μυρ.) (vac.)

γ[΄ εἰδ]έαc (δην. [μυρ.)

. . . .

6 δι΄   9–11 l. ἐγγεγραμμένην . . . χειρίζομεν   16 παντοᶜ   17 δαλμιᴷγυναικᶴταρcιᴷ
18 μεγαλᵒμετρα΄εἶ⊁∩ l. ἰδέαc (so also 19–26, 28–30)   19 ⊁∩ (and so throughout)   21 αναβολ΄ομο·αεἶ
24 cτιχομο·αεἶ   27 φακιαλ΄ομο·

'To Flavius . . ., logistes of the Oxyrhynchite nome, from the guild of Tarsian weavers of the same city, by agency of . . .

'We report at our own financial risk that the price entered below for the saleable goods which we handle has been in force during this month and we swear the divine oath that we have made no false statement.

'Viz: For the quaternion of every category of linen:

'Ladies' Tarsian sleeved tunics, large size, 1st quality (blank) myriads of denarii, 2nd quality (blank) myriads of denarii, 3rd quality (blank) myriads of denarii.

'Shawls likewise, 1st quality (blank) myriads of denarii, 2nd quality (blank) myriads of denarii, 3rd quality (blank) myriads of denarii.

'Tunics likewise, 1st quality (blank) myriads of denarii, 2nd quality (blank) myriads of denarii, 3rd quality (blank) myriads of denarii.

'Facecloths likewise, 1st quality (blank) myriads of denarii, 2nd quality (blank) myriads of denarii, 3rd quality (blank) myriads of denarii. . . .'

4 ταρcικαρίων. For bibliography see S. Lauffer, *Diokletians Preisedikt* 274, citing especially J. P. Wild, 'The *tarsikarios*, a Roman Linen-Weaver in Egypt', in *Hommages à M. Renard* ii 810–19. The nature of Tarsian woven goods is still not known. The yarn used was already identified as Tarsian, see P. Lips. 89, where λίνον λευκὸν ταρcικόν should mean 'white linen Tarsian yarn', because it is measured in λίτραι. The loom was also specialized, see the ἱcτὸc ταρcοϋφικόc in XIV **1705**. Wild suggests that it was a warp-weighted loom. In the price edict many linen goods are separated into five categories named after cities in or near Syria, namely Scythopolitan, Tarsian, Byblian, Laodicean, and Tarsico-Alexandrian. The order is invariable and the prices are in descending order. Each category may be divided into three qualities, as here. Presumably the last category was an Alexandrian imitation of Tarsian goods and judged inferior to the original. The goods meant here will probably have been equivalent or inferior to the edict's Tarsico-Alexandrian category.

16–17 ὀθόνηc παντοί(αc) τοῦ τετραλάccου, 'for the quaternion of every category of linen cloth'. The prices—unfortunately never entered—were to apply to a unit called the τετράλαccον, itself of unknown derivation, see S. Lauffer, *Diokletians Preisedikt* 277, 'unerklärt (Viererstück)'. Since Egypt exported a great deal of linen, it is just possible that the root is the Coptic word **Ⲗⲁⲥ**, 'flax'. Such a coinage, though it is hard to see the need for it, might have become widely enough known in some technical sense to have been employed in the price edict. I am indebted to Dr Colin Walters for drawing my attention to the Coptic word.

The Latin equivalent is *quaternio*, see M. Giacchero, *Edictum Diocletiani* §26. 257a–262, 266, 267, 268a–270, 271a–3, translated by the editor as 'un gruppo di quattro'. In the edict this unit of measurement appears in connection with two types of linen goods only, namely *sabana* (26. 257a–62) and *mantelia . . . sive mappae* (26. 266, 267, 268a–270, 271a–3), and some varieties even of these can be measured by the *tela* or ἱcτόc (*Sabana Gallica*, 254–6; *mantelia villosa Gallica sive mappae—formae primae*, 265–5a). The *tela* is the unit commonly applied to linen goods. In contrast, woollen and silk textile goods are priced by the item, see cap. 9 of the edict.

Surviving linen garments from Egypt were woven in one piece, the neck opening and sleeves being produced on the loom, so that the garment could be completed by two seams only, one along each side, either ending at the armholes, or, if there were sleeves, continuing from the armpit outwards along their lower edges, see L. M. Wilson, *The Clothing of the Ancient Romans* 55–6, and pl. xli, cf. H. Granger-Taylor, 'Weaving Clothes to Shape in the Ancient World', *Textile History* 13 (1982) 3–25, esp. 22. (I am grateful to Miss Gillian Eastwood of Manchester University for this last reference.) If the same was not usually true for silk and woollen garments, that might explain why the ἱcτόc is specified for linen goods only.

The word τετράλαccον has appeared only once before in the papyri, PSI VIII 971. 17–20, τετραλαccον λέντιόν μοι πέμψον ἱcχνὸν πρωτουφαγωτον (= πρωτοϋφαντον).

Compare also δίλαccον, which occurs in two papyri, BGU III 814. 23–5, ἡ μήτηρ Οὐαλερίου ἔπεμψε αὐτῷ ζεῦγοc ὑποζωνῶν καὶ . . . καὶ . . . καὶ δίλαccον καὶ διακοcίαc δραχμάc, and 816. 16–18, καὶ καταβένον (= καταβαίνων) δῦc (= δῇc for δόc) τὸ δίλα[c]ον (= δίλαccον) αὐτῷ̣ (= αὐτῷ) καὶ χιθῶνα (= χιτῶνα); 22, καὶ οὐκ ἔδωκέ μοι τὸ [δ]ίλαcον (= δίλαccον). If this were taken to mean 'pair', it would appear to be restricted to linen goods. Note the ζεῦγοc ὑποζωνῶν in BGU 814. 24.

A diminutive, διλάccιον, occurs in P. Heid. III 237. 9–11, ἐν οἷc ἦν ἱμάτιον . . . καὶ κερβικάριον . . . [κ]αὶ διλάccιο[ν καὶ] πλαίcιον.

Finally, in a bilingual text published by A. C. Dionisotti, *JRS* 72 (1982) 83–125, we find a boy who washes himself in the morning and then demands, δοc †πενταλαcον εγμαγιον (l. 11, p. 98) or *da sabanum extersorium*. In view of the edict and the papyri it looks as if πεντάλας⟨ς?⟩ον ἐγμαγεῖον is perfectly correct. Clearly the boy wants a towel and not a set of five of anything. The stem of these words may have come to denote a unit of square measure.

17 δαλμ⟨ατ⟩ικ(ῶν) γυναικ(είων). The edict's chapter on linen goods is arranged differently (Giacchero 26. 1–27. 5 = Lauffer 26. 1–28. 74, Supp. pp. 301–2, 303–4). It begins with στίχαι, cf. 24 below, not differentiated by sex, then follow dalmatics divided according to sex and quality, i.e. women's first class (5 categories), men's first class (5 categories), women's second class (5 categories), etc. Women's dalmatics were more expensive for the same quality than men's. Then come ἀναβολαῖα (78), followed by φακιάλια (99).

18 μεγάλο(υ) μέτρ(ου) appears to be the only plausible expansion of the abbreviations. Sizes are not given in the edict. The expression may suggest that women's dalmatics were longer than men's, which is perhaps also implied by the edict's higher prices for women's dalmatics and by the description of men's dalmatics as δαλματικῶν ἀνδρείων ἤτοι κολοβίων (26. 39, 49, etc.). This interpretation does not agree with that of Lauffer, who produces one authority to show that a dalmatic is a sleeved tunic (19. 9 n.), and another to show that a *colobium* is a long sleeveless tunic (26. 28–63 n.). However, ἤτοι should indicate that *colobium* is only another name for a man's dalmatic.

α′ (= πρώτης) εἰδ(έας). Here ἰδέα is the equivalent of *forma*/φόρμα, meaning 'quality', in the price edict, see R. A. Coles, *ZPE* 37 (1980) 235 n. 53.

21 ἀναβολ( ). The edict refers to ἀναβολαῖα, but this version has not yet appeared in the papyri, which have ἀναβολάδιον and ἀνάβολον as the names of garments. These are usually translated as 'cloaks', but may be rather narrow wraps like a Scotch plaid, see P. Beatty Panop. 2. 26 and n. Giacchero, *Edictum Diocletiani*, p. 296, translates it as 'scialli' = 'shawls', which I have copied.

24 στιχ( ). The form used in the price-edict is στίχη, which does not occur in the papyri, though they have στιχάριον frequently in the same sense.

3627. JUDICIAL PROCEEDINGS

49 5B.105/B(1)a,   69 × 25.5 cm   Late fourth century?
(2)a, and (3-4)a

At the end of this text judgement is delivered by a prefect with a name, Junius Olympus, which is the same as that of a man who served as *praeses Arabiae* in 262/3, see 8n. Probably about a hundred years separated them, but they may have been related in some way. The prefect is perhaps to be identified with the Olympus who served in 362-3.

A certain Asclepiades is accused of having taken possession wrongfully of a house belonging to the other party, apparently in distraint for debt. His adversary asks that Asclepiades should be compelled to attend an audit of accounts and to restore the house, or, if he refuses, that he should be brought to court. The prefect orders arbitrators to draw up an account, adding further conditional promises of satisfaction.

There is one puzzling feature. The form of the introduction of the judgement, Ἰούνιος Ὄλυμπος ὁ λαμπρό[τα]τος ἔπαρχος εἶπεν, leaves no reasonable doubt that Olympus was prefect of Egypt and that this section at least is from a report of court proceedings. However, the preceding section, with the address ἡγεμὼ[ν] κύριε (6) and with the closing formula καὶ διὰ παντὸς τ[ῇ ς]ῇ λαμπρότητι εὐχαριστήςω (7), has all the appearance of a petition. Moreover, ἡγεμών at this date should refer to a *praeses* and should not be addressed to the prefect of Egypt, see C. Vandersleyen, *La Chronologie des préfets* 100-1. Probably a petition to a *praeses* was cited in court before the prefect, because, if the penultimate section is a speech, ἡγεμὼ[ν] κύριε is addressed to a prefect and contradicts the conclusions of Vandersleyen. A more remote possibility is that the prefect's judgement is cited at the foot of the petition to a *praeses* which it is supposed to support. In that case, however, we would expect it to be preceded by some introductory formula.

There is a deep lower margin of *c.* 11 cm, above which are remains of nine very long lines, progressively more damaged as they are further from the foot. About twenty fragments and scraps in a fragile condition have remained unplaced; several are blank; none has enough legible letters to be worth printing. It is uncertain how much is lost. Possibly the entire text was contained in this one very wide column, of unknown height.

There is a pattern of seventeen vertical folds dividing the papyrus into eighteen panels, of decreasing width from left to right. The first panel on the left is *c.* 4.25 cm broad, the last on the right *c.* 2 cm. This pattern shows that the strip of roll bearing the text was pressed flat after being rolled up with the right edge inside, as usual.

There are four joins in the piece, roughly 6, 24, 42, and 60 cm from the left hand edge, that is, each sheet is close to 18 cm in width. The back is blank.

. . . . .

[*c.* 105 letters   ]. [. . .]. [. . . . . . .]. . .[. . . . .]. κε. .[. . . . .]

. . . .[. . . . .]. . . . .[. . . . . .]. . [.]. Ἀϲ[κλη]πιάδου πολιτευομένου

[*c.* 103 letters   ]ουτου πραγμ̣α̣τ[. . . . .]. αϲτίᾳ χρη[ϲ]άμενος [. . . . . . .

πε]ρὶ τὸ λογοθ[έϲ]ιον ἐποιει. . .[. . .]. . [. .]ται ὑπὸ πολλῆς ἀπανθρωπίας

φερόμενος

[*c.* 60 letters   ]. . . .[*c.* 40 letters   ]. . δροϲ διε̣.[. . . . .]. ω τὴν τοῦ λόγου

ϲύϲτ[αϲιν μετ]ὰ πίϲτεωϲ κ̇αὶ πάϲης ἀκρι[βεί]αϲ πρὸς αὐτὸν ϲυνάραϲθαι

πεποιθὼϲ ὡϲ οὐκ ἀν

[*c.* 35 letters   ]περ. . . .[. . . . .]. .[. . . . .]αρ αὐτοῦ ἀλλ. .[. . . . .]

. . . .[. . . . . .]. [.]. [. . . . .]. . . . . .[. . . . .]. ομαι. [. . . . .]. [.].

προϲ. . . .[.]την. [. . . . . .]. ον ἐξουϲίαν προϲ[. . Π]τολεμαίου καὶ

Ἀμβροϲίου [τ]ῶν πολιτευο-

5   [μένων *c.* 25 letters   ]. [.]. . . μου καὶ α. [.]. η. . . . . . .[. . . .] καταναγκα-

ϲθῆ[ν]αι τὸν προειρ[η]μένον Ἀϲκληπ[ιάδην] ἐπὶ τὸ λο[γ]οθέϲιον

παρελθεῖν καὶ μετὰ π[άϲ]ης πίϲτεωϲ κ[αὶ] ϲυνειδήϲεωϲ τὸν λόγον πρός με

ϲυνάραϲθαι πρὸς τὸ ἔξω ἐπηρ`ε΄ίαϲ

μ. . . .[*c.* 15 letters   ]. [. .]. [.]. . .[. .] μοι τὸ ἀϲφαλὲϲ δ[ιὰ] τὴν ϲήν,

ἡγεμὼ[ν] κύριε, κηδεμονίαν, ἔτ⟦ε⟧ι γε μὴν διὰ τῆϲ αὐτῆ[ϲ] β[οη]θίαϲ ἣν

πρὸ ⟦ϲ⟧ δίκης καὶ [πρὸ]ϲ βίαν ἀφ`ε΄ίλετό [μ]ου οἰκίαν ἀπ[ο]κ̣α[τ]αϲτῆϲαί

μοι ἢ ἔτι καὶ νῦν ἀναιϲχυντοῦντα τοῦτον πέμπεϲθαι

εἰϲ τὸ μεγα[λεῖον τὸ ϲὸν] καὶ διὰ παντὸϲ τ[ῇ ϲ]ῇ λαμπρότητι εὐχαριϲτήϲω.

(vac.)

Ἰούνιοϲ Ὄλυμποϲ ὁ λαμπρό[τα]τοϲ ἔπαρχοϲ εἶπεν, ʽοἱ αἰτηθέντεϲ μεταξὺ τῶν

μερῶν τὸν λόγο[ν] θήϲονται καὶ τῶν ἐξ ἀληθείαϲ χρεωϲτουμένων

καταβαλλομένων περετέρω τοῦ δικαίου ὀφλήματος οὐκ ἐνοχληθήϲει, ἀλλ᾽

ἐπιγιγνώϲκων τὰ

ὁριζόμενα τῆϲ ἐν[ο]χῆϲ τοῦ χειριϲμοῦ τῶν πραγμάτων κατὰ νόμουϲ

ἐλευθερωθήϲει.᾽

6 l. βοηθείαϲ; ἀναιϲχυντοῦντα: αι corr. from ε   8 αἰτηθέντεϲ: αι corr. from ε; l. περαιτέρω; ἐνοχληθήϲει: ει corr. from ω; αλλ᾽

5 ff. ʽ. . . (I request) that the aforesaid Asclepiades be compelled to attend the audit and with all good faith and conscience help to make up the account relating to me, so that without ill-treatment . . . security for me, lord governor, on account of your solicitude, and further, that through the same succour (he be compelled)

to restore to me the house which he took away from me before judgement and by violence, or, if even now he shows no shame, that this person be sent up to your highness, and I shall be for ever grateful to your magnificence.'

'Junius Olympus, the most glorious prefect, said, "The invited persons shall hold a reckoning between the parties and, if the sums which are truly owed are being paid, you shall not be troubled beyond the just debt, but (rather), if you acquiesce in the rulings being given, you shall be released in accordance with law from the obligation to the inventory of property."'

1 πολιτευομένου. Cf. 4. On the title see H. Geremek, *Anagennesis* 1 (1981) 231–47. She concludes that it means 'of the curial class', while βουλευτής means '*decurio*, member of the council'. This is the best indication of the date of the document. The title προπολιτευόμενος makes its appearance in the late third century, see A. K. Bowman, *Town Councils* 155–8, but πολιτευόμενος does not occur regularly till very much later. The notable exception is in XX **2266** 18–19, where the prefect of 266–7 makes use of it in an edict which is too damaged to be fully understood. In XII **1501** the reading πολ( ) is doubtful and the document is only assigned to the late third century. It may be later. The earliest of the references collected in J. Lallemand, *L'Administration* 126–7 n. 4, is of 342, and this is a doubtful restoration which leaves the context unsatisfactorily obscure (P. Flor. I 34, with BL I 137). The earliest certain reference, apart from **2266**, dates from 366 (P. Lips. I 13). The term is particularly characteristic of the late fourth century, see Lallemand, loc. cit., though it certainly occurs later.

2 Read probably δυ]γαϲτίᾳ (= -είᾳ) χρη[ϲ]άμενος, 'using violence'.

λογοθ[έϲ]ιον. Cf. 5. The neuter form is not given an independent entry in *LSJ* and Suppl. S. Daris, *Spoglio* s.v., cites XVII **2187** (AD 304). 9, 12, 17, 19, [20], 22, 23, 31; P. Erl. 52 (AD 314). 30, 32, 72—see also the partial new edition in *ZPE* 28 (1978) 231–7; PSI VII 767 (AD 331?). 49.

3 Read perhaps] ἀνδρός. After this we may have ἔ]χω preceded by an adverb or an adverbial phrase with διά and the genitive. The sense appears to be, '(I am willing, *vel sim.*) to assist in the composition of the account relating to him with all good faith and accuracy, in the persuasion that . . . (would?) not . . .' At the end of the line ἄν may, or may not, be the right articulation.

6 ἡγεμὼ[ν] κύριε. See introd.

8 Ἰούνιος Ὄλυμπος ὁ λαμπρό[τα]τος ἔπαρχος. Junius Olympus is a name known as that of a *vir perfectissimus* who was *praeses Arabiae* in 262/3 (*PLRE* i 648: Olympus 4). He may possibly have been an ancestor of this prefect of Egypt, whose term of office is to be set at the earliest in the second half of the fourth century, see 1 n. The prefect of Egypt received the new title of *praefectus Augustalis* probably in 382, see C. Vandersleyen, *La Chronologie des préfets* 146–7, J. Lallemand, *L'Administration* 55–7. The simple wording ὁ λαμπρότατος ἔπαρχος (cf. VIII **1101** 2) suggests, therefore, that this Olympus held office before 382. Unhappily this argument remains doubtful because there are no complete and unambiguous documentary references to an Augustalis so early as this. See, however, P. Strasb. 255. 9 τ]οῦ (read]ου?) ἐπάρχου αὐγουϲταλ[ίου (395, 397, or 403). On the other hand the λαμπροτάτων ἐπάρχων of 388 in P. Lips. I 63. 10–11 seem to be the praetorian prefects, who ranked above the Augustalis; cf. W. *Chr.* 281 (= P. Lips. I 64). 11 and note.

A prefect called Olympus is known from the festal letters of Athanasius and an acephalous chronicle to have governed Egypt in 362 and 363. The prefect of the same period is called Ecdicius in a rescript and some letters of the emperor Julian. One of two persons called Ecdicius who received letters from Libanius was probably a Cilician, while the prefect Olympus was from Tarsus in Cilicia. Modern authors refer therefore to Ecdicius Olympus or Olympus Ecdicius. Junius Olympus could well have been the same person, though he need not be. If he was, the name may have been of some such form as (Flavius?) Junius Olympus (*signo?*) Ecdicius. For the literature on Ecdicius/Olympus see *PLRE* i 647–8, s.v. Olympus 3; C. Vandersleyen, *La Chronologie* 18, 125, 135; J. Lallemand, *L'Administration* 245–6.

καταβαλλομένων. The present tense indicates that the debt was being paid back in instalments, alleged by Asclepiades to be in arrears.

9 χειριϲμοῦ τῶν πραγμάτων. The law provided that a person convicted of debt had to allow an inventory of his property to be made for the purpose of distraint, see A. Berger, *Encyclopedic Dictionary of Roman Law* s.vv. *inventarium, missio in possessionem*.

3628-3636. COMMODITY PRICES AND TAX ACCOUNTS

c. 176? (estimated) × 32 cm   Fifth century

All these items stood on the same opisthograph roll. They are of great interest for the financial administration of the Middle Egyptian province of Arcadia, and must reflect to some extent the procedures used all over the Eastern provinces of the Empire. The items are of two types, lists of commodity prices for six of the nine nomes of the province (**3628-33**), and summaries of various taxes for the whole province, giving, so far as they are preserved, the total assessment and notes of receipts forwarded to Alexandria and of arrears (**3634-6**). Blank spaces were left on the face of the roll for schedules of prices for the other three nomes and these spaces were never filled, see below. Probably the roll was compiled as a memorandum in a government office and for some reason never completed.

The commodity prices are prefaced by a general heading, which runs: 'Schedule of purchasable goods on sale in the market place, for each city in accordance with the schedules submitted by the *tabularii* of each city for the ninth indiction, viz.:'. There follow for each nome three lists of the prices of eleven staple commodities, one list for each of the three *quadrimenstrua* into which the indictional year was divided. It is obvious that there is some connection here with the *quadrimenstrui breves*, returns from the provinces to the praetorian prefects containing information upon which to base the next year's tax demands, see 5–6 n.

The figures can be best presented in a series of tables for each product, see below. The prices of silver bullion and unworked silver are given in terms of gold solidi, which means in effect that they are less prices than fixed ratios of silver to gold. For the sake of comparison all the other prices are given in the tables in myriads of denarii, which is the usual way the texts present them, although they occasionally use the same system as for silver, e.g. 13 artabas of wheat per solidus. In these cases the figures and calculations are given in round brackets, and the same brackets are used for the wine prices, which are given in the texts for either seven or eight sextarii, and are calculated for one sextarius in the tables.

Gold, den. myr. per sol.:

	Sept.–Dec.	Jan.–Apr.	May–Aug.
Cynopolite (**3628**)	4,000	3,900	3,900
Oxyrhynchite (**3629**)	3,800	[ ]	3,850
Uncertain (**3630**)	3,900	3,900	3,900
Uncertain (**3631**)	[ ]	[ ]	3,900
Arsinoite (**3632**)	4,000	[ ]	4,000
Aphroditopolite (**3633**)	3,900	3,900	[ ]

Silver: Steady everywhere at 5 sol. per lb.

Unworked silver: Steady everywhere at $4\frac{3}{4}$ sol. per lb.

Wheat, den. myr. per art.:

	Sept.–Dec.	Jan.–Apr.	May–Aug.
Cynopolite (**3628**)	$(307\frac{9}{13};\ \frac{4000}{13})$	$(300;\ \frac{3900}{13})$	$(325;\ \frac{3900}{12})$
Oxyrhynchite (**3629**)	$(316\frac{2}{3};\ \frac{3800}{12})$	[ ]	[ ]
Uncertain (**3630**)	450	500	500
Uncertain (**3631**)	[ ]	[ ]	450
Arsinoite (**3632**)	240	[ ]	240
Aphroditopolite (**3633**)	450	450	[ ]

Barley, den. myr. per art.:

	Sept.–Dec.	Jan.–Apr.	May–Aug.
Cynopolite (**3628**)	$(285\frac{5}{7};\ \frac{4000}{14})$	$(278\frac{4}{7};\ \frac{3900}{14})$	$(300;\ \frac{3900}{13})$
Oxyrhynchite (**3629**)	$(292\frac{4}{13};\ \frac{3800}{13})$	[ ]	[ ]
Uncertain (**3630**)	270	400	270
Uncertain (**3631**)	[ ]	[ ]	[ ]
Arsinoite (**3632**)	225	225	225
Aphroditopolite (**3633**)	225	[ ]	[ ]

Lentils, den. myr. per art.:

	Sept.–Dec.	Jan.–Apr.	May–Aug.
Cynopolite (**3628**)	$(400;\ \frac{4000}{10})$	$(433\frac{1}{3};\ \frac{3900}{9})$	[ ]
Oxyrhynchite (**3629**)	$(475;\ \frac{3800}{8})$	[ ]	[ ]
Uncertain (**3630**)	430	400	400
Uncertain (**3631**)	[ ]	400	400
Arsinoite (**3632**)	360	360	[ ]
Aphroditopolite (**3633**)	360	[ ]	[ ]

Chaff, den. myr. per lb.:

	Sept.–Dec.	Jan.–Apr.	May–Aug.
Cynopolite (**3628**)	$1\frac{1}{2}$	$1\frac{1}{2}$	$1\frac{1}{2}$
Oxyrhynchite (**3629**)	$1\frac{1}{2}$	$1\frac{1}{2}$	[ ]
Uncertain (**3630**)	$1\frac{1}{2}$	$1\frac{1}{2}$	$1\frac{1}{2}$
Uncertain (**3631**)	[ ]	$1\frac{1}{2}$	$1\frac{1}{2}$
Arsinoite (**3632**)	$1\frac{1}{2}$	$1\frac{1}{2}$	[ ]
Aphroditopolite (**3633**)	$1\frac{1}{2}$	[ ]	[ ]

Wine, den. myr. per sextarius:

	Sept.–Dec.	Jan.–Apr.	May–Aug.
Cynopolite (**3628**)	$(20\frac{5}{8};\ \frac{165}{8})$	$(20\frac{5}{8};\ \frac{165}{8})$	$(22\frac{1}{2};\ \frac{180}{8}?)$
Oxyrhynchite (**3629**)	$(\qquad ?)$	$(22\frac{1}{2};\ \frac{180}{8})$	[ ]
Uncertain (**3630**)	$(21\frac{3}{7};\ \frac{150}{7})$	$(23\frac{4}{7};\ \frac{165}{7})$	$(28\frac{4}{7};\ \frac{200}{7})$
Uncertain (**3631**)	[ ]	$(\ ?\ ;\ \frac{200}{?})$	[ ]
Arsinoite (**3632**)	$(20;\ \frac{160}{8})$	$(23\frac{3}{4};\ \frac{190}{8})$	$(27\frac{1}{2};\ \frac{220}{8})$
Aphroditopolite (**3633**)	$(28\frac{4}{7}?;\ \frac{200}{7}?)$	[ ]	$(28\frac{4}{7}?;\ \frac{200}{7}?)$

Meat, den. myr. per lb.:

	Sept.–Dec.	Jan.–Apr.	May–Aug.
Cynopolite (**3628**)	24	24	24
Oxyrhynchite (**3629**)	24	24	[ ]
Uncertain (**3630**)	30	30	30
Uncertain (**3631**)	[ ]	30	[ ]
Arsinoite (**3632**)	24	24	[ ]
Aphroditopolite (**3633**)	30	[ ]	30

Salt, den. myr. per art.:

	Sept.–Dec.	Jan.–Apr.	May–Aug.
Cynopolite (**3628**)	150	150	150
Oxyrhynchite (**3629**)	150?	150	[ ]
Uncertain (**3630**)	150	150	150
Uncertain (**3631**)	[ ]	150	150
Arsinoite (**3632**)	150	150	[ ]
Aphroditopolite (**3633**)	150	[ ]	150?

Radish oil, den. myr. per sextarius:

	Sept.–Dec.	Jan.–Apr.	May–Aug.
Cynopolite (**3628**)	80	80	80?
Oxyrhynchite (**3629**)	[ ]	80	[ ]
Uncertain (**3630**)	105	105	105
Uncertain (**3631**)	[ ]	105	[ ]
Arsinoite (**3632**)	75	75	75?
Aphroditopolite (**3633**)	105	[ ]	105

There is useful information here, but it will take a great deal of careful consideration by experts before it can be assimilated. The first great problem is to come to some sort of conclusion about how the figures relate to real transactions in the market-places. The variations seem to indicate that the market was in some sense free, but, if it was free, the prices cannot have remained fixed for four months in each case and then clicked up or down a notch only at the beginning of a *quadrimenstruum*. Possibly the prices are averages, or they might be records of some system of government price-fixing. Perhaps, even, they might be the prices for the compulsory purchase of goods by the state, the *coemptio* or ϲυνωνή, or the prices paid for *adaeratio*, the commutation for money of taxes payable in these commodities. Only new evidence can help us here. The same sorts of problem arise in connection with the declarations of prices by guilds, see **3624–6** introd., where I have favoured the idea that the market prices were required as a standard for the commutation of payments of *annona* and for the purchase of *annonariae species*.

We also learn another lesson about the difficulties of comparing isolated prices, to add to those in R. S. Bagnall and P. J. Sijpesteijn, *ZPE* 24 (1977) 114–16. Here, although the ratio of gold to silver is fixed, and some commodities remain very steady in money terms, notably chaff and salt, there is a fairly wide range of variation by season and even more by location, though the prices cover a comparatively small region, the nomes of Middle Egypt. R. P. Duncan-Jones, *Chiron* 6 (1976) 243–5, discussing variations in grain prices under the principate, talks chiefly of differences between Upper and Lower Egypt.

It is very unfortunate that the date of the roll is indicated only by the mentions of a ninth indiction, which had evidently just ended. The roll itself must have been written early in some tenth indiction. The list of nomes in **3636** 2 makes it clear that we are dealing with the province of Arcadia, see note. The earliest documentary reference to Arcadia comes from 411 (SPP XX 117; on which see R. S. Bagnall and K. A. Worp, *Mnemosyne*, ser. 4, 31 (1978) 287–93, cf. **3639** introd.). A *terminus post quem* is said to be supplied by *C. Theod.* i 14, 1 of 17 February 386, which is addressed to Florentius, *praefectus Augustalis*, and mentions tax collection in the Thebaid and Augustamnica, but not in Arcadia, cf. M. Gelzer, *Stud. z. byz. Verwaltung Ägyptens* 8–9. A certain amount of suspicion is cast on this date by problems connected with the list of Augustal prefects, see C. Vandersleyen, *La Chronologie des préfets* 164–81, but Vandersleyen accepts it as correct in the end. If this is near enough right, the earliest possible ninth indiction is 395/6.

Arguments for the date can be derived from the commodity prices themselves, but they are very flimsy, both because of the shortage of other information and because by the fifth century the period of continuous inflation was ending and it is not possible to be sure that higher prices always indicate a later date. The strongest argument of this kind seems to be one derived from the prices of radish oil. The rates here are higher than that specified in P. Mich. XI 613 of 415, which suggests that our roll is later, if we make the assumption that inflation was still continuing. There 150 solidi are delivered to the head of the administrative staff of the *praeses* of Arcadia as the price of 9,000 sextarii of radish oil which is to be bought by compulsory purchase for supplying the city of Alexandria. The rate is 60 sextarii per solidus. Our three prices for one sextarius of radish oil are 75, 80, and 105 myriads of denarii, so that 60 sextarii would cost 4,500, 4,800, or 6,300 den. myr., somewhat more than one solidus, which ranges here from 3,800 to 4,000 den. myr. The higher rates in our roll may, therefore, indicate a somewhat later date, and the next ninth indiction after 415 is 425/6.

The other prices are not of much help. Although there are useful supplements for the fourth century in R. S. Bagnall and P. J. Sijpesteijn, *ZPE* 24 (1977) 111–124, and *ZPE* 27 (1977) 161–4, the standard collection is still A. C. Johnson and L. C. West, *Byzantine Egypt, Economic Studies* 176–82. For wheat there are no well-dated examples between *post*-345 and 539 (p. 177); for wine no well-dated examples between *c*.350 and 454 (p. 178). This last, P. Lond. V 1773, supposedly gives a price of 50,000 talents for 100 cnidia, but it is unusable both because of uncertainty about the size of the cnidium—at 8 sextarii per cnidium (see A. H. M. Jones, *LRE* i 447, but cf. L. Casson, *TAPA* 94 (1939) 7, 11) the price is absurdly low—and because the fragmentary text is suspiciously ungrammatical, . . . τ̣άλαντα μυριάδας πέντε . . . Lentils, salt, chaff, and radish oil do not appear. One document of 390, XIV **1753**, gives prices for meat (?) and oil which may be compared with ours, see Johnson and West, pp. 182, 185, but with no very satisfactory results. There three and a half pounds of meat (?) cost 105 den. myr., so that one pound cost 30 den. myr. In our documents there are two rates, one precisely the same as this and one lower, 24 den. myr., see table above. However, it was the lower price which prevailed in the Oxyrhynchite nome, from which we might deduce that our document is before 390, but this is impossible if it is after 386 and refers to a ninth indiction. The words ὑπὲρ κρέως are restored in XIV **1753** 4, because the commodity is measured in pounds. No other supplement seems so likely, but some uncertainty remains. In **1753** 2 eighty sextarii of oil of some kind (ἔλαιον χρηϲτόν), perhaps olive oil, are reckoned at two solidi, which at our top rate of 4,000 den. myr. per solidus would be 100 den. myr. per sextarius, very close to the rates here of 75, 80 and 105, see table above. However, that was probably better than radish oil, see the story from the Apophthegmata Patrum (Migne, *Patrologia Graeca* 65, col. 145A), quoted in P. Mich. XI 613. 4n. and P. Ross.-Georg. II 41. 54 n., in which guests presented with radish oil (ῥαφανέλαιον) ask for χρήϲιμον ἔλαιον and receive the reply that the host knows no oil but radish oil. In AD 390, therefore, radish oil was probably cheaper than it was in our text, and our text should be later. This argument at least rests on an unrestored text and may be regarded as stronger than the other, but still the doubt remains.

For barley Johnson and West give us no fifth-century prices at all, and only one rather unhelpful price, for 388, which is at all near to the right period (p. 176). In P. Lips. I 63 the rate is 30 modii per solidus. We do not know the monetary value of the solidus in 388, so it will be best to convert this to artabas per solidus at 3⅓ modii per artaba. The rate is equivalent to 9 art. per sol. This is extremely expensive by the standards of our documents, which give rates of 14 and 13 art. per sol., see table, for the Cynopolite and Oxyrhynchite nomes. The reasons may lie in the location concerned, which is Coptos in the Thebaid, a less fertile area than Middle Egypt, and in the fact that this is an *adaeratio* of a levy payable in barley and so may be regarded as a penalty price.

For barley in the Oxyrhynchite nome a late fourth-century rate of 225 den. myr. per art. is given by XLVIII **3410**, part of an archive which ranges at least from 331 to 371 (XLVIII p. 74). Here 225 den. myr. is the price of an artaba in the Arsinoite and

Aphroditopolite nomes, but in the Oxyrhynchite the price is over 290 den. myr., which indicates that these documents are later than **3410**, but allows no more specific conclusion. Dr Shelton, in **3410** introd., has shown that it belongs in the later years of the archive by reference to a range of fourth-century barley prices, including especially P. Col. VII 182 and 184. These, dated 372, give barley prices equivalent to 75 and 90 den. myr. However, these prices are artificially low because the transactions purport to be sales in advance but are thought to be concealed loans (R. S. Bagnall, *GRBS* 18 (1977) 85–96, cf. *ZPE* 24 (1977) 118 (foot) with n. 28, cf. p. 117 n. 24). They are also from the Arsinoite nome, which has low grain prices here. However, all we can argue from these examples is that our documents are later than 372, which we had concluded already.

Palaeography also is of very little help. Indeed it is rarely useful when it is a question of assigning dates within close limits and in this case the difficulties are greater than usual. The fifth century continues to be poorly represented by papyri (R. S. Bagnall and K. A. Worp in R. Pintaudi (ed.), *Miscellanea Papyrologica* (Pap. Laur. VII), 13–23, esp. 22), and its palaeography is correspondingly unfamiliar (W. Schubart, *Griechische Paläographie* 90). The writing here, see Pl. VII, has the very upright stance found in so many fifth-century hands but no features which I can recognize as early or late. For a range of fifth-century scripts see P. Mich. XI 613 (pl. iii; AD 415); P. Mich. XV 730 (pl. xxii; AD 430); P. Wisc. I 10 (pl. iv; AD 468—on a larger scale in E. Boswinkel and P. J. Sijpesteijn, *Greek Papyri*, no. 45); P. Mich. XV 731 (pl. xxii; AD 499). It is especially chastening to look at P. Mich. XV pl. xxii and speculate how far these two hands could have been dated by palaeographical criteria, even though they are separated by over sixty years.

The original layout of the roll is not fully known. Six fragments survive. Two join physically to give what is clearly the beginning of the roll on the recto (**3628, 3629**—commodity prices), and therefore the end of the roll on the verso (**3635, 3636**—tax accounts). Three other fragments come together on the evidence of shared recto fibres. One of the two joins involved is confirmed on the verso by the texts of **3631** and **3632** (commodity prices), which are shared between two fragments both blank on the recto. The other fragment of this group, which contains **3630** on the recto and **3633** on the verso, both commodity prices, is linked only by the recto fibres, which show clearly, however, that it stood immediately on the left of the two already joined on the recto and therefore on the right of them on the verso. The final isolated fragment is blank on the recto and contains **3634** (tax account) on the verso. It does not physically join at any point, but **3634** is the same type of text as **3635** and **3636** and the wide blank margin surviving at the right of **3629** could be part of the sheet which ends at a sheet-join in the blank recto of **3634**, so that it is probably nearer to the first group than the second.

Having got this far we can see that the clerk started with a roll of a definite limited size, put it down before him in the usual orientation so that the sheet joins stepped down from left to right, see E. G. Turner, *Greek Papyri* 5, and began at the top left with the general heading in **3628**. After writing **3628** and **3629** he left a blank of unknown width, parts of which survive at the right of **3629** and on the recto of **3634**. He resumed writing either where **3630** begins or at a point before that where some papyrus is lost. After writing **3630** he left another large blank space which we can see on the rectos of **3631** and **3632**. The right edge of the roll is lost, but there need not have been, and probably was not, more than a width of about 10–15 cm of papyrus to accommodate the beginnings of lines of **3631** on the verso, since the blank spaces on the recto that we can see would probably have been sufficient to take the entries for the three nomes which are missing. After writing **3630** and leaving the end of the roll blank, therefore, he turned the roll over—from left to right or from right to left, but not from top to bottom or bottom to top—and began writing again from the top left on the verso. He wrote three items, **3631–3**, still commodity prices, continuously without leaving any blanks. There followed a portion of the roll now largely lost, but of which **3634** was part, a tax account like the final items **3635** and **3636**.

Two considerations, one textual, the other physical, imply that the gap in the middle of the roll is a fairly large one. The fact that **3634–6** all begin καὶ ἀπὸ λόγου suggests that we have lost an item of the same sort that began simply ἀπὸ λόγου or with some general heading followed by ἀπὸ λόγου. A sizable loss here is also implied by the fibres of the recto of **3634**, which has a sheet join down the middle. The fibres on the left of the join look similar enough to those on the right edge of **3629** to have been part of the same sheet, while those on the right of the join look utterly different from those on the left side of **3630**. If this is right, a whole sheet, *c.* 20–4 cm wide, of the original roll has been lost, probably containing a tax account on the verso and possibly containing a list of commodity prices on the recto.

Attempts to identify the uncertain nomes referred to in **3630** and **3631** have failed. We can see from the list of nine nomes in **3636** 2 that we are dealing with the province of Arcadia, see n., and the fact that blanks were left on the face of the roll suggests that a fixed order of nomes was in the writer's mind. We might have hoped to discover what this order was from **3636** 2 and the similar lists of the cities of the province in Hierocles, *Synecdemus* (ed. H. Gelzer, Bibl. Teubn.) 729. 2–730. 4, and Georgius Cyprius, *Descriptio Orbis Romani* (ed. H. Gelzer, Bibl. Teubn.) 745–751a. The result is this:

3628–36	Hierocles	Georgius	**3636** 2
Cynop. (**3628**)	Cynopolis	Oxyrhynchus (metropolis)	Cynop.
Oxy. (**3629**)	Oxyrhynchus	Heracleopolis	Oxy.
Blank	Heracleopolis	Cynopolis	Heracl.
(Blank/Uncertain?)	Arsinoe	Nilopolis	Nilop.
Uncertain (**3630**)	Theodosiopolis	Arsinoe	Aphrod.
Blank	Nilopolis	Theodosiopolis	Memph.
Uncertain (**3631**)	Aphroditopolis	Aphroditopolis	Letop.
Arsin. (**3632**)	Memphis	Memphis	Arsin.
Aphrod. (**3633**)	Letopolis	Letopolis	Theod.

Compare two more lists, which antedate the creation of the province of Arcadia and of the Theodosiopolite nome but concern the same area:

XLVII **3362**	P. Med. inv. 211 (*Aegyptus* 56 (1976) 76)
Cynop.	Letop.
Oxy.	Memph.
Oasis	Aphrod.
Heracl.	Nilop.
Nilop.	Arsin.
Arsin.	Heracl.
Aphrod.	Oxy.
Memph.	(Cynop. omitted or misplaced).
Letop.	

More or less clearly discernible in all, but least clearly in **3628–33,** is a geographical principle. All proceed from south to north except P. Med. inv. 211, which takes the reverse direction as well as omitting or possibly misplacing the Cynopolite. Unfortunately the Arsinoite and Theodosiopolite nomes lay outside the Nile Valley to the west and this allowed different ways of treating the geography to arise. In **3636** 2 the Nile Valley is treated first in strict order and the two westerly nomes are added at the end. Hierocles leaves the Nile Valley after Heracleopolis to include the westerly cities and returns to it at Nilopolis. P. Med. inv. 211 follows the same process in reverse. George of Cyprus leaves the Nile Valley after Nilopolis and returns to it at Aphroditopolis. (His beginning is odd first because he isolates Oxyrhynchus as the metropolis and secondly because in the archetype of the two chief manuscripts Cynopolis was probably left out. It remained missing in one manuscript, Coislinianus 219, and appears after Heracleopolis instead of before it in the second, Barocci 185.) XLVII **3362** follows this order too.

The order of the commodity prices cannot have been organized like the list in **3636** 2, because the Arsinoite occurs before the Aphroditopolite, and not at the end. Since the Nilopolite does not fall between the two, it cannot have been organized like Hierocles or P. Med. inv. 211. It is remotely possible that it could have been organized on a principle similar to that of George of Cyprus and XLVII **3362**, i.e. recto: Cynopolite (**3628**), Oxyrhynchite (**3629**), blank, [Heracleopolite], Nilopolite? (**3630**), blank; verso: Theodosiopolite? (**3631**), Arsinoite (**3632**), Aphroditopolite (**3633**), [Memphite, Letopolite, tax account?], **3634, 3635, 3636**. But this means that the blanks on the recto to assume before, because if two more lists of commodity prices, and possibly another tax account, occurred on the verso, the loss at the middle of the roll must have been as much as 40 or 60 cm, which had only one column *c.* 20 cm wide on the recto. Since no logical order seems to suit the conditions, we cannot easily guess which nomes were concerned in **3630** and **3631**.

3628. Commodity Prices

65   6B.39/E(3)a front   22 × 32 cm   Fifth century

On the back is **3636**.

     ✝ βρέουϊον ὠνίων πιπρασκομένων ἐν ἀγορᾷ ἑκάστῃ πόλει
     ἀκολούθως βρεουΐοις διδομένοις παρὰ τῶν τ[α]β[ο]υλαρίων
     ἑκάστης πόλεως τῆς θ″ ἰνδικ(τίωνος)   (vac.)
          (vac.)   ο(ὕτως)   (vac.)

            i

5   Κυνοπολίτου ἐπὶ μηνὸς Θώθ, Φαῶφι,
       Ἁθύρ, Χοιάκ
         ο(ὕτως)
   χρυσοῦ τοῦ νο(μ.) α   (δην. μυρ.) ͵δ
   ἀργύρου τῆς λί(τρ.) α   νο(μ.) ε
10   ἀργύρου ἀργ(οῦ) τῆς λί(τρ.) α   νο(μ.) δ (ἥμ.) (τέταρτ.)
   σίτου τοῦ νο(μ.) α   (ἀρτ.) ιγ
   κριθῶν τοῦ νο(μ.) α   (ἀρτ.) ιδ
   φακοῦ τοῦ νο(μ.) α   (ἀρτ.) ι
   ἀχύρου τῆς λί(τρ.) α   (δην. μυρ.)   α (ἥμ.)
15   οἴνου διὰ ξ(εστ.) η   (δην. μυρ.) ρξε
   κρέως τῆς λί(τρ.) α   (δην. μυρ.) κδ
   ἁλὸς τῆς (ἀρτ.) α   (δην. μυρ.) ρν
   ἐλαίου ῥεφ(ανίνου) τοῦ ξ(έστ.) α   (δην. μυρ.) π
         (vac.)
   ἐπὶ μηνὸς Τῦβι, Μεχείρ, Φαμενώθ,
20   Φαρμοῦθι
         ο(ὕτως)
   χρυσοῦ τοῦ νο(μ.) α   (δην. μυρ.) γ ⋌
   ἀργύρου τῆς λί(τρ.) α   νο(μ.) ε
   ἀργύρου ἀργ(οῦ) τῆς λί(τρ.) α   νο(μ.) δ (ἥμ.) (τέταρτ.)
25   σίτου τοῦ νο(μ.) α   (ἀρτ.) ιγ

1 βρεουϊον   2 βρεουϊοις?   3 ἰνδικ//   4 ο—, and so throughout   8 ℬ, ×⌒, and so
both throughout   9 λ, and so throughout   10 αργς, ∟ d′, and so all three throughout   15 ξ/,
and so throughout   17 ⊤, and so throughout   18 ρεφ/, and so throughout; l. ῥαφανίνου

ii

κριθῶν τοῦ νο(μ.) α   (ἀρτ.) ιδ
φακοῦ τοῦ νο(μ.) α   (ἀρτ.) θ
ἀχύρου τῆς λί(τρ.) α   (δην. μυρ.) α (ἥμ.)
οἴνου διὰ ξ(εcτ.) η   (δην. μυρ.) ρξε
30 κρέωc τῆc λί(τρ.) α   (δην. μυρ.) κδ
ἁλὸc τῆc (ἀρτ.) α   (δην. μυρ.) ρν
ἐλαίου ῥεφ(ανίνου) τοῦ ξ(έcτ.) α   (δην. μυρ.) π
    (vac.)
ἐπὶ μηνὸc Παχών, Παῦνι, Ἐ[πεί]φ,
    Μεcορή
35   ο(ὔτωc)
χρυcοῦ τοῦ νο(μ.) α   (δην. μυρ.) ,γ ⳨
ἀργύρου τῆc λί(τρ.) α   νο(μ.) ε
ἀργύρου ἀργ(οῦ) ⟨τῆc⟩ λί(τρ.) α   νο(μ.) δ (ἥμ.) (τέταρτ.)
cίτου τοῦ νο(μ.) α   (ἀρτ.) ιβ
40 κριθῶν τοῦ νο(μ.) α   (ἀρτ.) ιγ
φακοῦ τοῦ νο(μ.) α   (ἀρτ.) [
ἀχύρου τῆc λί(τρ.) α   (δην. μυρ.) α (ἥμ.) [
οἴνου διὰ ξ(εcτ.) η   (δην. μυρ.) ρπ[
κρέωc τῆc [λί(τρ.)] ạ   (δην. μυρ.) κδ[
45 ἁλὸc τῆc (ἀρτ.) α   (δην. μυρ.) ρν[
ἐλαίου ῥεφ(ανίνου) τοῦ ξ(έcτ.) α   (δην. μυρ.) .[

'Schedule of purchasable goods on sale in the market place, for each city in accordance with the schedules submitted by the *tabularii* of each city for the 9th indiction, viz.:

Cynopolite		For the months	Thoth, Phaophi, Hathyr, Choeac, viz.:	Tybi, Mecheir, Phamenoth, Pharmuthi, viz.:	Pachon, Payni, Epeiph, Mesore, viz.:
Gold per	sol.	den. myr.	4,000	3,900	3,900
Silver per	lb.	sol.	5	5	5
Unworked silver per	lb.	sol.	$4\frac{3}{4}$	$4\frac{3}{4}$	$4\frac{3}{4}$
Wheat per	sol.	art.	13	13	12
Barley per	sol.	art.	14	14	13
Lentils per	sol.	art.	10	9	[ ]
Chaff per	lb.	den. myr.	$1\frac{1}{2}$	$1\frac{1}{2}$	$1\frac{1}{2}$
Wine per	8 sextarii	den. myr.	165	165	180?
Meat per	lb.	den. myr.	24	24	24
Salt per	art.	den. myr.	150	150	150
Radish oil per sextarius		den. myr.	80	80	80?'

1-2 βρέουϊον, βρεουΐοιϲ. Cf. CPR V 10, P. Cair. Isid. 1. 9, 16, where the βρέουϊον is Diocletian's schedule of tax assessments mentioned in the edict of Aristius Optatus; 9 n. refers us to Diocletian, *Edict. de pret.*, *Praef.* ii, 10, mentioning the *subditi brevis*, 'the schedule given below', which is the famous list of prices. On *quadrimenstrui breves* see 5-6 n.

2-3 τ[α]β[ο]υλαρίων ἑκάϲτηϲ πόλεωϲ. For the *tabularius civitatis* see A. H. M. Jones, *LRE* i 600, ii 1248 n. 89. He was chiefly concerned with tax assessment.

3 The ninth indiction remains unidentified, see introd. Those falling in the fifth century are 410/11, 425/6, 440/1, 465/6, 480/1, 495/6.

5-6 These four months form the first third of the Egyptian year, which approximates to the indictional year, the first *quadrimenstruum* in fact. The others follow in 19-20 and 33-4, and these sub-headings appear again in **3629-33**. It seems obvious that there is some connection here with the *quadrimenstrui breves*, which were reports on taxation compiled by provincial administrations and returned to the praetorian prefects, who used the information contained in them to control the progress of the collection of taxes in the current year and to form the basis of the assessments for the following year, see A. H. M. Hones, *LRE* i 404-5, ii 1164 n. 81; see also the references collected in the index to C. Pharr, *The Theodosian Code* 639, svv. tax-lists . . . quadrimestral; tax-payments to be made in three installments. Cf. P. Lond. V 1663. 22, where the period January to April is described as 'the second *quadrimenstruum* (τῆϲ δευτέραϲ τετραμήνου) of the present 13th indiction', with R. S. Bagnall and K. A. Worp, *Chronological Systems* 24.

8 One gold solidus is equivalent to 4,000 den. myr. The same rate is attested in P. Mich. XV 740, where 2 sol. are equated with 8,000 den. myr. At one point 2 carats (i.e. $\frac{2}{24} = \frac{1}{12}$ of a solidus) are equated with 334 den. myr., which implies a rate slightly higher, that is 4,008 den. myr. per sol., but this is probably a question of rounding up the figures, since $\frac{1}{12}$ of 4,000 comes out inconveniently at $333\frac{1}{3}$. P. Mich. 740 is assigned to the sixth century on palaeographical grounds, see pl. xxvi, and may well be of that date, since the period of continuous inflation ends about the fifth century. The editor, P. J. Sijpesteijn, refers us to XIV **1729**, assigned to the fourth century, in which he says the solidus is worth 4,500 den. myr. According to my calculations the text implies that $\frac{3}{4}$ of a solidus (νόμιϲμα ἐν π(αρὰ) τέταρτον) equals a total of 3,535 den. myr., so that the solidus would be equal to $4,713\frac{1}{3}$ den. myr. For a survey of values of the solidus in money see A. H. M. Jones, *LRE* i 440, ii 1183-4 n.74, citing especially himself in *Econ. Hist. Rev.* 5 (1953) 307-9. Add XLVIII **3401** 6n. Unfortunately almost all the material can be dated only approximately.

In this year the solidus ranged from 3,800 to 4,000 den. myr., and varied by locality as well as season, see **3628-36** introd. for a table of all the rates given in these texts. However, the documents seem to imply that the rates were valid at least for a four-month period. It may have been so in the transactions—whatever they were—with which the documents are concerned, but we have two texts which show clearly that this was not always the case, see IX **1223** 31-3 ὁ ὁλοκόττινοϲ νῦν μυρ(ιάδων) βκ ἐϲτίν. κατέβη γάρ, 'The solidus stands now at 2,020 myriads; it has come down'; XLVIII **3401** 7-13 [ϲπο]ύ[δ]αϲον οὖν ἀπόϲτιλόν [μ]οι τὸ κέρμα ἐν τῇ αὔριον, ἐ[πεί]περ γέγονεν φήμη περὶ [το]ῦ χρυϲοῦ τῶν τιρόνων κα[ὶ π]άντεϲ ζητῖ (l. ζητοῦϲι) νομιϲμ[ά]τια καὶ καθ' ἡμέρα⟨ν⟩ ἀναβένι (l. ἀναβαίνει) ἡ [τι]μή, 'Make haste therefore to send me the money tomorrow, seeing that there has been a rumour about the gold for the recruits and everyone is looking for solidi and the price is going up every day'. Both these texts are undated but belong to the later part of the fourth century. The first might refer to the change of *quadrimenstruum*, but καθ' ἡμέρα⟨ν⟩ shows clearly that the second cannot.

9 The equation 1 lb. silver = 5 sol. remains stable throughout this series of documents. The same rate is specified in *C. Theod.* xiii 2. 1 of 19 February 397. This is a ratio of gold to silver of 1:14.4. Another order, *C. Theod.* viii 4. 27 of 19 June 422, specified a lower rate of four solidi per pound of silver (1:18) for *sportulae* paid to *duces* by *primipilares*. (*Primipilares* were members of the staffs of provincial governors, see J. M. Carrié, *Pap. Brux.* 19, 156-76, conveniently summarized by himself in *ZPE* 35 (1979) 219.) Since it is the earlier order which is taken up into Justinian's code (*C. Theod.* xiii 2. 1 = *CJ* x 78. l), this has caused some bewilderment, cf. L. C. West and A. C. Johnson, *Currency* 108, but it is perhaps best regarded as a special concessionary rate, cf. A. H. M. Jones, *LRE* ii 1184 n. 73. This rate for the commutation of taxes payable in silver actually occurs in a papyrus assigned to the fourth century, see West and Johnson, *Currency* 185-6. If we can regard it as a special rate applicable only to the commutation of some taxes payable in silver, it looks as if the rate for most official purposes was maintained at 1:14.4 from the late fourth century to the mid sixth.

10 ἀργύρου ἀργ(οῦ) τῆϲ λί(τραϲ) α νο(μ.) δ (ἥμ.) (τέταρτ.) This rate is maintained throughout **3628-33**.

The wording looks at first sight as if it might give the clue to the long-standing puzzle of P. Ant. I 38, a declaration of prices in 300 of two sorts of one substance, one κατερ[γα]ζομένου at 62 den. per lb., the other ἀργοῦ χυτοῦ at 31 den. per lb. In *ed. pr.* ἀργοῦ was presented as ἀργ⟨υρ⟩ίου (*sic*), so that the text has ever since bedevilled discussions of the monetary history of the period, but the prices show that the substance cannot be silver. We must still follow the clear statement of M. H. Crawford and J. M. Reynolds in *ZPE* 34 (1979) 164 and reject P. Ant. I 38 as irrelevant, though the puzzle remains unsolved. (The new section of I **85** published by R. A. Coles in *ZPE* 39 (1980) 117, declaring the prices of copper or bronze (χαλκοῦ), τοῦ μὲν ἐλατοῦ λί(τρας) τάλ(αντα) (m. 4) ϛ (δηνάρια) Ἀ, (m. 1) τοῦ δὲ χυτοῦ' λί(τρας) α τάλ(αντα) (m. 4) δ, makes an interesting comparison.)

I have not found any other references in the papyri to ἄργυρος ἀργός, and at first it seems surprising that it was considered a staple commodity on the same level as the others. The meaning of ἀργός here is not entirely clear. I presume that ἄργυρος in 9 refers to refined bullion, probably in the form of ingots, and that it is this which is referred to in Diocletian's Price Edict (ed. M. Giacchero) 28. 9, *de argento hoc est pusula primi*, 'of silver, that is, pure silver of first (quality)', cf. P. G. W. Glare, *Oxford Latin Dictionary* s.vv. *pusula* (2.b), *pusulatus*. I presume also that ἄσημον καθαρόν in receipts such as P. Col. VII 140 is the same, though ἄσημον is used of jewellery, e.g. BGU I 22. 32 ζεῦγος ψελλίω(ν) ἀργυρῶν ἀσήμου ὁλκῆς (δραχμῶν) μ̄, 'a pair of silver armlets, 40 dr. by weight of uncoined silver', and, at least in the diminutive form ἀσήμιν = ἀσήμιον, of plate, see P. Vind. G. 15452. 5-6, as revised by H. C. Youtie, *Scriptiunculae* i 260 = *TAPA* 87 (1956) 64, ὀλίγον ἀσήμιν ἕως πατελλικ[ί]ον (= -ίων) δύο, ἐμβαφίον (= -ίων) ὀκτώ, 'some silver plate, at least two dishes and eight saucers'. Obviously ἄργυρος ἀργός here is something less than pure silver. It seems very unlikely to be any rough form straight from the mine. It might be silver in the forms of plate and jewellery, and therefore alloyed to some extent, cf. *ZPE* 46 (1982) 247; or it might be cast silver made from melting down such objects, cf. P. Col. VII 141. 23-33, a receipt for cast copper which required refining, see XLVIII p. xvii (n. on XXXIII **2673** 22). These forms of silver could quite reasonably be tarifed at $\frac{18}{20}$ of the value of pure silver bullion and must have been quite commonly traded in the towns of Egypt.

11 The rate of 13 art. of wheat per sol. is one actually given in a story relating to the abbot Pachomius from the fourth century, see A. H. M. Jones, *LRE* i 445. The story implies that it was a normal one, though it was illicitly offered at a time when there was a famine and the prevailing price was 5 or $5\frac{1}{2}$ art. per sol.

See **3628-36** introd. for a table of all the wheat prices given in the documents. They show very clearly how impossible it is to give a normal price for wheat, see Jones, loc. cit. The low prices in the Arsinoite nome are particularly interesting. It is well known that Arsinoite villages which are familiar to us from the papyri, such as Theadelphia and Dionysias, were becoming depopulated in the early fourth century and were entirely abandoned not long after, cf. e.g. H. Braunert, *Binnenwanderung* 310-13, 328-33, yet the reason for the low prices in the Arsinoite nome here must surely be that there was still an abundance of wheat there. The same good agricultural circumstances are reflected in the Arsinoite prices of barley, lentils, and oil.

12 For a table of barley prices and discussion see **3628-36** introd.

13 Lentils were evidently more important in Egyptian agriculture than we might imagine nowadays, cf. M. Schnebel, *Landwirtschaft* 191. In Aulus Gellius, *NA* 17. 8. 2, drawn to my attention by Dr Holford-Strevens, Egyptian lentils are the main ingredient of a meal. It is not quite clear whether we can deduce from this that they were exported from Egypt to Greece in the second century AD. Perhaps a variety grown in Greece might have been called Egyptian. For a table of all the lentil prices in these documents see **3628-36** introd. The range of prices, 360-475 den. myr. per art., is not so extreme as in the case of wheat, 240-500 den. myr., but the observation that lentils were generally equated or nearly equated with wheat, see XLVII **3345** 46-7 n., is confirmed in broad terms. In individual cases it would hardly be possible to guess whether lentils were likely to be dearer or cheaper than wheat. Note especially how the age of the lentils affects the price in **3345**.

14 The price of chaff remains steady throughout these documents at $1\frac{1}{2}$ den. myr. per lb. In XLVIII **3424** 12 the charge of 2 den. myr. per lb. seems, therefore, to be the price, rather than a surcharge, especially since the date of that document may be 357 or 372. It is probably the *adaeratio* of a tax or levy payable in kind and thus a penalty price; see also 16 n.

See S. L. Wallace, *Taxation* 25 for the uses of chaff and for requisitions of chaff by the Ptolemaic and Roman governments. Add P. Beatty Panop. 2. 250-55, an interesting letter about arrangements to ship chaff upstream to the Thebaid, where there was a shortage of it. The descriptions of winnowing in J. E. Harrison, *JHS* 24 (1904) 241-54 and K. D. White, *Agricultural Implements* 32-5, do not stress the necessity of keeping the chaff, but Xenophon, *Oecon.* 18. 7, refers to an ἀχυροδόκη: ἂν δέ τις . . . λικμᾷ ἐκ τοῦ ὑπηνέμου ἀρχόμενος . . . εὐθὺς ἐν τῇ ἀχυροδόκῃ ἔσται τὰ ἄχυρα, 'if one winnows . . . from the upwind (side of the threshing-floor) . . . the chaff will at once be found in the receptacle for chaff'. Many references to ἄχυρον and its cognates, e.g. ἀχυροθήκη, ἀχυροπράκτωρ, in the papyri show that its importance in ancient times was much greater than would readily come to mind nowadays.

15 διὰ ξ(εϲτ.) η. Cf. XVI **1896** 19 ϲηκώματα ὀκτάξεϲτα, and note, referring to P. Lond. inv. 2115 οἴνου ϲηκωμ[άτων] ὀκταξεϲτιέων (= -ιαίων), also P. Mich. XV 734. 16 ὀκταξεϲτιαίω[ν ϲηκωμάτων?]. The first and third of these texts are from the Oxyrhynchite nome. In this series of documents the prices are for 8 sextarii in three nomes, Cynopolite (**3628**), Oxyrhynchite (**3629**), and Arsinoite (**3632**), for 7 sextarii in two nomes, one unidentified (**3630**), the other the Aphroditopolite (**3633**), and for a measure apparently called the δι(πλοῦν) μέγα in the other unidentified nome (**3631** 6, 17). It appears that the κνίδιον could be either μέγα or μικρόν (XVI **1893** 14 n.) and that the κνίδιον was sometimes the same as the διπλοῦν (XVI **1951** 3, 5). In XVI **1920** 5 there is a διπλοῦν of 8 sextarii, in XIV **1720** 5 διπλᾶ and ϲηκώματα are equated, and in XVI **1896** 22 ὑπὲρ ἑκάϲτου κνιδίου seems to refer back to the ὀκτάξεϲτα ϲηκώματα of 19, cf. 20. It is a possibility that in this case the δι(πλοῦν) μέγα was one of 8 sextarii, answering to a διπλοῦν μικρόν of 7 sextarii. For a measure of 7 sextarii see P. Cair. Masp. I 67104. 12 (sc. ἑκάϲτου ἀγγείου) ἐκ ξεϲτῶ⟨ν⟩ ἑπτά. Cf. πενταξεϲτιαῖον (PSI VIII 881. 5), ἑξαξεϲτιαῖον (= διπλοῦν; P. Mich. XIII 674. 5, cf. 10; P. Flor. I 65. 6-7), with P. Mich. XIII 667. 17 ἄγγια (= -εια) πεντήκοντα ἀπὸ ἑξαξέϲτων ἑκάϲτου ἀγγίου (= -είου) and P. Vatic. Aphrod. 12. 5, 12 (οἴ(νου) ἀγγ(εῖα) . . . ἑξαξεϲτ(ιαῖα)?). For more details, which demonstrate how great the variations in measure and price were, and so how uncertain modern calculations are likely to be, see L. Casson, *TAPA* 70 (1939) 1-16.

From the table of wine prices in **3628-36** introd. we can see that new wine is meant, because the prices tend to be cheaper in the autumn after the vintage and dearer in summer.

16 See **3628-36** introd. for a table of the meat prices in this series, which show only two levels, 24 and 30 den. myr. per lb., and also for a discussion of what appears to be a high price of 30 den. myr. per lb. for meat in 390 (XIV **1753** 4). In XLVIII **3424**, perhaps of 357 or 372, the charge of 26 den. myr. per lb. looks like a price rather than a surcharge, and is probably the *adaeratio* of a tax payable in kind; see also 14 n. All these prices are high by the standards suggested by A. H. M. Jones, *LRE* i 446. He points out, however, that Egypt is not rich in pasture and that Egyptian meat prices can be expected to be high.

17 Salt remains fixed throughout at 150 den. myr. per art. J. Karayannopulos, *Finanzwesen* 235, regards salt as the only commodity subject to a fiscal monopoly. However, A. H. M. Jones, *LRE* ii 826, tells us that monopolies are not heard of till the latter part of the fifth century, and seems to regard the *mancipes salinarum* exclusively as a guild of the city of Rome, i 357, 705. The steady price here is not necessarily the result of a monopoly, as is proved by the case of chaff; cf. 14 n. For instances of the supply of salt to the army see P. Beatty Panop. 2. 248, 288 (AD 300), P. Laur. III 111 (late vi AD). The first two are for *salgamum*, on which see XXXI **2561** 17 n., A. H. M. Jones, *LRE* i 631-2.

18 On radish oil see P. Mich. XI 613. 4 n. For a discussion of the price see **3628-36** introd.

43 After ρπ[, where the pi is damaged but not really uncertain, there may have been another digit lower than ten.

45 ρν[. This price for salt is steady throughout, so that there is no likelihood that a digit has been lost after the break.

3629. Commodity Prices

65 6B.39/E(7)a front   25.5 × 17 cm   Fifth century

On the back is **3635**.

i

Ὀξυρυγχίτου ἐπὶ μηνὸς

Θώθ, Φαῶφι, Ἀθύρ, Χοιάκ

ο(ὕτως)

χρυσοῦ τοῦ νο(μ.) α   (δην. μυρ.)   ͵γω

5   ἀργύρου τῆς λί(τρ.) α   νο(μ.)   ε

ἀργύρου ἀργ(οῦ) τῆς λί(τρ.) α   νο(μ.)   δ (ἥμ.) (τέταρτ.)

cίτου τοῦ νο(μ.) α   (ἀρτ.)   ιβ

κριθῶν τοῦ νο(μ.) α   (ἀρτ.)   ιγ

φακοῦ τοῦ νο(μ.) α   (ἀρτ.)   η

10   κρέως τῆς λί(τρ.) α   (δην. μυρ.)   κδ

ἀχύρου τῆς λί(τρ.) α   (δην. μυρ.)   α (ἥμ.)

οἴ[ν]ου διὰ ξ(εcτ.) η   (δην. μυρ.)   ρ. [

[ἁλὸς τῆς (ἀρτ.)   (δην. μυρ.)]ρν[

.   .   .   .   .

ii

κρέως τῆς λί(τρ.) α   (δην. μυρ.)   κδ

15   ἀχύρου τῆς λί(τρ.) α   (δην. μυρ.)   α (ἥμ.)

οἴνου διὰ ξ(εcτ.) η   (δην. μυρ.)   ρπ

ἁλὸς τῆς (ἀρτ.) α   (δην. μυρ.)   ρν

ἐλαίου ῥεφ(ανίνου) τοῦ ξ(έcτ.) α   (δην. μυρ.)   π

(vac.)

ἐπὶ μηνὸς Παχών, Παῦνι, Ἐπείφ, Μεcορή

20   ο(ὕτως)

χρυσοῦ τοῦ νο(μ.) α   (δην. μυρ.)   ͵γων

ἀργύρου τῆς λί(τρ.) α   νο(μ.)   ε

ἀργύρου ἀργ(οῦ) τῆς λί(τρ.) α   νο(μ.)   δ (ἥμ.) (τέταρτ.)

cίτου τοῦ ν]ο[(μ.) α

.   .   .   .   .

'Oxyrhynchite		For the months	Thoth, Phaophi, Hathyr, Choeac, viz.:	Tybi, Mecheir, Phamenoth, Pharmuthi, viz.:	Pachon, Payni, Epeiph, Mesore, viz.:
Gold per	sol.	den. myr.	3,800	[ ]	3,850
Silver per	lb.	sol.	5	[ ]	5
Unworked silver per	lb.	sol.	$4\frac{3}{4}$	[ ]	$4\frac{3}{4}$
Wheat per	sol.	art.	12	[ ]	[ ]
Barley per	sol.	art.	13	[ ]	[ ]
Lentils per	sol.	art.	8	[ ]	[ ]
Meat per	lb.	den. myr.	24	24	[ ]
Chaff per	lb.	den. myr.	$1\frac{1}{2}$	$1\frac{1}{2}$	[ ]
Wine per	8 sextarii	den. myr.	100 +	180	[ ]
Salt per	art.	den. myr.	150?	150	[ ]
Radish oil per sextarius		den. myr.	[ ]	80	[ ]'

1–4 The beginnings of ll. 1, 2 and 4—οξ, part of θ, part of χ—stand on the right-hand edge of the fragment chiefly occupied by **3628**, so that the join here is certain.

13 It seems quite safe to restore this line as for salt in spite of the scantiness of the remains, cf. 16–17 and the table showing a steady price for salt in **3628–36** introd.

3630. COMMODITY PRICES

65 6B.39/E(1)a front   22 × 31 cm   Fifth century

On the back is **3633**.

i

	] . λ( ) ἐπὶ μηνὸς	
	Θώθ,] Φαῶφι, Ἁθύρ, Χοιάκ	
	] ο(ὕτωϲ)	
	χρυϲοῦ] τοῦ νο(μ.) α	(δην. μυρ.) ,γ λ
5	ἀργύρου] τῆϲ λί(τρ.) α	νο(μ.) ε
	ἀργύρου ἀ]ργ(οῦ) τῆϲ λί(τρ.) α	νο(μ.) δ (ἥμ.) (τέταρτ.)
	ϲίτου τῆ]ϲ (ἀρτ.) α	(δην. μυρ.) υν
	κριθῶ]ν τῆϲ (ἀρτ.) α	(δην. μυρ.) ϛο
	φακοῦ τ]ῆϲ (ἀρτ.) α	(δην. μυρ.) υλ
10	ἀχύρου τ]ῆϲ λί(τρ.) α	(δην. μυρ.) α (ἥμ.)
	οἴνου] διὰ ξ(εϲτ.) ζ	(δην. μυρ.) ρν
	κρέωϲ τ]ῆϲ λί(τρ.) α	(δην. μυρ.) λ
	ἁλὸϲ τῆ]ϲ (ἀρτ.) α	(δην. μυρ.) ρν
	ἐλαίου ῥε]φ(ανίνου) τοῦ ξ(έϲτ.) α	(δην. μυρ.) ρε
	(vac.)	

15 ἐπὶ μηνὸς Τ]ῦβι, Μεχείρ, Φαμεν‘ώ′θ,
     Φα]ρμοῦθι
      ο](ὕτως)
     χρυσοῦ] τοῦ νο(μ.) ᾳ   (δην. μυρ.) ,γ ϡ
     ἀργύρου τ]ῆς λί(τρ.) ᾳ   νο(μ.) ε
20 ἀργύρου ἀρ]γ(οῦ) τῆς λί(τρ.) α   νο(μ.) δ (ἥμ.) (τέταρτ.)
     σίτου τῆς] (ἀρτ.) α   (δην. μυρ.) φ
     κριθῶν] τῆς (ἀρτ.) α   (δην. μυρ.) υ

ii

     φ[α]κ[οῦ] τῆς (ἀρτ.) α   (δην. μυρ.) υ[(vac.)?] (vac.)
     ἀχύρου τῆς λί(τρ.) α   (δην. μυρ.) α (ἥμ.)
25 οἴνου διὰ ξ(εστ.) ζ   (δην. μυρ.) ρξε
     κρέως τῆς λί(τρ.) α   (δην. μυρ.) λ
     ἁλὸς τῆς (ἀρτ.) α   (δην. μυρ.) ρν
     ἐλαίου ῥεφ(ανίνου) τοῦ ξ(έστ.) α   (δην. μυρ.) ρε
          (vac.)
     ἐπὶ μηνὸς Παχών, Παῦνι, Ἐπείφ, Μεσορή
30   ο(ὕτως)
     χρυσοῦ τοῦ νο(μ.) α   (δην. μυρ.) ,γ ϡ
     ἀργύρου τῆ[ς] λί(τρ.) α   νο(μ.) ε
     ἀργύρου ἀργ(οῦ) τῆς λί(τρ.) α   νο(μ.) δ (ἥμ.) (τέταρτ.)
     σίτου τῆς (ἀρτ.) α   (δην. μυρ.) φ
35 κριθῶν τῆς (ἀρτ.) α   (δην. μυρ.) ςο
     φακοῦ τῆς (ἀρτ.) α   (δην. μυρ.) υ
     ἀχύρου τῆς λί(τρ.) α   (δην. μυρ.) α (ἥμ.)
     οἴνου διὰ ξ(εστ.) ζ   (δην. μυρ.) ς
     κρέως τῆς λί(τρ.) ᾳ   (δην. μυρ.) λ
40 ἁλὸς τῆς (ἀρτ.) α   (δην. μυρ.) ρ̣ν̣
     ἐλαίου ῥεφ(ανίνου) τοῦ ξ(έστ.) ᾳ   (δην. μυρ.) ρε

'...		For the months	Thoth, Phaophi, Hathyr, Choeac, viz.:	Tybi, Mecheir, Phamenoth, Pharmuthi, viz.:	Pachon, Payni, Epeiph, Mesore, viz.:
Gold per	sol.	den. myr.	3,900	3,900	3,900
Silver per	lb.	sol.	5	5	5
Unworked silver per	lb.	sol.	$4\frac{3}{4}$	$4\frac{3}{4}$	$4\frac{3}{4}$
Wheat per	art.	den. myr.	450	500	500
Barley per	art.	den. myr.	280	400	280
Lentils per	art.	den. myr.	430	400	400
Chaff per	lb.	den. myr.	$1\frac{1}{2}$	$1\frac{1}{2}$	$1\frac{1}{2}$
Wine per	7 sextarii	den. myr.	150	165	200
Meat per	lb.	den. myr.	30	30	30
Salt per	art.	den. myr.	150	150	150
Radish oil per sextarius		den. myr.	105	105	105'

1]．λ( ). The mark of abbreviation is an oblique stroke rising to the right after lambda. There is a ligature joining the lambda from the left, but this does not exclude omicron as the preceding letter, since in this roll it is often made as a continuous clockwise loop with a ligature into the next letter. The possibilities, therefore, are Ἡρακλεοπ]ϙλ(ίτου), hardly Ἡρα]ϙλ(εοπολίτου), Ν(ε)ιλοπ]ϙλ(ίτου), hardly Ν(ε)]ιλ(οπολίτου), Λητοπ]ϙλ(ίτου), and Θεοδοσιοπ]ϙλ(ίτου). In the visible cases the name of the nome is set out about the space of two or three letters before the normal left-hand edge (χρυσοῦ κτλ.), so that we expect to restore eight or nine letters here. This may permit us to regard the shorter names, Ν(ε)ιλοπ]ϙλ(ίτου) and Λητοπ]ϙλ(ίτου), as less likely. The order of the nomes does not allow any firm conclusions, see **3628-36** introd., **3636** 2 n. The prices show no overall or consistent similarities that would link them closely with any of the surviving nomes.

22-3 This price for barley is by far the highest in the series. The traces and the spaces in both lines have been carefully checked and seem to justify the text as given. Perhaps the clerk inadvertently copied the figure for lentils instead of barley in 22.

3631. COMMODITY PRICES

64 6B.41/D(2)a back (col. i)　　　　　13 × 27 cm　　　　　Fifth century

The first column of this item is lost, including the name of the nome to which it refers. On the same fragment stand the beginnings of **3632** col. i, which join directly to the rest of that item on another fragment. Both the fragments are blank on the front, see **3628-36** introd.

φακοῦ τῆς (ἀρτ.) α　　　　　　　　(δην. μυρ.) υ
ἀχύρου τῆς λί(τρ.) α　　　　　　　　(δην. μυρ.)　α (ἤμ.)
κρέως τῆς λί(τρ.) α　　　　　　　　(δην. μυρ.)　λ
ἁλὸς τῆς (ἀρτ.) α　　　　　　　　(δην. μυρ.) ρν
5　ἐλαίου ῥεφ(ανίνου) [τ]οῦ ξ(έcτ.) α　(δην. μυρ.) ρϛ
οἴνου δι(πλοῦ)? μεγάλ(ου)　　　　　(δην. μυρ.) ϲ
　　　(vac.)

ἐπὶ μ]ηνὸς Παχών, Παῦνι,
    Ἐπείφ, Μεcορή
    ο(ὕτωc)

10 χρυcοῦ τουc νο(μ.) ạ   (δην. μυρ.) ,γ ⟩
    ἀ]ργύρου τῆc λί(τρ.) ạ   νο(μ.) ε
    ἀ]ργύρου ἀργ(οῦ) . . .   νọ(μ.) δ (ἥμ.) (τέταρτ.)
    c]ίτου τῆc (ἀρτ.) α   (δην. μυρ.) υṿ
    φακοῦ τῆc (ἀρτ.) α   (δην. μυρ.) υ
15 ἀχύρου τῆc λί(τρ.) α   (δην. μυρ.) α (ἥμ.)
    ἁλὸc τῆc (ἀρτ.) ạ   (δην. μυρ.) ρν
    οἴνου δι. [
    κρέωc τ[ῆc λί(τρ.)] ạ [
    ἐλαίο[υ ῥεφ(ανίνου) τοῦ ξ(έcτ.) α

.   .   .   .   .

6 δι[(ν.)?]μεγαλ´   7 παῦνι

'. . .		For the months	Thoth, Phaophi, Hathyr, Choeac, viz.:	Tybi, Mecheir, Phamenoth, Pharmuthi, viz.:	Pachon, Payni, Epeiph, Mesore, viz.:
Gold per	sol.	den. myr.	[ ]	[ ]	3,900
Silver per	lb.	sol.	[ ]	[ ]	5
Unworked silver per	lb.	sol.	[ ]	[ ]	4¾
Wheat per	art.	den. myr.	[ ]	[ ]	450
Barley per	art.	den. myr.	[ ]	[ ]	[ ]
Lentils per	art.	den. myr.	[ ]	400	400
Chaff per	lb.	den. myr.	[ ]	1½	1½
Wine per	?	den. myr.	[ ]	200	[ ]
Meat per	lb.	den. myr.	[ ]	30	[ ]
Salt per	art.	den. myr.	[ ]	150	150
Radish oil per sextarius		den. myr.	[ ]	105	[ ]'

6 After δι there is a narrow gap in the papyrus before μεγαλ´. There may have been a mark of abbreviation there, cf. 17 n.

12 The normal entries have ἀργ(οῦ) τῆc λί(τραc) α. Probably τῆc was omitted here. The remains are very scanty, but ⟨τῆc⟩ λί(τραc) ạ seems acceptable, cf. **3628** 38, **3632** 27.

14-15 An entry for barley is expected between these two lines. Either it was omitted entirely or added after 19, cf. **3632** 14 n.

17 The remains after δι are confused. They may be from an abbreviation mark of some kind, or from mu, cf. 6 and n., or from both together. They do not seem to favour διὰ [ξ(εcτῶν) or διὰ ξ(εcτῶν) [, which are versions of the form found in the other items.

3632. COMMODITY PRICES

64 6B.41/D(2)a back (col. ii)　　　　　13 × 27 cm　　　　　Fifth century
64 6B.41/D(1)a back　　　　　　　　21 × 28 cm

For the low prices of agricultural products in the Arsinoite nome see **3628** 11 n.

i

$Ἀρϲι(νοΐτου)$ $ἐπὶ$ $μηνὸϲ$
　$Θώθ,$ $[Φα]ῶφι,$ $Ἀθύρ,$ $Χο[ι]άκ$
　　$[ο](ὕτωϲ)$
　$χρυϲοῦ$ $[τοῦ]$ $ν[ο](μ.)$ $α$　　　　　　$(δην.$ $μυρ.)$ $,δ$
5　$ἀργύρου$ $τῆ[ϲ$ $λ]ί(τρ.)$ $α$　　　　　$νο(μ.)$ $ε$
　$ἀργ[ύ]ρου$ $ἀρ[γ(οῦ)$ $τ]ῆϲ$ $λί(τρ.)$ $α$　　$νο(μ.)$ $δ$ $(ἥμ.)$ $(τέταρτ.)$
　$ϲίτου$ $τῆϲ$ $(ἀρτ.)$ $α$　　　　　　$(δην.$ $μυρ.)$ $cμ$
　$κριθῶν$ $τῆϲ$ $(ἀρτ.)$ $α$　　　　　$(δην.$ $μυρ.)$ $cκε$
　$οἴνου$ $διὰ$ $ξ(εϲτ.)$ $η$　　　　　　$(δην.$ $μυρ.)$ $ρξ$
10　$ἐλαίου$ $ῥεφ(ανίνου)$ $τοῦ$ $ξ(έϲτ.)$ $α$　$(δην.$ $μυρ.)$ $οε$
　$κρέω[ϲ$ $τῆϲ$ $λί(τρ.)]$ $α$　　　　　$(δην.$ $μυρ.)$ $κδ$
　$ἁλὸϲ$ $[τῆϲ]$ $(ἀρτ.)$ $α$　　　　　　$(δην.$ $μυρ.)$ $ρν$
　$ἀχύρου$ $τῆϲ$ $λί(τρ.)$ $α$　　　　　$(δην.$ $μυρ.)$ $α$ $(ἥμ.)$
　$φ]ακ[οῦ]$ $τ[ῆϲ]$ $(ἀρτ.)$ $α$　　　　$(δην.$ $μυρ.)$ $τξ$
　　　　$(vac.)$
15　$ἐ[πὶ$ $μηνὸϲ$ $Τῦβι,]$ $Μεχείρ,$ $Φ[α]μενώ'θ',$

.　　.　　.　　.　　.

ii

　$κριθῶν$ $τῆϲ$ $(ἀρτ.)$ $α$　　　　　$(δην.$ $μυρ.)$ $cκε$
　$φακοῦ$ $τῆϲ$ $(ἀρτ.)$ $α$　　　　　$(δην.$ $μυρ.)$ $τξ$
　$οἴνου$ $διὰ$ $ξ(εϲτ.)$ $η$　　　　　$(δην.$ $μυρ.)$ $ρρ$
　$ἐλαίου$ $ῥεφ(ανίνου)$ $τοῦ$ $ξ(έϲτ.)$ $α$　$(δην.$ $μυρ.)$ $ρε$
20　$κρέωϲ$ $τῆϲ$ $λί(τρ.)$ $α$　　　　　$(δην.$ $μυρ.)$ $κδ$
　$ἁλὸϲ$ $τῆϲ$ $(ἀρτ.)$ $α$　　　　　$(δην.$ $μυρ.)$ $ρν$
　$ἀχύρου$ $τῆϲ$ $λί(τρ.)$ $α$　　　　$(δην.$ $μυρ.)$ $α$ $(ἥμ.)$
　　　　$(vac.)$

ἐπὶ μηνὸς Παχών, Παῦνι, Ἐπείφ, Μεσορή
    ο(ὕτως)

25   χρυσοῦ τοῦ νο(μ.) α   (δην. μυρ.) ͵δ
       ἀργύρου τῆς λί(τρ.) α   νο(μ.) ε
       ἀργύρ[ου ἀρ]χ(οῦ) ⟨τῆς⟩ λί(τρ.) α   νο(μ.) δ (ἥμ.) [(τέταρτ.)]
       σίτου τῆς (ἀρτ.) α   (δην. μυρ.) σμ
       κριθῶν τῆς (ἀρτ.) α   (δην. μυρ.) σκε
30   οἴνου διὰ ξ(εστ.) η   (δην. μυρ.) σκ
       ἐλαίου ῥεφ(ανίνου) [τοῦ ξ(έστ.) α   (δην. μυρ.) ο]ε
       κριθῶν [
       ἁλὸς τῆ[ς
       ἀχύ]ρου [

·   ·   ·   ·   ·

'Arsinoite		For the months	Thoth, Phaophi, Hathyr, Choeac, viz.:	Tybi, Mecheir, Phamenoth, Pharmuthi, viz.:	Pachon, Payni, Epeiph, Mesore, viz.:
Gold per	sol.	den. myr.	4,000	[ ]	4,000
Silver per	lb.	sol.	5	[ ]	5
Unworked silver per	lb.	sol.	$4\frac{3}{4}$	[ ]	$4\frac{3}{4}$
Wheat per	art.	den. myr.	240	[ ]	240
Barley per	art.	den. myr.	225	225	225
Wine per	8 sextarii	den. myr.	160	190	220
Radish oil per	sextarius	den. myr.	75	75	75?
Meat per	lb.	den. myr.	24	24	[ ]
Salt per	art.	den. myr.	150	150	[ ]
Chaff per	lb.	den. myr.	$1\frac{1}{2}$	$1\frac{1}{2}$	[ ]
Lentils per	art.	den. myr.	360	360	[ ]

14 Lentils usually stand earlier in the lists, after wheat and barley, as in 17 here, but they are displaced again, or omitted, in the list for the third *quadrimenstruum*, 23-34. A similar displacement of barley may have occurred in **3631**, see **3631** 14-15 n.

32 There is a satisfactory entry for barley in 29. The order of the entries suggests that the clerk miscopied κρέως as κριθῶν, cf. 10-12, 19-21.

3633. COMMODITY PRICES

65　6B.39/E(1)a back　　　　　　　　　22 × 31 cm　　　　　　　　　Fifth century
On the front is **3630**.

i

Ἀφρο[δ(ιτοπολίτου) ἐ]πὶ μηνὸ[ς] Θώθ, Φαῶφι,
　　　Ἀθύρ, Χοιάκ, ο(ὕτως)
　　　　　　(vac.)

χρυσοῦ τοῦ νο(μ.) α	(δην. μυρ.) ͵γ ⳥
ἀργύρου τῆς λί(τρ.) α	νο(μ.) ε
5　ἀργύρου ἀργ(οῦ) τῆς λί(τρ.) α	νο(μ.) δ (ἥμ.) (τέταρτ.)
cίτου τῆς (ἀρτ.) α	(δην. μυρ.) υν
κριθῶν τῆς (ἀρτ.) α	(δην. μυρ.) cκε
φακοῦ τῆς (ἀρτ.) α	(δην. μυρ.) τξ
ἀχύρου τῆς λί(τρ.) α	(δην. μυρ.)　α (ἥμ.)
10　ἐλαίου ῥεφ(ανίνου) τοῦ ξ(έcτ.) α	(δην. μυρ.) ρε
κρέως τῆς λί(τρ.) α	(δην. μυρ.)　λ
ἁλὸς τῆς (ἀρτ.) α	(δην. μυρ.) ρϟ
οἴνου διὰ ξ(εcτ.) ζ	(δην. μυρ.) ς
(vac.)	
ἐπὶ μηνὸς Τῦβι, Μεχε[ίρ, Φ]αμενώθ,	
15　　Φαρμοῦθι	
ο(ὕτως)	
χρυσοῦ τοῦ νο(μ.) α	(δην. μυρ.) ͵γ ⳥
ἀργύρου τῆς λί(τρ.) α	ν̣[ο(μ.)] ε
ἀργύρου ἀργ(οῦ) τῆς λί(τρ.) α	νο(μ.) δ (ἥμ.) (τέταρτ.)
20　cίτου τῆς (ἀρτ.) α	(δην. μυρ.) υν

ii

κ̣ρ̣ιθῶν τῆς (ἀρτ.) α	[
φακοῦ τῆς (ἀρτ.) α	[
ἀχύρου τῆς λί(τρ.) α	[
κρέως τῆς λί(τρ.) α	[

25   ἁλὸϲ τῆϲ (ἀρτ.) α   [

     οἴνου διὰ ξ(εϲτ.) ζ   [

     ἐλαίου ῥεφ(ανίνου) τοῦ ξ(έϲτ.) α   (δην. [μυρ.)

                    (vac.)

     ἐπὶ μηνὸϲ Παχών, Παῦνι, Ἐπ[είφ,

                    Μεϲορή

30   ο(ὕτωϲ)

     χρυϲοῦ τοῦ νο(μ.) α   (δην. [μυρ.)

     ἀργύρου τῆϲ λί(τρ.) α   νο(μ.)[

     ἀργύρου ἀργ(οῦ) τῆϲ λί(τρ.) α   νο(μ.)[

     ϲίτου τῆϲ (ἀρτ.) α   (δην. μυρ.) [

35   κριθῶν τῆϲ (ἀρτ.) α   (δην. μυρ.) . [

     φακοῦ [τῆϲ] (ἀρτ.) α   (δην. μυρ.) . [

     ἀχύρου τῆϲ λί(τρ.) α   (δην. μυρ.) . [

     ἁλὸϲ τῆϲ [(ἀρτ.) α]   (δην. μυρ.) ρ[

     ἐλαίου ῥεφ(ανίνου) [τοῦ ξ(έϲτ.) α]   (δην. μυρ.) ρε[

40   κρέωϲ τῆϲ λί(τρ.) ạ   (δην. μυρ.) λ[

     οἴ[ν]ου διὰ ξ(εϲτ.) ζ   (δην. μυρ.) ϛ[

'Aphroditopolite		For the months		Thoth, Phaophi, Hathyr, Choeac, viz.:	Tybi, Mecheir, Phamenoth, Pharmuthi, viz.:	Pachon, Payni, Epeiph, Mesore, viz.:
Gold per	sol.		den. myr.	3,900	3,900	[ ]
Silver per	lb.		sol.	5	5	[ ]
Unworked silver per	lb.		sol.	4¾	4¾	[ ]
Wheat per	art.		den. myr.	450	450	[ ]
Barley per	art.		den. myr.	225	[ ]	[ ]
Lentils per	art.		den. myr.	360	[ ]	[ ]
Chaff per	lb.		den. myr.	1½	[ ]	[ ]
Radish oil per sextarius			den. myr.	105	[ ]	105
Meat per	lb.		den. myr.	30	[ ]	30
Salt per	art.		den. myr.	150	[ ]	150?
Wine per	7 sextarii		den. myr.	200	[ ]	200?'

3634. Tax Accounts

65　6B.39/E(7)b back　　　　　　　　　11.5 × 31.5 cm　　　　　　　Fifth century

The front is blank.

καὶ ἀπὸ λόγου ναύλων ἀρουρατεί[ωνος
ἀφ' ὧν ἐλογίσθ(η) τῇ ἐπαρχ(ίᾳ) ἐν Ἀ[λεξανδρείᾳ
τοῖς ὀρρίοις τῆς αὐτῆς λ[
καὶ τελεῖται ἐν Ἀλε[ξανδρείᾳ
5　καὶ ἀπεστάλ(η) [
　　　[　　　　　　o(ὕτως)?
　　　Χ[οιάκ] .　δι(ὰ) Φοιβάμ[μωνος
　　　Φαμενὼθ ι　δι(ὰ) Ἀνουβί[ωνος
　　　Παχὼν　γ̄　δι(ὰ) Ἰωνᾶ [
10　Ἐπεὶφ　ᾱ　δι(ὰ) Κασίου π[αραπομποῦ
　　　Μεσορὴ　ια　δι(ὰ) Ἰωνᾶ [
　　　Φαῶφι　ιϛ̄　δι(ὰ) Ἰωνᾶ [
　　　　　(vac.)
καὶ κατεβλήθ(η) ἐν Ἀλεξανδρείᾳ . [
　　　　(vac.)　　　　　　　　[
　　　　(vac.)　　γί(νονται?) ,α[
　　　　(vac.)　　　　　　　　[
15　καὶ ἀπὸ λόγου γαλαθηνῶ[ν
　　　ἀφ' ὧν ἐλογίσθ(η) ἐν Ἀλεξα[νδρείᾳ
　　　τοῖς ὀρρίοις τῆς αὐτῆ[ς
　　　καὶ ἀπεστάλ(η) ἐν Ἀλεξ
　　　　　　　　　[ανδρείᾳ?
　　　　(vac.)　　　. [

1 l. ἀρουρατίωνος　　2 ελογιϲθ, επαρχ　　5 απεϲταλ/　　7-12 δι/　　13 κατεβληθ
14 χ!?　　16 ελογιϲθ　　18 απεϲταλ/

'And from the account of freight charges on *aruratio* ...
'From which have been credited to the province in Alexandria ... the granaries of the same ... and there are being paid(?) in Alexandria ... and there have been sent ...
　Viz.:

Choeac　　*n*th through Phoebammon ...
Phamenoth　10 through Anubion ...
Pachon　　3 through Jonas ...
Epeiph　　1 through Casius, escort (?), ...
Mesore　　11 through Jonas ...
Phaophi　　16 through Jonas ...

'And there have been paid in Alexandria . . .

Total(?) 1,000(+ ?).

'And from the account of sucklings . . .'

'From which have been credited in Alexandria . . . the granaries of the same . . . and there have been sent to(?) Alexandria . . .'

1-5 The structure of 1-5, which is very similar to that in 15-18, is not certain, but it can be compared with **3635** 1-3 and **3636** 1-4, where the assessed total is given and then followed directly by ἀφ' ὧν ἀπεcτάλ(η) εἰc . . . Ἀλεξάνδρειαν. Here the assessed total seems to have been divided into a sum 'credited' or 'charged' (cf. 2 n.) to the province of Arcadia in Alexandria and a sum 'payable' (cf. 4 n.) in Alexandria, although what precisely these terms mean is not clear to me. Only after this division of the assessed total do we find ἀπεcτάλη κτλ., followed by a list of various persons who escorted payments from Arcadia to the capital, as in **3636**.

1 The word ἀρουρατίων has appeared only three times before, see XLVIII **3397** 22 n. In P. Cair. Masp. III 67329 ii 8 it refers to taxes assessed in proportion to the total area of the lands of a village (καθ' ὁμοιότητα πάcηc τῆc ἀρουρατίονοc τῆc αὐτῆc κώμηc). The date is *c*.529-30. In P. Lips. I 62 ii 21 (AD 385) and XLVIII **3397** 22 (late iv AD) a tax called χρυcόc or χρυcίον (τῆc) ἀρουρατίωνοc is mentioned. A tax for the freight charges of seagoing ships is known to have been assessed by arurage, see XVII **2113** (cf. A. C. Johnson, L. C. West, *Byzantine Egypt* 160-1), XLVIII **3424** 3-4, so that it looks as if the same tax is involved here. For other levies assessed by a similar method see R. S. Bagnall, 'Bullion Purchases and Landholding', *CÉ* 52 (1977) 322-36.

2 ἐλογίcθ(η). It is not clear whether this should be translated as 'credited' or 'charged', cf. *CÉ* 49 (1974) 166 n. 1.

ἐν Ἀ[λεξανδρείᾳ. Cf. 16.

3 Cf. 18, τοῖc ὁρρίοιc τῆc αὐτῆ[c. For the Latin word in the papyri see S. Daris, *Lessico latino* 80. These *horrea* are presumably the state granaries in or around Alexandria, cf. A. Calderini, *Diz. geogr.* i 1. 135, P. Turner 45. 4-5 n. This last document, dated AD 374, has τοῖc κατ' Ἀλεξάνδρειαν θείοιc θηcαυροῖc, while later parallels have τοῖc ὁρρίοιc (XXIV **2408** 9; AD 397) and τοῖc ὁρ(ρίοιc) κατὰ τὴν Ἀλεξ(άνδρειαν) (P. Ryl. IV 652. 10; late iv or early v). This word might lead us to expect accounts of taxes in grain, but ναύλων ἀρουρατεί[ωνοc seems likely to be a tax in gold, cf. 1 n., 7 n., and γαλαθηνῶ[ν to be a tax payable in kind, i.e. in animals, see 15 n., or in money or bullion. In the first case we might guess that the freight charges were applied to grain taxes and were therefore payable at the granaries, but it is harder to see how sucking pigs are connected with granaries.

λ[. I take τῆc αὐτῆc to refer back to Ἀ[λεξανδρείᾳ in 2, and λ[as separate. It is not alpha for Ἀ[λεξανδρείαc or mu for μ[εγαλοπόλεωc.

4 τελεῖται. Cf. **3636** 3, 5, 11. The present tense creates a difficulty. Perhaps the meaning is 'are payable' rather than 'are being paid', see **3636** 3 n. In **3636** 3, 11, the subject is νο(μίcματα) ιδ.

7 Φοιβάμ[μωνοc. Cf. **3636** 11. Jonas, see 9, 11, and 12, also appears in **3636** 10, 12 (twice), and his name is distinctive. It is likely, therefore, that ναύλα ἀρουρατίωνοc were payable in gold solidi like the tax for πλατυπήγια, as the references to χρυcόc or χρυcίον (τῆc) ἀρουρατίωνοc also suggest, see 1 n., cf. 3 n., and that the same persons escorted shipments of gold deriving from various taxes on their journeys from Arcadia to Alexandria.

10 π[αραπομποῦ. Cf. **3635** 3 n. This word was probably abbreviated to παρ' or παραπ', see **3636** 7-12.

13 This line may answer to ἐλογίcθ(η) in 2 or to τελεῖται in 4. Presumably it does not just give the total of the payments in 7-12, since that is given very succinctly at the end of the list in **3636** 5.

14 Palaeographically χί(νονται) ͵α[, 'total 1,000(+ ?)', seems attractive, but it is far from certain, especially because we miss the units of payment, which in this case ought to be gold solidi, $\overset{o}{\nu}$ = νο(μίcματα), cf. 7 n.

15-18 This passage is similar to 1-5, see n., but it looks as if it did not have the section represented by 4.

15 Cf. Diocletian, *Edict. de pret.*, 4. 46 (ed. S. Lauffer or M. Giacchero), where γαλαθηνοῦ ἀπὸ γάλακτοc translates *porcelli la{n}ctantis*. A Megarian copy of the Greek has χοίρου γαλακτοπότου in his place. Sucking pigs seem likely to be meant here, cf. A. C. Johnson, L. C. West, *Byzantine Egypt* 206-7, but the only occurrence of γαλαθηνόc in the papyri is as an adjective agreeing with ἐρίφουc, 'kids' (P. Cair. Zen. III 59429. 17; iii BC).

There is no other record of such a tax or levy. We may guess that the pigs were needed to supply meat to Alexandria on a system like that by which Rome was supplied with live pigs from Campania, Samnium, and Lucania, see A. H. M. Jones, *LRE* i 702-3.

16 Cf. 2 n.

17 Cf. 3 n.

18 ἐν Ἀλεξ[ανδρείᾳ? We expect rather εἰς Ἀλεξάνδρειαν, cf. **3635** 2, **3636** 4, but it cannot be read. Probably this is a clerical error induced by memories of ll. 2, 4, 13, and 16.

3635. Tax Accounts

65 6B.39/E(7)a back   25.5 × 17 cm   Fifth century

On the front is **3629**.

καὶ ἀπὸ λόγου ἐρέας—ὁ κ(ανὼν)   (vac.)   λί(τρ.) ͵ηφνδ

ἀφ' ὧν ἀπεστάλ(η) εἰς τὴν μεγαλόπολιν Ἀλεξάνδρειαν διὰ

διαφόρων παραπ(ομπῶν)   (vac.)   λί(τρ.) ͵δψξζ χρ(υσοῦ) λί(τρ.) β

                                                (οὐγκ.) δ γρ(αμμ.) κ

    λοιπαὶ   (vac.)   λί(τρ.) ͵γψπζ

5   (vac.)   ο(ὕτως)   (vac.)

    Ἀφροδ(ιτοπολίτου) λί(τρ.) ψμβ   Μεμφίτου   λί(τρ.)   χρε

    Λητοπολ(ίτου)   λί(τρ.) φξε   Ἀρσινοείτου   λί(τρ.)   ͵αφκ

    Κυνοπολ(ίτου)   λί(τρ.) ϲκ   Ἡρακλεοπολ(ίτου) λί(τρ.)   με

                                                (vac.)

καὶ ἀ[πὸ λό]γου κηροῦ – ὁ κ(ανὼν)   λί(τρ.) [.] . μθ

· · · · ·

1 κ/, ⟨, and so throughout   2 απεσταλ/   3 παραπ/, χρ⟨ βΕδυρκ   5 ο—   6 αφροδ/

7 λητοπολ/; l. Ἀρσινοΐτου   8 κυνοπολ/, ηρακλεοπολ/   9 κ/

'And from the account for wool: The assessment: lb. 8,554.

'From which there have been sent to the great city of Alexandria through different escorts, lb. 4,767: gold lb. 2, oz. 4, scr. 20.

'Remaining, lb. 3,787,

Viz.:

Aphroditopolite lb. 742, Memphite lb. 695, Letopolite lb. 565, Arsinoite lb. 1,520, Cynopolite lb. 220, Heracleopolite lb. 45.'

'From the account for wax: The assessment: lb. [?]?49. . . .'

1 For levies of wool in Egypt see A. H. M. Jones, *LRE* i 837, ii 1351 n. 32. Cf. XLVIII **3420** 37–9, **3428** 19, P. Turner 47. 5, 9, 10.

For the abbreviation representing λίτρα cf. P. Lond. IV p. 601. In **3628–33** the abbreviation is different, λ.

2 μεγαλόπολιν. Cf. VIII **1130** 6 n.

3 παραπ(ομπῶν). These are obviously official escorts of tax payments, Latin *prosecutores*, cf. e.g. *C. Theod.* viii 5. 18, viii 5. 40, viii 5. 47–8, x 24. 3, xii 6. 13, xii 8. 1, xiii 9. 4. Outside this group of documents, see **3634** 10, **3636** 4, 6–11, the word appears in only three papyri, I **127** 4, 11, XVI **1844** 1, 5, and SB VI 9139. 12, all of which are undated but plausibly assigned to the sixth century or later. Earlier the words καταπομπός and προπομπός were used in the same sense, cf. L **3576** 6 n.

The significance of the sum of 2 lb. 4 oz. 20 scr. of gold is not clear. The figures of wool in pounds work out correctly as read and the readings seem convincing, though there are various patches of damage. Since the amount in gold, equal to 692 scruples, and the sums in pounds do not possess common factors, it seems unlikely that the gold is simply the value of one of the amounts of wool.

6–8 It seems that the assessments for the Oxyrhynchite, Nilopolite, and Theodosiopolite nomes had been delivered in full and were included in the amount of 4,767 pounds given in l. 3. This amount may also have included contributions from the nomes listed here as owing the amounts against their names.

9 κηροῦ. Cf. XLVIII **3412** introd., P. Turner 47. 2, 6. Very little is known about such levies. The one in **3412** was apparently destined for Alexandria, but the wording there is extremely puzzling.

3636. Tax Accounts

65　6B.39/E(3)a back　　　　　　　　22 × 32 cm　　　　　　　　Fifth century

On the front is **3628**.

καὶ ἀπὸ λόγου [π]λατυπηγίων—ὁ κ(ανὼν) τῆς αὐτῆς θ𝕾″ νο(μ.)　,αϙ

2　Κυν(οπολίτου) νο(μ.) ξβ (ἤμ.) (τρίτ.), Ὀξυρ(υγχίτου) νο(μ.) ϲϙη,
　　　Ἡρακλ(εοπολίτου) νο(μ.) ϲνα (ἕκτ.), Νιλ(οπολίτου) νο(μ.) ϙο
　　　(δίμοιρ.), Ἀφ(ροδιτοπολίτου) νο(μ.) ϙβ, Μεμφ(ίτου) νο(μ.)
　　　λζ (δίμοιρ.), Λητ[(οπολίτου)] νο(μ.) ζ (ἤμ.), Ἀρσι(νοΐτου)
　　　νο(μ.) ρξγ, Θεοδ(οσιοπολίτου) νο(μ.) ιχ (ἕκτ.).′

3　‵τελ(εῖται) νο(μ.) ιδ.′
　　ἀφ′ ὧν [ἀ]πεστάλ(η) ε[ἰ]ϲ τὴν μεγ[α]λόπ[ο]λιν Ἀλεξάνδρειαν διὰ διαφόρων

5　παραπομπῷ[ν] ϲ[ὺ]ν τῶν τελουμένων ἐν αὐτῇ　　　νο(μ.)　,αλα (δίμοιρ.)
　　　　(vac.)　　　　　οὕτωϲ　　　(vac.)

　　Μεϲορὴ ⁻ δι(ὰ) Πτολεμαίου παραπ(ομποῦ)　νο(μ.) χιβ
　　Θὼθ　ε̄ δι(ὰ) Ἰωάννου παρ(απομποῦ)　νο(μ.) π
　　Φαῶφι　ε̄ δι(ὰ) Μακαρίου παρ(απομποῦ)　νο(μ.) οζ (ἤμ.) (τρίτ.)
10　Ἀθὺρ　ῑθ̄ δι(ὰ) Ἰωνᾶ παραπ(ομποῦ)　νο(μ.) ρν
　　Χοίακ　κ⁻ δι(ὰ) Φοιβάμμωνοϲ παρ(απομποῦ) νο(μ.) κε (ἤμ.) (τρίτ.),
　　　　　　　　　　　　　　καὶ τελεῖται νο(μ.) ιδ
　　Μεϲορὴ ιᾱ δι(ὰ) Ἰωνᾶ παραπ(ομποῦ)　　νο(μ.)　λ , Φαῶφι ιϛ
　　　　　　　　　　　δι(ὰ) Ἰωνᾶ νο(μ.) μβ.
　　λοιπ[ὰ] πρὸϲ κανόνα　　　(vac.)　　　νο(μ.) νη (τρίτ.)
　　　　(vac.)　　　ο(ὕτωϲ)　　　(vac.)
15　[Μ]εμφίτου　　　νο(μ.) λζ (δίμοιρ.) Λητοπολ(ίτου) νο(μ.) ζ (ἤμ.)
　　Θεοδοϲιοπολ(ίτου) νο(μ.) ιγ (ἕκτ.)　　(vac.)
　　　　　　　　(vac.)

1 κ/　　2 κυνℓξβℓγ″οξυρ/, ηρακλ/ℓϲναϲ″νιλ/ℓρϙℓϲαφ/, μεμφ/ℓλζℓℓϲλητ[/?]ℓζℓ αρϲⁱ, θεοδ/ℓιγϛ″
3 τελ/　4 [α]πεϲταλ/　5 ℓ,αλαℓϲ　6 δι/, and so throughout, παραπ/　8 παρ/
9 παρ/　ℓοζℓ γ″　10 παραπ/　11 παρ/, ℓκεℓ γ″　12 παραπ/　13 ℓνηγ″　14 ο—
15 ℓλζℓϲ, λητοπολ/ ℓζℓ　16 θεοδοϲιοπολ/ ℓιγϛ″

καὶ ἀ]π̣ὸ̣ [λ]ό̣γο̣υ ὄνων καὶ βοῶν καὶ μιcθ(οῦ?) ἀρτοκ(όπων?) τῆc
μεγαλοπόλεωc Ἀλεξανδρείαc
τῆc αὐτῆc] θϛʹʹ (vac.) ὁ κ(ανὼν) νο(μ.) ρι (ἥμ.) (δωδέκατ.) κα̣ὶ
ἀργυρ(ίου?) (μονάδ.?) κ καὶ (δην.μυρ.?) ͵δφ
(vac.) ο(ὕτωc) (vac.)
. . . .] ὄνων καὶ βοῶν νο(μ.) μθ (τρίτ.), μιcθ(οῦ?) ἀρ̣τ̣ο̣κ̣(όπων?) (μονάδ.?)
ι̣α̣. ἀπεcτάλ(η) πλῆρ(εc).
. . . .] ὄνων καὶ βοῶν νο(μ.) ξα (τέταρτ.), μιcθ(οῦ?) ἀρ̣τ̣[ο]κ̣(όπων?) . .
͵δφ. ἀπεcτάλ(η) πλ(ῆρεc).

17 μιcθαρτοκ/ 18 κ/ ϑρι∟ι̅β̅, αργυρ/∩κ, μ̆ ͵δφ 19 ο— 20 ϑμθγʹʹμιcθαρτ̣ο̣κ̣/∩ι̣α̣ απεcταλ/πληρ/ 21 ϑξαd/μιcθαρ̣τ̣[ο]κ̣/. . ͵δφ απεcταλ/πλ/ /

'And from the account for flat-bottomed boats: The assessment for the same 9th (indiction): sol. 1,090.

'Cynopolite sol. $62\frac{5}{6}$, Oxyrhynchite sol. 298, Heracleopolite sol. $251\frac{1}{6}$, Nilopolite sol. $170\frac{2}{3}$, Aphroditopolite sol. 72 (?), Memphite sol. $37\frac{2}{3}$, Letopolite sol. $7\frac{1}{2}$, Arsinoite sol. 163, Theodosiopolite sol. $13\frac{1}{6}$ (?). Sol. 14 are being paid (?).'

'From which there have been sent to the great city of Alexandria through different escorts, with those that are paid in it (?), sol. $1{,}031\frac{2}{3}$,

viz.:

Mesore	. . ., through Ptolemaeus, escort	sol. 612 (?)
Thoth	5, through John	sol. 80
Phaophi	5, through Macarius, escort	sol. $77\frac{5}{6}$
Hathyr	19, through Jonas, escort	sol. 150
Choeac	2 (?), through Phoebammon, escort	sol. $25\frac{5}{6}$, and there are being paid (?) sol. 14
Mesore	11, through Jonas, escort	sol. 30 (?), Phaophi 16, through Jonas sol. 42.

'Remaining, by reference to the assessment, sol. $58\frac{1}{3}$,

'Viz.:

Memphite sol. $37\frac{2}{3}$, Letopolite sol. $7\frac{1}{2}$, Theodosiopolite sol. $13\frac{1}{6}$.

'And from the account for donkeys and oxen and bakers' wages (?) for the great city of Alexandria for the same 9th (indiction): The assessment: sol. $110\frac{7}{12}$ and in money (?) monads (?) 20 and den. myr. (?) 4,500,

viz.:

Donkeys and oxen sol. $49\frac{1}{3}$, bakers' wages (?) monads (?) 11; they were sent in full.
Donkeys and oxen sol. $61\frac{1}{4}$, bakers' wages (?) . . . 4,500; they were sent in full.'

1 On payments for the maintenance of flat-bottomed boats see R. Rémondon, *Revue de philologie* 80 (ser. 3, vol. 28; 1954) 204–6. The text of the papyrus published by Rémondon has appeared again as SB VI 9614 and as P. Sakaon 77. It is assigned to *c.* AD 283. The word *πλατυπήγιον* has also appeared in XIV **1652** a 2, b 2, XXXI **2615** 1 (both iii AD) and in P. Thead. 59 (= P. Sakaon 75). 3 (iv AD). The written form in the papyri is invariably *πλατυπηγ-*, as if deriving from *πήγνυμι*, but it must be compared with Strabo iv 4. 1 *πλατύπυγα δὲ ποιοῦcι καὶ ὑψίπρυμνα καὶ ὑψίπρῳρα διὰ τὰc ἀμπώτειc, δρυΐνηc ὕληc, ἧc ἐcτιν εὐπορία*, 'they'—the Veneti of Gaul—'make flat-bottomed boats with high sterns and high prows because of the tides, out of oak timber, of which there is an abundance'. On the frequent interchange of hypsilon and eta in the papyri see F. T. Gignac, *Grammar* i 262–7, esp. 266–7.

2–3 These lines were added on a smaller scale, but apparently by the same hand, after 4 had been written. They are set out into the left-hand margin and 3 is so short that it is entirely in the margin under the beginning of 2.

2 This list of nine territories is to be compared with Hierocles, *Synecdemus* 729. 1–730. 4, *Ἐπαρχία Ἀρκαδίαc, ὑπὸ ἡγεμόνα, πόλειc θ̅: Κυνῶν, Ὀξύρυγχοc, Ἡρακλεύc, Ἀρcενοίτηc, Θεοδοcιούπολιc, Νικόπολιc,*

Ἀφροδιτῶ, Πέμφις, Λίττους, which may be paraphrased, if we ignore the bad spelling and the inconsistencies, as follows: 'Province of Arcadia, under a *praeses*, 9 cities: Cynopolis, Oxyrhynchus, Heracleopolis, Arsinoe, Theodosiopolis, Aphroditopolis, Memphis, Letopolis'. Compare also the very similar list in George of Cyprus, *Descriptio Orbis Romani* 744–751a, which specifies Oxyrhynchus as the μητρόπολις or provincial capital. Both these authorities also mention a Theodosiopolis in the Lower Thebaid (Hier. 730. 7, Geo. Cypr. 763), see below.

Clearly, therefore, this whole roll relates to the province of Arcadia. The date of the creation of the province is discussed in **3628–36** introd.

The distinction between the Arsinoite and Theodosiopolite assessments gives the first unambiguous proof that Theodosiopolis was not simply another name for Arsinoe, as Grenfell and Hunt thought, see P. Tebt. II pp. 363–5. They allowed, however, that there was, or might be, some evidence for a separate territory, p. 364, a proviso which practically disappears in the summary in A. H. M. Jones *CERP²*, 343. H. Gauthier, *Les Nomes d'Égypte* 202–5, though entitling his chapter 'Le nome Théodosiopolite', came to the conclusion that there were, at different times, two Theodosiopolite territories, one carved out of the old Arsinoite nome, the other out of the Hermopolite. The second area has been discussed recently by M. Drew-Bear, *Le Nome Hermopolite* 48, 111–12. She maintains the distinction between the two Theodosiopolite territories (48) against P. J. Sijpesteijn, who allowed only one nome of that name and took it to be the one near Arsinoe, see P. Wisc. I (= Pap. Lugd. Bat. XVI) 10 introd., pp. 40–1. That document, of 10 October 468, is of great importance to the problem. One of the parties, though temporarily resident in Oxyrhynchus, came, according to the *ed. pr.*, ἀπὸ κώμης Κέρκε τοῦ ἄνω Θεοδοσιοπολίτου (5–6). In Egyptian topography ἄνω means 'southern', and κάτω 'northern'. This was taken to indicate a division of the nome into two sections. The obvious alternative, that there were two nomes of the same name so distinguished, was rejected, but we may compare the same terms used of the two Cynopolite nomes, see H. Gauthier, *Les Nomes* 193–4, A. H. M. Jones, *CERP²* 493 n. 66, XLVII **3345** 50 n., XLIX **3477** 5 and n. If there were two nomes of this name in 468, the 'southern' Theodosiopolite must clearly have been the one cut out of the Hermopolite. The village name Κέρκε is unattested. The editor claimed that the reading 'cannot be doubted' (p. 40) and this claim is repeated in A. Calderini, *Dizionario dei nomi geografici* i 2. 98. The papyrus is illustrated in pl. iv of P. Wisc. I, and on a larger scale, though still reduced, in E. Boswinkel–P. J. Sijpesteijn, *Greek Papyri, Ostraca and Mummy Labels*, no. 45. The body of the document, ll. 1–17, has epsilons of two kinds, one with a strong diagonal projection to the upper right, the other very rounded; both are large letters. The final letter of the village name is tiny, but clearly recognizable as an alpha. There are numerous similar ones in the text, but the beginning of καταμένοντι in l. 6 provides a good comparison. The village name Κερκᾶ is also unattested, but it may well be a variant of the well-known Hermopolite village of Κιρκᾶ, see M. Drew-Bear, *Le Nome Hermopolite* 140–1. The change of iota to epsilon is attested, see S.-T. Teodorsson, *The Phonology of the Ptolemaic Koine* 100–1, and this case may also have been affected by numerous village names beginning with the element Κερκε-, cf. J. Yoyotte, 'Le problème des Kerké', *Revue d'Égyptologie* 14 (1962) 86. The village of Κιρκᾶ is now known to have belonged to a Theodosiopolite nome in the Byzantine period from P. Vat. gr. 2653, as reported by R. Pintaudi, *ZPE* 48 (1982) 101 n. 15, ἀπὸ κώμης Κιρκᾶ τοῦ Θεοδοσιοπολίτου νομοῦ.[1]

There is no doubt that two places called Theodosiopolis existed contemporaneously for a long period. They were obviously named after one or both of the two emperors called Theodosius (379–95; 402–50). There may have been a period at the beginning during which one existed without the other. The one near Hermopolis is still mentioned in the papyri as late as 614, if SB I 4669. 6 is correctly restored with τοῦ [Θεοδο]σιουπολίτου νομοῦ, cf. P. Ross.-Georg. V 42 (AD 604). The one near Arsinoe is referred to as late as 600, see P. Lond. i 113. 5 c (p. 212).

There are various patches of damage which mean that we cannot be one hundred per cent sure that the figures are correctly read, but as offered they satisfy the arithmetic and the traces. The sum for the Theodosiopolite is confirmed by 15–16, from which it seems almost certain that all three nomes concerned were in arrears for the full amounts of their assessments. The second figure of the Nilopolite assessment was perhaps obscured by a riser from 4 (the eta of τήν) and then inked over, but ο = 70 is by far the best of the possibilities, which are α to θ, plus ς = 6, κ to π, plus ρ = 90. The worst damage affects the assessment for the Aphroditopolite, but the arithmetic indicates that it should be either οβ = 72 or πς = 86, depending on whether or not the fourteen solidi of 3 were part of the total assessment or not. The most prominent trace is

[1] The same correction of the reading in P. Wisc. 10 and the same identification of the village have now been made independently by M. Drew-Bear, *CÉ* 54 (1979) 299–303, *RÉA* 83 (1981) 29 n. 27.

a diagonal which looks as if it was part of beta, beginning where the waist swells out into the lower curve of the right-hand side.

The figures are of some importance because this money tax was quite probably divided among the city territories in proportion to their economic strength. The Oxyrhynchite territory pays the most (298 sol.), which suits the fact that George of Cyprus calls Oxyrhynchus the metropolis of the province, see above. Then follow the Heracleopolite (251⅙), Nilopolite (170⅔—if rightly read), Arsinoite (163), Aphroditopolite (72—if rightly read), Cynopolite (62⅝), Memphite (37⅔), Theodosiopolite (13½), and Letopolite (7½). The vast differences are very striking and perhaps at first sight seem to contradict the idea that they are proportionate to the economy of the territories, but at least we can see that they fit with the evidence from later Byzantine times that the Oxyrhynchite and the Cynopolite territories were lumped together (XVI **1909**; vii AD), as were the Arsinoite and the Theodosiopolite (cf. P. Tebt. I, p. 363).

3 τελ(εῖται) νο(μ.) ιδ. Cf. 5 and especially 11 for the expansion of τελ/. Compare also **3634** 4 and n. From 5 and **3634** 4 it becomes clear that we need to understand ἐν Ἀλεξανδρείᾳ with τελ(εῖται) here and in 11. The literal translation, therefore, is 'fourteen solidi are being paid (in Alexandria)', but this is very far from being clear in meaning. The sense may be that the sum is payable in Alexandria, that is, not to be collected in Arcadia and transported to Alexandria by *prosecutores*, see **3635** 3 n., but to be paid in Alexandria itself. If the figures in 2 are correctly read, see n., these fourteen solidi do not form part of the sums assigned to the city territories but are assessed on the province as a whole without being divided. This seems rather implausible at first sight, but perhaps we may guess that there were persons legitimately resident in Alexandria who were registered as provincials of Arcadia and obliged to pay this tax on the spot in Alexandria.

5 παραπομπῷ[ν]. Cf. **3635** 3 n.

ϛ[ὺ]ν τῶν τελουμένων. The writer probably thought that he had written μετά rather than ϲύν, though there is a possibility that the error is connected with the suppression of the dative, see J. Humbert, *La Disparition du datif*. There are some few examples of ϲύν with the genitive in the papyri and elsewhere, see *LSJ* s.v., and the genitive also occurs occasionally after ἐν, see CPR V 15 3 n.

The τελούμενα ἐν αὐτῇ are the fourteen solidi mentioned already in 3, see n., and again, as an element of this section of the account, in 11.

17 ὄνων καὶ βοῶν . . . Ἀλεξανδρείας. From XVI **1905** 17–19 we know that this tax was calculated on land area, cf. J. Karayannopulos, *Finanzwesen* 125 n. 10, A. C. Johnson and L. C. West, *Byzantine Egypt* 209. The damaged state of **1905** hardly justifies the figures given by Johnson and West.

μιϲθ(οῦ?) ἀρτοκ(όπων?) . . . Ἀλεξανδρείας. This is an unknown tax, but it was presumably part of the arrangements for the food supply of Alexandria. We may compare the measures to control the bakers of Rome and Constantinople, see A. H. M. Jones, *LRE* ii 699–701.

18 ἀργυρ(ίου?) (μονάδ.?) κ καὶ (δην. μυρ.?) ,δφ. The interpretation remains questionable for the moment. The sign ∩ usually means μυριάς, see XVI **1905** 21 n. It is frequent in **3628–33** in the combination ×∩ (δηναρίων μυριάδες). But 20 den. myr. is less than the price of a pound of meat in this period and looks absurdly small in the context of an assessment for the whole province, so that there is a great incentive to look for an alternative meaning for the sign. Perhaps it might represent μο(νάϲ), with mu over omicron in vestigial forms. It has recently been suggested that a μονάϲ is not a pound of silver, as previously thought, but a myriad of myriads of denarii, i.e. 100,000,000, see XLVIII **3402** 5 and n. The text there is damaged but the reading and interpretation seem convincing. Here 2,000,000,000 denarii would be the equivalent of fifty solidi, taking 4,000 myriads of denarii as a convenient exchange rate for a solidus, see **3628–36** introd. This sum would be quite appropriate in its place, though so indeed would 20 pounds of silver, the equivalent of one hundred solidi. The great objection to this hypothesis, which is put forward tentatively, is that it would be extremely confusing to have the same symbol representing values so immensely different.

Before ,δφ there is a clear mu surmounted by a shallow bowl that could easily be a hypsilon. In P. Mich. XV 740, to take just one example, this appears frequently as the abbreviation for μυ(ριάϲ), i.e. a myriad of denarii, so there is no difficulty in taking it so here, even though in **3628–33** this sum is always represented by ×∩. This seems to reinforce the previous argument that ∩κ must be something larger than 20 den. myr.

20–1 Though there are difficulties in the calculations, see below, it appears that the whole assessment was divided into two categories, one for each line here. The lost beginnings of the lines would have told us what these categories were. A blank margin of *c*. 3.5 cm at the foot suggests that the paragraph is complete, so that if ια in 20 is right, we expect ∩θ καὶ μ̄ ,δφ in 21 to make up the sum specified in 18. The remains seem far too short for that. They might suit ∩θ ,δφ, i.e. ∩θ ⟨καὶ μ̄⟩ ,δφ.

3637. OFFICIAL LETTER

54 1B.26(E)/B(6)a   17 × 42 cm   19 (?) October 623

The mention of a shipment of gold coin to the 'king of kings' allows us to assign this letter, dated by indiction, month, and day, to the last Persian occupation of Egypt.

The recipient is one Marinus, whose titles suggest that he may have been a *scholasticus*, possibly a man known from other documents, see 20 n. He is informed that his secretary has paid to the sender the large sum of 3,962 gold solidi in respect of 'the first instalment for the twelfth indiction', and is requested to send the balance within three days, since a shipment of gold is to be dispatched to the Persian king. It is a pity that we do not learn the circumstances of the shipment. The 3,962 solidi, coined at seventy-two to the libra, must have weighed just over fifty-five Roman pounds, a figure which can be compared with two assessments for compulsory bullion purchases of the early fourth century of twenty-eight pounds and thirty-eight pounds for the whole of the Oxyrhynchite nome (XVII **2106**, XLIII **3120**). Evidently a tax or levy was involved here too, and we must reckon, even though the country was in the hands of the Persians, that 'the first instalment' refers to the customary payment of taxes in three instalments, see J. Karayannopulos, *Finanzwesen* 189–91, E. R. Hardy, *Large Estates* 55–6, so that the figure mentioned is likely to be less than one-third of the amount payable. However, though the sum is a large one, it should also be compared with those in XVI **1909**, where we have a list of assessments which may represent the full obligations of at least three cities for a year in the seventh century. Oxyrhynchus and Cynopolis are assessed jointly at 59,500 *sol.*, Heracleopolis at 57,500 *sol.* Part of an entry for Nilopolis also survives. Possibly this list would have contained originally assessments for all nine cities of the province of Arcadia, cf. **3636** 2 n.

The letter comes from an unnamed 'us' (ἡμῖν 5, 11, 16, cf. θέλομεν 18), but the plural may well be a Byzantine formality, since Marinus is called ἡ ὑμετέρα μεγαλοπρεπὴς σοφία. In spite of the polite forms the tone is that of a superior to a subordinate.

Orders relating to the gold has been issued by a high Persian official, 'our master the all-praiseworthy Saralaneozan', who is mentioned also in BGU II 377. 1. That papyrus is supposed to come from the Arsinoite nome, indicating that the Persian's authority may have covered a wider area than that of the city territory of Oxyrhynchus. It may have extended to the province of Arcadia or even to the whole of the country.

A useful new bibliography relating to the Persian occupation has appeared in the second edition (1978) by P. M. Fraser of A. J. Butler, *The Arab Conquest of Egypt* (1902), pp. xlvi–xlviii (Greek papyri), liii–liv (Pahlavi papyri—add now P. Rainer Cent. 13, pp. 215–28), lviii–lix (modern works).

The main text (1–19) is written across the fibres of the recto of a piece cut from a roll, including three sheet-joins 9.25, 20.5, and 32 cm from the top. While it was rolled up the piece suffered some damage which has produced an undulating left-hand edge, but very little of the writing has been lost. The address and endorsement, of one line each (20–1), are written along the fibres of the verso.

In format this letter is very like XVI **1843** (18.3 × 43.3 cm), which is in the same hand and related in subject, though complications arise when we try to define the relation closely. That letter is from an unnamed 'us' to a person referred to as ἡ ὑμετέρα μεγαλοπρεπὴς καὶ πάνσοφος φιλία. It is dated to Hathyr 9 (= 5 or 6 November) of a twelfth indiction and acknowledges receipt of 2,016 solidi, half of which sum is to make up the first instalment of the twelfth indiction for Oxyrhynchus, while half is for the same instalment of the same indiction for Cynopolis. The money was delivered by a secretary with the same name and title as the man in our text.

I am inclined to believe that **1843** is also addressed to Marinus, cf. 20–1 n., and is the next stage or a succeeding stage in the same transaction. In that case Marinus has not obeyed the instruction to pay within three days. It has taken nearly three weeks, 19 (?) October to 6 November 623. That seems not too improbable. Also Marinus may have done more than he was asked, if our 3,962 solidi were all for Oxyrhynchus and he was asked to pay only the remaining 1,008, i.e. 4,970 in all. On the other hand, our 3,962 may be for both cities, and he may be asked in our letter to pay the remaining 2,016, i.e. 5,978 in all for both cities. Also there is the possibility of a payment, or more than one payment, in the interim, though ὑπὲρ cυμπληρώcεωc seems to imply that the sum was completely paid by the date of **1843**, so that we need not reckon with subsequent payments. But, of course, the payment acknowledged in our letter need not have been the first. Exact calculations, therefore, are out of the question. What we gain chiefly is a vivid impression of tax-collecting activity at a fairly high level of the provincial administration.

+

+] καταλαβὼν τὰ ἐνταῦθα Γεώργιος
  ὁ περίβλεπτος χαρτουλάριος τῆς
  ὑμ]ετέρας μεγαλοπρεποῦς cοφίας
5 κ]ατέβαλεν ἡμῖν ὑπὲρ τῆς πρώτης
  καταβολῆς δωδεκάτης ἰνδ(ικτίωνος) νομίcματα
  τρι]cχίλια ἐννακόcια ἑξήκοντα δύο
  πλήρης Ἀλεξανδρείας καὶ πρὸς τῷ
  αὐ]τὴν εἰδέναι ἐcήμανα. cπουδάcῃ δὲ
10 κ]αὶ ἐντὸς ἡμερῶν τριῶν τὴν cυμπλήρ(ωcιν)
  τ]ῆς πρώτης καταβολῆς πέμψῃ ἡμῖν.
  ἰ]δοὺ γὰρ καὶ τὰ περὶ τούτου γεγράφηκεν αὐτῇ

  6 ἰνδ/   7 l. ἐνακόcια   8 l. τό   10 cυμπληρ/

ὁ δ]εcπότης ἡμῶν ὁ πανεύφημος

C]αραλανεοζᾶν. λοιπὸν καὶ αὐτὴ cπουδάcῃ

15 δι]ὰ cυντομίαc τὴν cυμπλήρωcιν τῆc

π]ρώτης καταβολῆς πέμψαι ἡμῖν,

ἐ[π]ειδὴ τὴν ἐκπομπὴν τοῦ χρυcίου

θ]έλομεν ποιήcαcθαι πρὸc τὸν δεcπότην

ἡ]μῶν τὸν βαcιλέα τῶν βαcιλέων. +

20 Back. + τῷ τὰ πά(ντα) μ(ου) cοφ(ωτάτῳ) τι(μῆc) ἀξί῾ῳ' (vac.) Μαρίνῳ . [

(m. 2) Φαῶφι ϟα, ἰ(νδικτίωνοc) ιβ, νο(μίcματα) Γ ϡξβ ὑ(πὲρ) (πρώτηc)

κατα(βολῆc) (m. 3) Ῥαcβαϟα . [

20 ᾱμ̄cοφ/τϟαξΐ   21 ϟιβ β̄/, ῥϟκᾱ

'On his arrival here George, the admirable secretary of your magnificent wisdom, paid down to us in respect of the first instalment for the twelfth indiction three thousand nine hundred and sixty-two solidi in full by the Alexandrian standard, and I notify you for your information. Make haste to send us also, within three days, the balance of the first instalment. For remember, you have also had written instructions about this matter from our master the all-praiseworthy Saralaneozan. Now you yourself make haste immediately to send us the balance of the first instalment, since we wish to make the shipment of the gold to our master the king of kings.'

Back. 'To my in all respects most learned (and) worthy of honour Marinus . . .'

'Phaophi 21 (?), indiction 12, 3,962 *solidi* for the first instalment. Rasbana . . .'

2 καταλαβὼν τὰ ἐνταῦθα. Cf. XVI **1856** 5; in **1829** 18–19 restore probably καταλαμβάνοντοc [τὰ], instead of [καὶ?], ἐνταῦθα.

2–3 Cf. XVI **1843** 3 Γεωργίου τοῦ περιβλέπτου . . . χαρτουλαρίου, who is very likely the same, see introd. A George with the same title occurs in XVI **1864**, which is addressed to a Marinus like **3637**, though his title there is τῷ ἐνδοξ(οτάτῳ), and which also mentions a twelfth indiction. Cf. 20 n.

4 μεγαλοπρεποῦc cοφίαc. Cf. cοφ(ωτάτῳ), 20, and n.

6 The twelfth indiction must be that of 623–4, because no other falls in the period of the Persian occupation, AD 619–28, cf. R. S. Bagnall, K. A. Worp, *Chronological Systems* 92–3.

8 Indeclinable πλήρηc is normal, see W. Crönert, *Mem. Gr. Herc.* 179 n. 2.

Ἀλεξανδρείαc. Sc. ζυγῷ, see L. C. West and A. C. Johnson, *Currency* 140–56. They conclude, p. 155, that this is an accounting term indicating that the money must reach Alexandria free of all deductions.

8–9 πρὸc τὼ (= τὸ) [αὐ]τὴν εἰδέναι ἐcήμανα. Cf. **1843** 11–12 πρὸc τὼ (same error) τὴν ὑμετέραν μεγαλοπρεπῆ καὶ πάνcοφον φιλίαν εἰδέναι ἐcήμανα.

9–11 cπουδάcῃ . . . πέμψῃ. In 14 below, cπουδάcῃ, which is a jussive subjunctive of which the understood subject is ἡ ὑμετέρα μεγαλοπρεπὴc cοφία, is followed by an infinitive (πέμψαι 16) as expected, see B. G. Mandilaras, *The Verb* §558. Here it is followed by a second jussive subjunctive, cf. ibid. §554(3).

14 Cf. BGU II 377. 1. Γνῶcιc τῶν δοθ(έντων) εἰc τὸ μαγειρ(εῖον) τοῦ δεcπό(του) ἡμῶν τοῦ πανευφήμ(ου) Cαραλακεοξαν (sic). Dr G. Poethke kindly confirmed from the original that Cαραλανεοζᾶν should be read there also. The Berlin inventory and the publication record that the papyrus came from the Arsinoite nome. If so, this person exercised power in both the Arsinoite and Oxyrhynchite nomes, see introd. The Cαραλαν( ) who appears in SPP X 251(a). 2 might possibly be the same, but there is no strong indication that that person is of very high rank.

It is not clear whether Saralaneozan is a name or a title. Having learnt from A. J. Butler, *The Arab Conquest* 75, that there is a Persian word 'Salar' meaning 'chief', I wondered whether this was the first element, with the common confusion of lambda and rho, see F. T. Gignac, *Grammar* i 102–10. I put this suggestion to Dr Ilya Gershevitch of Jesus College, Cambridge, who is inclined to accept it, though only tentatively. He writes:

'It is indeed likely that, as you suggest, *Saralaneozan* contains *sālār*, "chieftain". By this token there is a prima facie case for not regarding the word as a proper name, but as a title. *Sālār* (or its older form *sardār*) is well attested in titles, but invariably as the second compound-term governing the first, e.g. *spāh-sālār*, "army-chief", or *artēštārān-sālār*, "chief of the warriors", where *artēštārān* is plural of *artēštār*. It is therefore not very likely that in your compound *saral* governs what follows. What may be conceivable is that what follows is an epithet juxtaposed to *saral*. But the division of the words is a headache. Does the second compound-term begin with *a*? Or is its first letter *n*, the preceding *a* being merely a euphonic vowel? Or should one divide *saralan-eozan*, treating the first term as the plural *sālārān* or *sālār*? On this last supposition let me venture a suggestion. In Avestan (spoken in the sixth century BC) the adjective *aiwi.aojah-* occurs, meaning "die Übermacht gewinnend über" (with accusative), see C. Bartholomae, *Altiranisches Wörterbuch* col. 88. This spelling shows that the Old Iranian form of the word was **abi-aujah-*, from which in Middle Persian (spoken from the third century BC to the seventh AD) **ayōz* is to be expected, and in New Persian (from the seventh century onwards) **yōz*. The loss of the *a* of **ayōz* in *late* Middle Persian would be acceptable. Semantically an adjective starting off as 'overpowering' could well, after a millennium, have ended up as 'most powerful'. Since *-ān* is well attested as a suffix in Persian, **yōzān* would not need to differ in meaning from **yōz*. Your Saralaneozan, as **sālārān-yōzān*, would then amount to meaning "most powerful of commanders". I give you this *jeu d'esprit* for what it is worth. No later form of Avestan *aiwi.aojah-* has been identified anywhere.'

The accentuation of Ϲαραλανεοζᾶν is based on Dr Gershevitch's statement that he would 'expect the long word to have borne two stresses, one each on the final syllable of its components, **sālārānyōzân*'.

λοιπόν. For the use of this word in a temporal sense, as the equivalent of ἤδη, see D. Tabachovitz, *Études sur le grec de la basse époque* 32.

15 δι]ὰ ϲυντομίαϲ. Cf. **1843** 14–15 διὰ ϲυντομίαϲ πάϲηϲ.

19 On the title 'king of kings' in this period see E. K. Chrysos, 'The Date of Papyrus SB 4483 and the Persian Occupation of Egypt', *Dodone* 4 (1975) 343–8, esp. 344–5, id., 'The Title Βαϲιλεύϲ in Early Byzantine International Relations', *Dumbarton Oaks Papers* 32 (1978) 29–75, esp. 35–6, cf. G. Rösch, Ὄνομα Βαϲιλείαϲ 156, items no. 2 and 3 with n. 93, R. S. Bagnall and K. A. Worp, *CÉ* 56 (1981) 131, eid., *Regnal Formulas*, 82.

20 ϲοφ(ωτάτῳ) Cf. 3–4 τῆϲ [ὑμ]ετέραϲ μεγαλοπρεποῦϲ ϲοφίαϲ. Marinus ought perhaps to be identified with the *scholasticus* who was the recipient of XVI **1862, 1863** and possibly also **1864**, see A. Claus, Ὁ ϲχολαϲτικόϲ (Diss. Köln, 1965), 155 and n. 3. In PSI VIII 894 there is a *scholasticus* of the same name who has a secretary, whose name, however, is not George but Theodore, cf. ibid., 155. That document, with an invocation of Jesus Christ, but without *intitulatio*, is also dated to a twelfth indiction and may well be of the same year as this one, cf. *CÉ* 56 (1981) 124–31, esp. 129–30.

The last letter of the line is a rounded one, so that it is possible that we should read and restore ϲ[χολαϲτικῷ.

20–1 Line 20 is written in the highly artificial and difficult upright style normal in addresses of this period. It is different in appearance from the body of the letter, but is best taken to be by the same writer. The first half of 21—as far as κατα(βολῆϲ)—is in a small angular hand. It probably belongs to the recipient or a clerk in his employ, the date being the date of the receipt of the letter. The rest of 21 is in a different rounded style.

A photograph of the back of **1843**, which is now itself in Cairo, shows that the address there is the same for the first five words, + τῷ τὰ πά(ντα) μου ϲοφ(ωτάτῳ). After that, before a blank space, there is something which I cannot read and which is different from τι(μῆϲ) ἀξίῳ. After the blank space the writing is mostly lost in a hole; only feet remain in most cases. I cannot fit them to the name of Marinus, but I believe that the other factors indicate that he was the addressee. In the second line of the address there the letters given in the *ed. pr.* as . . .ραϲ Βαγα. . . are clearly part of the same combination as Ῥαϲβαγα. [here. In P. Rainer Cent. 13. 22, l. 4, there occurs a Persian name transliterated from the Pahlavi as Razbānag (p. 223). It seems a possibility that this or some similar name should be recognized here. The final letter does not look like gamma, or kappa, which may be a phonetic alternative, but rather a rounded letter such as sigma. The photograph of **1843** is too indistinct at this point to offer help. Dr Holford-Strevens informs me that Middle Persian *-ag* becomes Modern Persian *-ah*, pronounced *-e*, and suggests that we might reasonably take Ῥαϲβανᾶϲ as a Hellenization of *Razbāna(gh)* with the final consonant already weakening.

II. PRIVATE DOCUMENTS

3638. Cession of a Share of a Vineyard

27 3B.44/H(1–2)a   17 × 35.5 cm   11 September 220

The vineyard in question here was held by the seller in common with his full siblings, of whom there were at least two. By this deed he sold a half of his share to his half-sister by the same father, while the father provided the price of one thousand drachmas and acted for his daughter, who was a minor. Evidently the father was making provision for his daughter by buying for her property from which she could derive an income. The sale is called a cession because the land was part of the allotment made to a military settler of the Ptolemaic period, originally inalienable and held from the king in return for military service, cf. XLIX **3482** introd. For a short bibliography see O. Montevecchi, *La papirologia* 210–11. The best Oxyrhynchite parallels are IX **1208**, XIV **1636**, XXXIV **2723**, XLIX **3498**, and P. Wisc. I 9. The back of the sheet is blank.

I have derived great assistance from a transcript and notes by Sir Eric Turner, and from reading the document with a pupil, Jane Rowlandson.

Μᾶρκος Αὐρήλιος Χαιρήμων υἱὸς Ἑρμίου ἀγορανομήσαντος β[ουλευτοῦ τῆς Ὀξυ-
ρυγχειτῶν πόλεως μητρὸς Ταύριος ἀπὸ τῆς αὐτῆς πόλεως τῇ ὁμοπατρί[ᾳ ἀδελφῇ Αὐρηλίᾳ Τετσείρι μητρὸς Τανετβέως ἀπὸ τῆς αὐτῆς πόλεως οὐδέπω οὔσῃ τῷ[ν ἐτῶν διὰ τοῦ
πατρὸς Αὐρηλίου Ἑρμίου χαίρειν. ὁμολογῶ παρακεχωρηκέναι σοι διὰ τ[οῦ πατρὸς
5   ἡμῶν ἀπὸ τοῦ νῦν εἰς τὸν ἅπαντα χρόνον ἥμισυ μέρος τοῦ ἐπιβάλλον[τός μοι μέρους
περὶ κώμην Σιναρὺ τῆς κάτω τοπαρχίας τοῦ αὐτοῦ νομοῦ ἐκ τοῦ Ῥοδ[ίππου κλήρου
ἀμπελικοῦ κτήματος καὶ τῶν φοινίκων καὶ φυτῶν καὶ ἀκροδρύων κα[ὶ τῆς προσούσης
                                              καλα-
μείαν καὶ ὑδρευμάτων καὶ τῆς ἐπικειμένης αὐτοῖς μηχανῆς καὶ ἐποικίου καὶ λη[νοῦ καὶ
                                              πίθου
καὶ στεμφυλουργικοῦ ὀργάνου καὶ ἡλιαστηρίου καὶ ἑτέρων χρηστηρί[ων καὶ συγ-
10   κυρόν[τ]ων πάντων πάντα ὅσου ἐστὶν ἀρουρηδοῦ κοινωνικῶν πρ[ὸς τοὺς ὁμογνη-
σίου[ς] μου ἀδελφούς, ὧν πάντων γείτονες νότου ὠνημέ[νη c. 12 letters] . .
κᾳὶ ἄλλω[ν], βορρᾶ χ[ύ]ῃς, ἀπηλιώτου πλευρισμός, λιβὸς Τῶμις ποταμό[ς, τὰς δὲ
                                              συμπεφωνημέ-
νας πρὸς [ἀ]λλήλους ὑπὲρ τειμῆς καὶ παραχωρητικοῦ τοῦ αὐτοῦ πωλουμένου σοι καὶ
                                              παραχω-
ρουμένου ὑπ' ἐμοῦ ἡμίσου⟨ς⟩ μέρους τοῦ ἐπιβάλλοντός μοι μέρους τοῦ αὐτοῦ ἀμπελικοῦ
                                              κτή-

1 ϋιος   1–2 l. Ὀξυρυγχιτῶν   3 l. Τετσείρει   7–8 l. καλαμείας   13 l. τιμῆς

15 ματος καὶ τ[ῶν c]υνωνομασμένων αὐτῷ πάντων ἀργυρίου Cεβαστοῦ νομίσματος δραχμὰς
χειλίας αὐ[τό]θι ἀπέσχον παρὰ coῦ τοῦ πατρὸς Ἑρμίου διὰ χειρὸς ἐκ πλήρους, ἃc καὶ

προφέ-
ρῃ ἐντεῦθεν ἀποχαρίζεcθαι τῇ αὐτῇ θυγατρί cου κατὰ χάριν ἀναφαίρετον. διὸ ἀ-
πὸ τοῦ νῦν cὲ τὴν Τετcεῖριν κρατεῖν καὶ κυριεύειν cὺν ἐκγόνοις καὶ τοῖc παρὰ coῦ μεταλημψομένοις τοῦ αὐτοῦ ἡμίcους μέρους τοῦ ὡς πρό{c}κειται ἐπιβάλλοντός μοι μέρους
20 τοῦ τε ἀμπελικοῦ κτήματος καὶ κ[α]λαμείας καὶ τῶν ἄλλων cυνωνομαcμένων πάντων
καὶ τελείαν γενομένην ἐξουcίαν ἔχειν χρᾶcθαι καὶ οἰκονομεῖν περὶ αὐτοῦ ὃν ἐὰν αἱρῇ τρόπον, ὅπερ καὶ ἐπάναγκον παρέξομαί coί τε καὶ τοῖc παρὰ coῦ μεταλημψομένοις ὡ-
αύτως διὰ παντὸς βέβαιον ἀπὸ πάντων πάcῃ βεβαιώcει καὶ καθαρὸν ἀπό τε γεωργί-
ας βαcιλικῆς καὶ οὐcιακῆς γῆς καὶ παντὸς εἴδους καὶ ἀπὸ ἀπεργαcίας καὶ ὑδροφυλακίας

χωμά-
25 των πλὴν μόνων τοῦ αἱροῦντος μέρους τῶν τοῦ κτήματος χωμάτων, ὁμοίως δὲ ἀπὸ
ὀφειλῆ[c] καὶ κατοχῆς πάcης δημοcίας τε καὶ ἰδιωτικῆς καὶ ἀπὸ δημοcίων καὶ

ἐπιμεριcμῶν πάν-
των τῶ[ν] μέχρι τοῦ διελθόντος [κ]αὶ αὐτοῦ τοῦ διελθόντος γ (ἔτους) διὰ τὸ τὰ ἀπὸ τοῦ
ἐνεcτῶτος δ (ἔτους)
πρόcφορα εἶναι coῦ τῆς ὠνουμένη[c], πρὸς ὃν καὶ εἶναι ⟨τὰ⟩ ἀπὸ τοῦ αὐτοῦ ἐνεcτῶτος
ἔτους δημόcια.
κυρία ἡ παραχώρηcις διccὴ γραφεῖcα, ἥνπερ ὁπήνικα ἐὰν αἱρῇ ποιήcομαί coι καὶ διὰ
30 καταλογείου μηδὲν ἕτερον λαμβάνων παρὰ coῦ, τῶν τελῶν καὶ γραμματικῶν ὄντων πρὸς
cὲ τὴν Τετcεῖριν. περὶ δὲ τοῦ ταῦτα ὀρθῶς καὶ δικαίως γε[νέ]cθαι ἐπερωτηθεὶς ὑπὸ coῦ
διὰ τοῦ αὐτοῦ πατρὸς ἡμῶν ὡμολόγηcα. (ἔτους) δ Αὐτοκράτορος Καίcαρος Μάρκου
Αὐρηλίου Ἀντων[ί]νου Εὐcεβοῦς Εὐτυχοῦς Cεβαστοῦ, Θὼθ ιδ‾.
(m. 2) Αὐρήλιος Χαιρήμων Ἑρμίου πέπρακα καὶ παρεχώρηcα τῇ
35 [ὁ]μοπατρίᾳ μου ἀδελφῇ Αὐρηλίᾳ Τετcείρει οὐδέπω οὔcῃ τῶ(ν)
[ἐ]τῶν διὰ τοῦ πατρὸς Αὐρηλίου Ἑρμίου ἥμιcυ μέρος τοῦ ἐ-
πιβάλλοντός μοι μέρους περὶ κώμην Cιναρὺ ἐκ τοῦ Ῥοδίππου κλήρου ἀμπελικοῦ κτήματος καὶ καλαμίας καὶ
τῶν ὡς πρόκειται cυνονομαcμένων πάντων καὶ ἀπέ-
40 cχον τὰc τῆς τιμῆς καὶ παραχωρητικοῦ δραχμὰς χειλίας
καὶ βεβαιώcω ὡς πρόκειται ⟨καὶ⟩ ἐπερωτηθεὶc ὡμολόγηcα.

16 l. χιλίας	18 τετ᾿ceιριν	26 ἰδιωτικης	28 l. πρὸс ἤν	31 τετ᾿ceιριν	35 τῶ
38 l. καλαμείας	39 l. cυνωνομαcμέων	40 l. χιλίας	41 l. ἐπερωτηθείς		

'Marcus Aurelius Chaeremon, son of Hermias former agoranomus councillor of the city of the Oxyrhynchites, mother Tayris, from the same city, to his paternal half-sister Aurelia Tetseiris, mother Tanetbeus, from the same city, not yet of legal age, through their father Aurelius Hermias, greeting. I declare that I have ceded to you through our father from the present for all time a half-share of the share which falls to me in the village of Sinary in the Lower toparchy of the same nome from the allotment of Rhodippus of a vineyard estate and the dates and plants and fruit-trees and the adjoining reed-bed and wells and the irrigation machine installed in them and farmstead and treading-trough and vat and pressing-machine and drying-ground and all other appurtenances and attributes in all respects, of whatever acreage it is, held in common with my full siblings, of all which the boundaries are: on the south bought land of . . . and others, on the north an embankment (?), on the east a side-embankment (?), on the west the Tomis river, and I received on the spot the sum agreed between us in respect of the price and cession-fee for the same half-share being sold to you and ceded by me of the share which falls to me of the same vineyard estate and all the things named along with it, namely one thousand drachmas of money of the coinage of the Augustus from you (our) father Hermias in cash in full, which you also declare that you are henceforth granting to your same daughter as an unreturnable favour. Therefore I declare that from the present you Tetseiris own and possess with your descendants and successors the same half-share of the share falling to me, as aforesaid, of the vineyard estate and reed-bed and all the other things named along with it and on reaching your majority have power to use and dispose of it in whatever way you may choose, and I shall necessarily deliver it to you and your successors likewise perpetually guaranteed against all claims by every guarantee and free of liability for cultivation of imperial and domain land and every impost and for work on dikes and control of water in dikes excepting only the appropriate share of the dikes of the estate, and likewise free of debt and all distraint public and private and from state taxes and all allocations up to and including the past third year, because from the current fourth year the revenues belong to you the buyer, at whose charge lie also the state taxes from the current year. The cession, written in two copies, is enforceable, and I shall also make it for you through the office of the archidicastes whenever you may choose without receiving anything else from you, though the taxes and the scribal fees shall be at the charge of you Tetseiris. To the question posed by you through our same father concerning the correct and lawful transaction of these affairs I gave my assent. Year 4 of Imperator Caesar Marcus Aurelius Antoninus Pius Felix Augustus, Thoth 14.' (2nd hand) 'I, Aurelius Chaeremon son of Hermias, have sold and ceded to my paternal half-sister Aurelia Tetseiris, not yet of legal age, through our father Aurelius Hermias a half-share of the share which falls to me in the village of Sinary from the allotment of Rhodippus of a vineyard estate and reed-bed and all the things also named as aforesaid and I received the thousand drachmas of the price and the cession-fee and I shall guarantee as aforesaid and in answer to the formal question I gave my assent.'

1 For the use of the *praenomen* with Aurelius as a status symbol see D. Hagedorn, *BASP* 16 (1979) 47–59. The persons are unidentified. Hermias does not appear in the list of councillors in A. K. Bowman, *Town Councils* 140–7.

6 Ῥοδ[ίππου. Cf. 37–8. This allotment is not in the list by P. Pruneti, *Aegyptus* 55 (1975) 159–244.

7 προσούσης. Cf. XIV 1631 7, XLVII 3354 7. However, the restoration is comparatively long; it might be better to omit this word and leave it comparatively short.

8 For ληνοῦ καὶ πίθου cf. XXXIV 2723 9.

9 στεμφυλουργικοῦ ὀργάνου. Elsewhere only in P. Osl. III 145. 3, XXXIV 2723 9, cf. στεμφυλουργεῖον in BGU II 531 ii 12, PSI VI 669. 9. Possibly this was a press which operated on the residue left by the treading of the grapes, cf. C. Ricci, 'La coltura della vite e la fabbricazione del vino nell'Egitto greco-romano', *Studi della Scuola papirologica* (Milan, 1926) iv 1. 57.

10 ὅσου ἐςτὶν ἀρουρηδοῦ. Cf. H. H. July, *Die Klauseln hinter den Maβangaben* 40–7, esp. 42–3.

11 The writing down to the end of ἀδελφούς is rather larger and more widely spaced than usual. It looks as if a gap was left between πρός (10) and ὧν πάντων and was subsequently filled up by the same writer.

ὠνημέ[νη. Cf. XLII 3047 13 n.

12 χ[ύ]ης. The reading is by J. Rowlandson; cf. e.g. XLIX 3482 22 n. The meaning is still in doubt, but it appears to have been some sort of embankment, cf. *ZPE* 31 (1978) 94.

πλευρισμός is also some sort of channel or embankment, see M. Schnebel, *Landwirtschaft* 36, but its nature is imperfectly understood. The root meaning, 'rib', suggests that it was an offshoot from a larger drainage feature of the same kind.

Τῶμις ποταμός. This is the ancient name for the Bahr Yusuf, cf. P. Coll. Youtie II pp. 462-3. Dr Z. Borkowski suggested privately some time ago that Sinary is to be identified with Shinara, see Survey of Egypt map (1930; scale 1:100,000), Maghāgha section, *c.* N 28° 47′ E 30° 46′. The names resemble one another and the location of Shinara in the northernmost part of the territory of Oxyrhynchus corresponds with the known fact that Sinary was in the Lower, i.e. northernmost, toparchy. The map shows Shinara on the eastern bank of the Old Bahr Yusuf, which agrees very well with this new information that land at Sinary was bounded on the west by the river Tomis.

12-13 For the restoration τὰς δὲ cυμπεφωνημέ]νας cf. X 1276 9.

16-17 This passage suggests that we should read in 2723 18 ἃc κ]αὶ [ἐν]τεῦθεν προφέρε[τ]α[ι ἀποχαρίζ]εcθαι τῷ . . . υἱῷ, 'which he also declares that he is granting henceforth to his son'.

25 μόνων. Read perhaps μόνον—a phonetic equivalent—as an adverb, or μόνου agreeing with μέρους.

3639. LEASE OF AN OIL-FACTORY

65 6B.36/J(1-3)b   13.5 × 21 cm   11 September 412

The consular date clause differs from the modern fasti and agrees with two other clauses from papyri in attributing to Honorius a ninth consulship in 411; see *Mnemosyne* 31 (1978) 287-93 for a discussion of the evidence. This papyrus adds nothing except confirmation of the regular form of the clause at this time.

A plausible explanation, based on the state of confusion after Alaric's sack of Rome in 410, is advanced by Professor Alan Cameron in *BASP* 16 (1979) 175-7, cf. now 18 (1981) 69-72. According to this it was decided to cancel an abortive ninth consulship of Honorius in 411 and announce it anew for 412, and a trace of an original date clause of 411 seems to survive in the Theodosian Code. What we still conspicuously lack is an explanation of the use of the post-consular formula in the papyri as late as September 412, if the decision to cancel and reannounce the ninth consulship was taken in, say, October or November 411, as suggested in *BASP* 16 (1979) 177. Not that this is an isolated phenomenon. The persistence of post-consular formulae into the second half of the year is common in fifth-century papyri, see *BASP* 17 (1980) 32-3. Perhaps we should look for a single administrative cause, though it is hard to imagine one, rather than a series of explanations based on current events connected with each particular instance.

Other leases of oil-factories are CPR I 242 = SPP XXII 173 (AD 40), P. Lond. II 280, pp. 193-4 = W. *Chr.* 312 (AD 55), P. Aberd. 181 (Claudius or Nero), P. Sorb. inv. 2371 (AD 104/5; ed. D. Bonneau, *Scritti . . . O. Montevecchi* 49-57), P. IFAO III 53 (AD 102-16—a fragment, perhaps not actually the lease itself), PSI IX 1030 (AD 109), SPP XXII 177 (AD 137), P. Amh. II 93 = W. *Chr.* 314 (AD 181), P. Fay. 95 (ii AD), P. Flor. III 285 (AD 552). Two of these, P. IFAO III 53 and P. Fay. 95, are from Dionysias; P. Sorb. inv. 2371 is from from Theadelphia, PSI 1030 from Oxyrhynchus, relating to a village, P. Flor. 285 from Aphrodite in the Antaeopolite nome; all the others concern property in Socnopaeu Nesus. Most are fairly badly damaged and offer few clues to the restoration of the lost portions to the right and at the foot here. What remains of the technical terminology is interesting, though far from easy to understand.

We may compare also W. *Chr.* 176 and BGU XI 2066, petitions about disputes arising out of leases of oil factories, also in Socnopaeu Nesus. BGU 2066 introd. contains a useful short bibliography.

The back is blank so far as it is preserved.

μετὰ τὴ]ν ὑπατίαν τῶν δεϲπο[τῶν ἡμῶν Ὀνωρίου
τὸ] θ΄΄ καὶ Θεοδοϲίου τὸ δ΄΄ τῶ[ν αἰωνίων Αὐγούϲτων
     (vac.)   Θὼθ ιδ. (vac.) [

Φλαουΐῳ Λιμενίῳ λαμπροτάτ[ῳ ἀπὸ τῆϲ λαμ(πρᾶϲ) καὶ λαμ(προτάτηϲ)
5 Ὀξυρυγχιτῶν πόλεωϲ παρὰ Αὐρηλίου Πέτρο[υ   *c.* 12 letters
    ἀπὸ τῆϲ αὐτῆϲ πόλεωϲ ἐλαιουργοῦ. ἑκουϲίωϲ ἐπι[δέχομαι μιϲθώ-
    ϲαϲθαι ἀπὸ τοῦ ὄντοϲ μηνὸϲ Θὼθ τοῦ ἐν[εϲτῶτοϲ ἔτουϲ
    π̄θ̄η̄΄΄ τῆϲ παρούϲηϲ ἐνδεκάτηϲ ἰνδικ[τίωνοϲ ἀπὸ τῶν
    ὑπαρχόντων ϲοι ἐν τῇ αὐτῇ πόλει ἐπ᾽ ἀμφ[όδου   *c.* 8 letters
10 Παρεμβολῆϲ ὁλόκληρον ἐλαιουργιο[ν] ε[*c.* 15 letters
    ον ἓν ϲὺν ϲτροβίλῳ καὶ καλαθ[.].....[*c.* 12 letters
    κοπικὸϲ ϲὺν θυείῃ καὶ ὦμοι δύο καὶ ...[*c.* 15 letters
    καὶ ἐπαύλειϲ καὶ τόποι{.} καὶ φρέαρ καὶ ..[*c.* 15 letters
    πάντα καὶ τελέϲω ὑπὲρ φόρου ἐνιαυϲίωϲ .[*c.* 12 letters
15 ἐλαίου ῥεφανίνου ξέϲταϲ ἑκατὸν εἴκοϲ[ι   *c.* 12 letters
    καθαροῦ ἀρτάβαϲ ἑκατὸν εἴκοϲι .[*c.* 12 letters
    ...κ[*c.* 10 letters]..κ..[*c.* 20 letters

.   .   .   .   .

1 l. ὑπατείαν   3 φλαουϊω   8 ἰνδικ[τιωνοϲ   10 l. ἐλαιουργεῖον   15 l. ῥαφανίνου

'After the consulship of our masters Honorius, for the 9th time, and Theodosius, for the 4th time, the eternal Augusti, Thoth 14.

'To Flavius Limenius, *vir clarissimus*, of the glorious and most glorious city of the Oxyrhynchites, from Aurelius Petrus . . . of the same city, oil-manufacturer. I willingly undertake to lease from the present month of Thoth of the current year 89 (and) 58, of the present eleventh indiction, out of property belonging to you in the same city in the district of . . . Camp, a complete oil-factory (in working order?), in which there is one mill (?) with *strobilus* and *calathus*, and a (stone for crushing vegetable matter?) with a mortar, and two arms (?) and . . . and courtyards and outhouses (?) and a well and . . . and all . . ., and I shall pay in respect of rent yearly . . . 120 (+?) sextarii of radish oil and 120 (+?) artabas of pure . . .'

2]θ΄΄. The trace is an arc, almost amounting to a quadrant, from the lower right of a large rounded letter, clearly theta and not eta.

4 Flavius Limenius has not been identified elsewhere. Three papyri from Oxyrhynchus of about the right date also contain the name Limenius and may refer to the same man, XIV **1752** (AD 390), PSI VIII 884 (AD 391), and PSI IX 1081 (iii-iv).

5 The end of the line probably contained the filiation of Aurelius Petrus.

8 For the Oxyrhynchite eras see R. S. Bagnall and K. A. Worp, *Chronological Systems* 36–42. Eras 89 and 58 = AD 412/13 = indiction 11.

9 At the end restore Ἄνω, or Ἱππέων, or Λυκίων, cf. H. Rink, *Straßen- und Viertelnamen* 52.

10 ἐλαιουργῖο[ν] = ἐλαιουργεῖον. The word here denotes a building, as for instance in P. Mich. V 322a. 8–9, οἰκίας τρὶς (= τρεῖς) . . ., μία μὲν δίϲτεγοϲ λεγομένη ἐλεούργιν (= ἐλαιουργεῖον).

10–11 Restore probably ἐν ᾧ μυλαῖ]|¹¹ον ἐν ϲὺν ϲτροβίλῳ καὶ καλάθ[ῳ]. If the last surviving epsilon in 10 belongs to ἐν, the line was rather shorter than 6–8, where twelve to fourteen letters are missing. More likely it belongs to an intervening word, such as ἐ[νεργόν, 'in working order', cf. P. Amh. II 93 (= W. *Chr.* 314). 8, *Scritti . . . O. Montevecchi*, 50 (l. 6).

For μυλαῖ]ον cf. P. Mert. I 39. 9, μυλαῖον ϲὺν τῷ ϲτ⟨ρ⟩οβίλλου (l. ϲτροβίλῳ, cf. 6, 10). For ϲτρόβιλοϲ and κάλαθοϲ as parts of a mill see XVI **1983**, where a κάλαθοϲ (or κάλαθον neuter?; see 15, τὸ αὐτὸ κάλαθον) needed for a tenant's μυλαῖον was supplied along with a ϲτρόβιλοϲ. This was a grain mill, see ἀρτοποείαϲ (20). *Strobili* also occur in the fragmentary bakery leases P. Rein. II 108 and SPP XX 131. In XIV **1704** 11 it has been supposed to be part of an irrigation machine, 'winch, windlass', but the text is suspicious, [καὶ το]ῦ ἐν αὐτῆϲ (l. αὐταῖϲ) μοι (l. μου) ἀ[ν]τλετικοῦ (l. ἀντλητικοῦ) ϲὺν ϲτροβίλῳ, which invites the interpretation μοιλ[αίου (the phonetic equivalent of μυλαίου)] ἀλετικοῦ. A photograph of **1704**, itself now in Cairo, shows that the space favours this, and the remains are suitable though not very clear on the photograph. Compare μηχανὴ ἀλετική P. Cair. Isid. 64 (= SB VI 9168). 20; cf. P. Ryl. II 321. 5, P. Mil. Vogl. II 53 (= SB VI 9265). 11. In XVI **1890** 8 λίθοϲ ἀλετικόϲ should be read, and ϲτεγικόϲ should be deleted from *LSJ* Suppl. and S. Daris, *Spoglio lessicale.*

Other references to ϲτρόβιλοϲ in the same sense are P. Cair. Isid. 137. 12 (in an inventory with κοπτούρα, 'mortar') and XVI **1912** 145, τιμ(ῆϲ) ϲτροβίλ{λ}[ου   *c.* 13   ] εἰϲ τὸ μυλαῖον, where the gap may have contained καὶ καλάθου (ten letters). Add P. Laur. IV 164, a lease of something ϲὺν ϲτροβίλοιϲ . . . καὶ θυείῃ.

Unfortunately the meaning of these terms is still not known, though **3641** now helps by showing that they were made by a μυλοκόποϲ and that they were of stone. Tentatively I suggest that the *strobilus* is the cone- or bell-shaped lower stone of a donkey-mill, the *meta*, as described and discussed in L. A. Moritz, *Grain Mills and Flour in Classical Antiquity* 74–96, cf. K. D. White, *Farm Equipment of the Roman World* 15, and that the *calathus* is the upper stone, the *catillus.*

In this machine the lower millstone was a free-standing pillar about one metre high, firmly founded in the floor, with the top shaped like a bell or dome with a blunt point. The shaped top does not much resemble a pine-cone, but it is very like the bottom of a child's whipping-top, also called *strobilus*, see those illustrated in W. M. Flinders Petrie, *Objects of Daily Use*, pl. l.

The upper stone was in the shape of a tall waisted drum. The top and bottom of the drum were each drilled out to the shape of a funnel, and the tips of these funnels met and communicated inside the waist, so that the lower half of the hollow interior would fit over the *meta* and grind the grain against it, while the upper half served to funnel the grain down between the grinding surfaces. The exterior shape might be thought to resemble a waisted basket. This is not exactly the shape attributed to the *calathus* in K. D. White, op. cit., 70–3, but some of the illustrations in the article on the calathus in Daremberg and Saglio, *Dictionnaire des antiquités* i 2. 812–14, namely figs. 998, 999, and 1001, show shapes quite like the *catilli* illustrated in Moritz, op. cit., pls. 4 and 5 (opp. pp. 64 and 65), p. 75 (fig. 8), pl.7 (opp. p. 77), pl. 9b (opp. p. 86), pl. 10 (opp. p. 92), and in R. Meiggs, *Roman Ostia*, pl. xxviiib.

A system of overhead beams supported the upper stone and another beam projected horizontally from its waist, against which a donkey could push to rotate the stone. Donkey-mills were in use in Egypt, see VI **908** (AD 199). What can only be the *meta* of such a mill was uncovered at Caranis and is illustrated in A. E. R. Boak and E. E. Peterson, *Karanis: Topographical and Architectural Report, 1924–8* (University of Michigan Humanistic Series XXV, 1931), pl. xxix, fig. 57. The top is worn much flatter than those illustrated in Moritz, op. cit., pl. 6, for instance, but the resemblance is unmistakable.

This sort of mill would not be suitable for dealing with olives, which required a quite different apparatus to avoid crushing the stones, see A. G. Drachmann, *Ancient Oil Mills and Presses*; K. D. White, op. cit., 225–33. However, Egypt was poor in olives and ἔλαιον in the papyri usually means vegetable oil, of which there were many kinds, such as sesame, saffron, castor, linseed, and radish oil, see T. Reil, *Beiträge zur Kenntnis des Gewerbes* 136–8. Here part of the rent is in radish oil, see 15 and cf. 11–12 n. The mill concerned must have been in use for grinding oil-bearing seeds, cf. M. Schnebel, *Landwirtschaft* 197–200, 204. That mills with *strobilus* and *calathus* were used in bakeries, on farms, and in oil-factories is now shown by **3641** 8–10.

In the same photograph as the Caranis *meta* are shown three or four drum-shaped stones, which may well have been used for grinding, and the heavy stone base, or *ara*, of a press, briefly described in Boak and Peterson, op. cit. 37, cf. Pl. XXVIII, fig. 56. The presence of the press could indicate that this area was used for the manufacture of oil.

It is worth noting that there were two adjacent places on the south coast of the Gulf of İzmit in the Sea of Marmara, near modern Yalova, which were called *Cτρόβιλος* and *Κάλαθος*, see J. and L. Robert, *RÉG* 92 (1979) 514-15, no. 548, referring to S. Şahin, *Bithynische Studien* 29-48, esp. 29-39 (in Turkish), cf. L. Robert, *Journal des savants* 1979, 270ff., *ZPE* 47 (1982) 50 and n. 18. It seems very likely that these names should be interpreted as Nether Millstone and Upper Millstone. L. Robert has already concluded that there were two levels to the site, 'Il y avait donc deux agglomérations de Pylai'—the name of the same place towards the end of the eighth century AD—'Pylai d'En-Haut et Pylai d'En-Bas' (*RÉG* loc. cit.). Presumably the peculiarities of the topography gave the names a special force.

11-12 The traces are very scanty and faint. Restore perhaps *καλάθ[ω] καὶ λ[ίθος λαχανο-]|¹²κοπικὸς cὺν θυείη*, though the only parallel known is XVI **1913** 65 *ὑπὲρ τιμ(ῆς) λίθων λαχανοκοπικ(ῶν) ἀγορασθ(έντων) καὶ δοθ(έντων) εἰς τὸ γεουχικ(ὸν) ἐλαιουργῖον τοῦ κτήμ(ατος)* . . . This would presumably be an apparatus for crushing oil-bearing vegetable matter, seeds of, for example, radish, since the rent is partly in radish oil, cf. above 10-11 n. The items *λίθος ςιτοκοπικὸς cὺν θυείη* and *λίθος ἀλετικός* (cf. above 10-11 n., para. 2) *cὺν θυείη* in XVI **1890** 8-9 show that a 'stone' and 'mortar' go together suitably. Presumably in our case the apparatus is not for grain, i.e. not *ςιτο]κοπικός*.

12 *ὦμοι δύο*. What is meant is not clear. Two passages show that they were of wood and probably that they were solid hewn wood and not complicated pieces of carpentry. These are: SB VI 9406. 45-6 *τέκτονι ποιοῦντι δίφρους καὶ ἄλοτρον* (l. *ἄροτρον*) *καὶ κόψαντι ὄμους* (l. *ὤμους*) *(δύο) εἰς χρείαν τοῦ ἐλαίου*; P. Ryl. II 236. 22-6 *ποίηςον δὲ ἐξαυτῆς ὤμους δύο κοπῆναι ἵνα χωρήςωςι εἰς τὸ ἐλαιουργῖον*. Four passages in all—ours, the two just quoted, and P. Flor. II 233. 3-8-refer to pairs of timbers. In P. Sorb. inv. 2371 (*Scritti . . . O. Montevecchi* 50). 7-8 we find *θ[υῖαι?] δύο καὶ τριβῖς* (= *τριβεῖς*) *δύο*, which may possibly be relevant. It is also possible that P. Fay. 110. 29 *τὰς ὠλένας τοῦ ἐλαιουργίου* could be relevant.

. . . . [. A possible reading might be *πύελ[ος* (or -*οι*), see the *χαλκίον* in P. Fay. 95. 11, cf. T. Reil, *Beiträge zur Kenntnis des Gewerbes* 140. The remains do not suit *π(ε)ίλα*, 'mortar', which might be appropriate, cf. White, op. cit., 9; XVI **1890** 12, P. Mert. I 39. 10, P. Rein. II 108. 4.

13 *ἐπαύλεις*. Though it appears to be a plural, this may be the phonetic equivalent of *ἔπαυλις*, singular. *τόποι{.}*. The final letter looks like an anomalous sigma or epsilon, or like omicron with an oblique projection upwards to the right. Possibly it has been cancelled and we should read [[.]]. The translation has 'outhouses (?)' only as a stopgap; it is not clear whether these are areas in the open air or rooms indoors, cf. *WB* s.v. *τόπος* (i).

13-14 The *πάντα* at the beginning of 14 suggests that some word meaning 'appurtenances' preceded, e.g. *ἀνήκοντα, χρηστήρια, cυγκύροντα, ἐπιτήδεια*. None of these fits the traces in 13, but it is not very likely that there was room for another item after the well.

14 At the end of the line there perhaps stood a term for the payment of the rent each year, i.e. in such and such a month. There would be several crops of vegetables each year, so that there is no way of guessing which month was specified.

15 *ἐλαίου ῥεφανίνου*. See P. Mich. XI 613. 4 n. for a bibliography. The radish seed produced the oil. On the spelling see F. T. Gignac, *Grammar* i 280.

At the end of the line restore perhaps *καὶ λαχανοςπέρμου*, cf. PSI IX 1030. 12-13 *καδ' ἐνιαυτὸν* (= *κατ' ἐ*) *ἀμιςθὶ λαχανοςπέρμ[ο]υ ἀρτάβα[[τα]]ς ὀκτώ*.

3640. RECEIPT FOR ROPES

54 1B.26(E)/D(6)a   15.5 × 9.5 cm   20 July 533

The two ropes or coils for which this is a receipt were to replace old ropes on an irrigation machine. Similar documents are I **147** (= SPP III 281) and XVI **2015**, cf. E. R. Hardy, *Large Estates* 128-9 and n. 1. All three documents emanate from monasteries. In this case the monastery is the hitherto unknown one of Apa Hierax. From the fact that its head, called an archimandrite, is a deacon and not a priest we may surmise that it was a small house; see P. Baden II 55. 2–3, P. Ross.-Georg. III 48. 2 for the combination 'priest and archimandrite'.

The writing runs across the fibres of a piece of papyrus which shows no sheet join. The back is blank.

+   ἐδόθ(η) δι(ὰ) Ἰωάννου διακ(όνου) καὶ ἀρχιμανδρ(ίτου) μοναϲτηρ(ίου) Ἄπα
                                                                    Ἱέρακοϲ

Φοιβάμμωνι καταμείν(αντι) ἔξω τῆϲ πύληϲ εἰϲ τὴν μηχ(ανὴν) ἀντλοῦϲαν
εἰϲ τὸ μικρ(ὸν) πωμάρ(ιον) ἐγγὺϲ Εὐτρυγίου ἀντὶ τῶν παλαιωθέντων
[ϲ]χ[ο]ινίων ϲχοινία ἤτοι κρίκια δύο, γί(νεται) ϲχοιν(ία) ἤτοι κρίκ(ια)
                                                                   β̄ μόνα{ϲ}.
5   (ἔτουϲ) ϲθ ροη, Ἐπεὶφ κϛ ἰνδ(ικτίωνοϲ) ἐνδεκάτηϲ.   (vac.)
     (vac.)   / γί(νεται) ϲχοιν(ία) ἤτοι κρίκια δύο//.

1 εδοθ\Ϛδι/, διακ/, αρχιμανδρ/, μοναϲτηρ/   2 καταμειν\Ϛ, μηχϚ   3 μικρ/πωμαρ/   4 γι/ϲχοινϚ,
κρικ/   5 ∟ϲθροη, ινδ/   6 /γι/ϲχοινϚ

'There were supplied through John, deacon and archimandrite of the monastery of Apa Hierax, to Phoebammon, sub-tenant (?) outside the gate, for the irrigation machine which draws water for the little orchard at Eutrygius', in place of the decayed ropes, two ropes or coils, total 2 ropes or coils only. Year 209, 178, Epeiph, 26, indiction 11.'

'Total two ropes or coils.'

1 ἀρχιμανδρ(ίτου). Cf. F. Cabrol, H. Leclercq, *Dictionnaire d'archéologie chrétienne et de liturgie* i, cols. 2739–61; P. Strasb. 679 introd.

2 Other occurrences of καταμείναϲ indicate that it had some technical sense which is not clear to us. These are discussed by I. F. Fikhman, *Proceedings of the XII International Congress of Papyrology* 127–9, where it is suggested that it meant a sub-tenant holding land from a tenant-in-chief serving as an official in the administration of a large estate.

ἔξω τῆϲ πύληϲ. It is clear that this has nothing to do with the ἐξωπυλῖται discussed by H. C. Youtie, *Scriptiunculae* i 96 = *TAPA* 71 (1940) 656, but is connected with an adjunct of sixth-century Oxyrhynchus, the προάϲτιον ἔξω τῆϲ πύληϲ (PSI III 193. 2, P. Wisc. II 66. 2, XVI **1925** 44, cf. perhaps **1913** 34), cf. P. Pruneti, *I centri abitati* 156. G. Husson, *Rech. Pap.* 4 (1967) 192–6, has shown that it was a palatial residence of the Apion family, presumably close outside one of the city gates of Oxyrhynchus, with associated vineyards and other cultivated ground. From **1913** 1, 6, 16, 20, 21, 45, 50, 63, 68, we learn that there were at least three orchards there, of which our 'little orchard' (3) may have been one, if these monks were supplying ropes for the Apion estate; we learn too that there were gardens there, and that irrigation was carried on, as well as pottery and brick-making.

3 ἐγγύϲ = 'chez', see D. Tabachovitz, *Études sur le grec de la basse époque* 62–3, though in this case the personal name may have been fossilized into a place-name, as so often. Clearly the λαχανία Εὐτρυγίου of **1913** 17, also 'outside the gate', may be connected.

4 ϲχοινία ἤτοι κρίκια. Cf. I **147** 2 ϲχοιν(ίον) ἤτοι κρίκον ἕνα, XVI **2015** 3–4 ϲχοινί(ον) ἤ[το]ι κρίκ(οϲ) α (ἥμιϲυ). The second document indicates that a ϲχοινίον, κρίκοϲ, or κρίκιον was a coil of rope of a standard length. A photograph confirms that the symbol after κρίκ(οϲ) α—or κρίκ(ιον) α, as we now see—is the sign for one-half which resembles an ∟ with the foot descending obliquely to the right. Otherwise one might have suggested that the term 'coil' referred to the rope quoits on which the pots of the modern sakiyeh are seated, see L. Ménassa, P. Laferrière, *La Sāqia* (Bibliothèque d'étude 67, 1974) 19–20 (figs. 18–20); cf. 42 (fig. 39d–e)—a similar quoit used in the harness of a draught animal.

5 For the Oxyrhynchite eras see R. S. Bagnall, K. A. Worp, *Chronological Systems of Byzantine Egypt* 36–42. A photograph of I **147** shows that the date was wrongly read as ϲλα καὶ ϲ. It is ϲλβ καὶ ϲα. The beta is somewhat damaged, but certain; the remains of the alpha, which was very small, are scanty. This removes the contradiction remarked in *ed. pr.* between the era and indiction numbers. Year 232 and 201 = AD 555/6 = indiction 4, and the date of the document is 7 April AD 556.

The same photograph gives reason to doubt the unintelligible εὐμά(νου) after the total in 2. This is based in turn on **146** 3, which is supposed to have γί(νεται) μονεῖ(ον) ᾱ εὐμάνου in full. In fact a photograph shows that **146** 3 has ἓν μόνον (possibly μῶνον) fairly clearly, and **147** 2 may be read in the light of it as ἓν μόνον, which is very rapidly written but probably written in full. The first writer certainly wrote κρίκον ἕνα in 2, but the second writer chose to think of the object as neuter, perhaps thinking of the alternative name ϲχοινίον, or perhaps of κρίκιον, as here.

6 Very often such repeated formulae are in a different hand and constitute a countersignature. In this case I can detect no difference.

The initial oblique stroke, somewhat arched upwards towards the left, appears to be the sign that often represents (γίνεται) or (γίνονται) by itself. If so, it is superfluous.

3641. Contract of a Millstone-cutter

318/1   22 × 30.5 cm   7 February 544

A stone-worker specializing in the cutting of millstones concluded this contract with the large landowner Flavius Apion II. The workman was to provide, for the duration of his life, new parts, called *strobili* and *calathi*, at 2½ gold solidi each, or possibly at that price for each pair. He was not to withdraw his labour for any reason, except illness, upon penalty of a fine of 24 solidi, and this sum was also to be paid by Apion if he sought to dismiss the workman without cause.

The chief interest of the piece lies in the unmistakable implication that these mill parts, about which little is known for certain, were of stone, see 6 n., with **3639** 10–11 n. It is also stated that mills with these components were used in bakeries and in oil-factories, see 8–10 n.

✝ βασιλείας τοῦ θειοτάτου καὶ εὐϲεβεϲτάτου ἡμῶν δεϲ]πότου Φλαουΐου Ἰουϲτινιανοῦ τοῦ αἰωνίου

Αὐγούϲτου καὶ Αὐτοκράτοροϲ ἔτουϲ ι]ζ, τοῖϲ τὸ δ μετὰ [τὴν] ὑπατίαν Φλαουΐου Βαϲιλίου τοῦ λαμ(προτάτου), Μεχεὶρ ιβ, ἰνδ(ικτίωνοϲ) ζ.

Φλαουΐῳ Ἀπίωνι τῷ ὑπερ]φυεϲτάτῳ ὑ[πάτ]ῳ ὀρδιναρίῳ γεουχοῦντι καὶ ἐνταῦθα τῇ λαμπρᾷ

Ὀξυρυγχιτῶν πόλει διὰ Μ]ηνᾶ [οἰ]κέτου τοῦ ἐπερωτῶντοϲ καὶ προϲπορίζοντοϲ τῷ ἰδίῳ

5   δεϲπότῃ τῷ αὐτῷ ὑπε]ρφ[υ]εϲτάτῳ ἀνδρὶ τὴν ἀγωγὴν καὶ ἐνοχήν, Αὐρήλιοϲ Ϲερῆνοϲ

μυλοκόποϲ τὴν τέ]χνην υἱὸϲ Ἡλίο[υ ὁ]ρμ[ώμ]ενοϲ ἀπὸ τῆϲ Ὀξυρυγχιτῶν πόλεωϲ

χαίρειν. ὁμολογ]ῶ διὰ ταύτηϲ μου τῆϲ ἐγγρ[ά]φ[ο]υ ἀϲφαλείαϲ ἑτοίμωϲ ἔχω ἐργάϲαϲθαι

ἀπὸ .[. . . .] . . . ἐπὶ τὸν τῆϲ ζωῆϲ μ[ο]υ χρόνον εἰϲ πάνταϲ τοὺϲ μυλαίουϲ ϲτροβίλλουϲ τε

κ[α]ὶ καλάθουϲ τοὺϲ ὄνταϲ ἐν ἑκάϲ[τῳ] τόπῳ τῆϲ ὑμετέραϲ οὐϲίαϲ ἔν τε κριβανείῳ τε

10   καὶ πᾶϲιν τοῖϲ κτήμαϲιν καὶ ἐν ἐλαι[ου]ργίοιϲ τῆϲ ὑμετέραϲ ὑπερφυείαϲ ἀόκνωϲ

καὶ ἀκαταγνώϲτωϲ εἰϲ τὸ μηδε[μ]ίαν μέμψιν ἢ ἀμέλειαν ἢ κατάγνωϲιν ἢ ῥαθυμία⟨ν⟩

τινὰ περὶ ἐμὲ γενέϲθαι δίχα ἀρρ[ωϲτ]ίαϲ καὶ πόνου τινὸϲ καὶ δέξαϲθαί με παρὰ τῆϲ

ὑμετέραϲ ὑπερφυείαϲ ὑπὲρ ἑκάϲτου ϲτροβίλλου νέου καὶ καλάθου νέου

χρυϲοῦ νομιϲμάτια δύο ἥμιϲ[υ ἰ]διωτικῷ ζυγῷ νομιτ[ε]υόμενα, ἐμοῦ λαμβάνοντοϲ

15   τοὺϲ παλαιοὺϲ λίθουϲ, καὶ μη[*c.* 10 letters] . . ἀποϲτῆναι ἀπὸ τῆϲ ὑμετέραϲ [χρείαϲ

ἢ ἀπὸ τῶν ὀφειλόντων γενέ[ϲθα]ι [ἔ]ργων. εἰ δὲ [τοῦ]το ποιήϲω, ἐπὶ τῷ με δοῦναι

τῇ ὑμετέρᾳ ὑπερφυείᾳ λόγῳ προϲτίμου χρυϲοῦ νομιϲμάτια εἴκοϲι τέϲϲαρα. εἰ δὲ

---

1 φλαουϊουϊουϲτινιανου   2 l. ὑπατείαν; φλαουϊου, λαμϛ, ινδ/   3 ϋ[πατ]ω   4 ϊδιω
6 υϊοϲ   7 εγγρ[α]φ[ο]υ; l. ἔχειν   8 ϲτροβιλ'λουϲ; l. ϲτροβίλουϲ   9 ϋμετεραϲ; 1st τε for τῷ
10 l. ἐλαιουργείοιϲ; ὑμετεραϲ?, ὑπερφυειαϲ   13 ϋμετεραϲϋπερφυειαϲϋπερ, ϲτροβιλ'λου; l. ϲτροβίλου
15 ϋμετεραϲ   17 ϋμετεραϋπερφυεια, τεϲ'ϲαρα

ἡ ὑμετέρα ὑπερφύεια διὰ τῶν αὐτῆς διοικητῶν ἐκβάλῃ με ἐκτὸς καταγνώςεως
ἢ ῥαθυμία⟨ς ἢ⟩ οἱαςδήποτε αἰτίας, ὑποκεῖςθαι καὶ αὐτὴ τῷ ἴςῳ προςτίμῳ.
ὑποθέμενος

20 εἰς τὸ δίκαιον τούτου τοῦ ςυναλλάγματος ἅπαντά μου τὰ ὑπάρχοντα καὶ
ὑπάρξοντα ὅςα τε νῦν ἔχω
κạὶ [ὅςα ἄλλα μ]ετὰ ταῦτα ἐπικτήςομαι ἰδικῶς καὶ γενικῶς ἐνεχύρου λόγῳ καὶ
ὑποθήκης δικαίῳ.
κύριο[ν τὸ ςυ]νάλλαγμα διςςὸν γραφὲν καὶ ἐπερωτηθεὶς ὡμολόγηςα. ✝ (m. 2)
Αὐρήλιος Ϲερῆνος,
μυλοκ[όπ]ọς τ[ὴ]ν̣ τέχνην, υἱὸς Ἡλίου ὁ προγεγραμμένος πεποίημαι τοῦτο τὸ
ςυνάλλαγμα
κ[ατ]ὰ̣ τọ̀ν̣ προκείμενον τρόπον καὶ ςυμφωνεῖ μοι πάντα ὡς πρόκειται.
Αὐρήλιος

25 c. 5 υἱὸς τ]ọῦ μακαρίου Ἰςὰκ ἀξιωθ(εὶς) ἔγραψα ὑπὲρ αὐτοῦ ἀγραμμάτου
ὄντος. ✝

(vac.)
(m. 3) ✝ di' em(u) Iust(u) apo diacon(on) etelioth(e) . . . . ✝
Back, downwards along the fibres:
(m. 1?) [5–10 letters   Ϲερή]ν̣ọ[υ] μ[υ]λ[ο]κόπου τὴν τέχνην υἱοῦ Ἡλίου
ἀπὸ τῆς Ὀξυρυγχ(ιτῶν) πόλεως.

---

18 ὑμετεραϋπερφυεια   19 ὑποκεισθαι, ἴςω, ὑποθεμενος   20 ςυναλ'λαγματος, ὑπαρχοντα,
ὑπαρξοντα   21 ἰδικως, ὑποθηκης   23 υϊος   25 ϊςακαξιωθ⟨, ὑπερ
26 dieῆiusᶠ apodiaconetelioth   27 υϊου, οξυρυγχϛ?

'In the 17th year of the reign of our most godly and most pious master Flavius Iustinianus the eternal
Augustus and Imperator, in the 4th year after the consulship of Flavius Basilius, *vir clarissimus*, Mecheir 12, of
the 7th indiction.

'To Flavius Apion the most excellent *consul ordinarius*, landowner here also in the glorious city of the
Oxyrhynchites, through Menas, slave, putting the question and providing for his own master the same most
excellent man the liability and responsibility, Aurelius Serenus, millstone-cutter by trade, son of Elias, from the
city of the Oxyrhynchites, greeting. I acknowledge through this my written assurance that I am ready to work
from . . . for the period of my lifetime on all the milling *strobili* and *calathi* that are in every location of your
estate, both in the bakery and on all the farmsteads and in the oil factories of your excellency, without
reluctance and without reproach so that no condemnation or negligence or reproach or inefficiency may
attach to me, except in case of illness or pain, and that I am to receive from your excellency in respect of every
new *strobilus* and new *calathus* two and a half solidi of gold tested by the private scale, myself receiving the old
stones, and that I am not . . . to withdraw from your service or from the works which require to be done. If I do
this, I am to give to your excellency by way of fine twenty-four solidi of gold. If your excellency, through your
administrators, ejects me without reproach or inefficiency or any cause whatsoever, you too shall be subject to
the same penalty. I pledge for the legal force of this contract all my belongings now and in the future, such as I

now hold and such others as I shall acquire after this, in particular and in general, by way of security and by right of mortgage. The contract, written in two copies, is enforceable, and in answer to the formal question I gave my assent.'

(2nd hand) 'I, Aurelius Serenus, millstone-cutter by trade, son of Elias, the aforementioned person, have made this contract according to the aforesaid fashion and it satisfies me in all respects as aforesaid. I, Aurelius . . ., son of the late Isaac, on request wrote on his behalf because he is illiterate.'

(3rd hand) 'Drawn up through me, Justus, ranked as deacon . . .'

(1st hand?) 'Contract (?) of Serenus, millstone-cutter by trade, son of Elias, from the city of the Oxyrhynchites.'

2 The figures of the regnal year and the consulship are damaged, but the remains are very suitable and they may be regarded as certain because they are confirmed by elements which are certain. Mecheir 12 (= 6 or 7 February) of a seventh indiction in the reign of Justinian with a post-consulship of Basilius can only be 7 February 544 (leap year) or 6 February 559, see the synoptic table in R. S. Bagnall, K. A. Worp, *Chronological Systems* 88–9. The regnal year must therefore be either 17 or 32, and the post-consular number must be 3 (new style 4) or 18 (new style 19). The second figure of the regnal year number has a long trailing finial sloping and curving down to the right, clearly the ζ of ιζ = 17, and the post-consular number is rounded on the left, that is δ = 4 rather than γ = 3, ι[η] = 18, or ι[θ] = 19, all of which would be angular on the left.

3 For Flavius Apion II see the stemma in P. Oxy. XVI, p. 6; cf. *PLRE* ii 1325 (stemma 27), where he is called Flavius Strategius Apion. The article on him is reserved for *PLRE* iii.

6 μυλοκόπος. Cf. 23, 27. A μυλοκόπος is a worker in stone, see T. Reil, *Beiträge zur Kenntnis des Gewerbes* 27, with 14–15 here, ἐμοῦ λαμβάνοντος τοὺς παλαιοὺς λίθους. Therefore the objects upon which he works, the ϲτρόβιλοι and κάλαθοι, are stone parts of a mill; see 8–10 n. and 3639 10–11 n. for what is known and speculated about their nature. Hence the translation 'millstone-cutter'.

Ἠλίο[υ. Cf. 27. In XVI 1983 of 535, a document addressed to Flavius Strategius I, the father of Flavius Apion II, who is addressed in this document, a *strobilus* and *calathus* are delivered διὰ Ἠλίου τοῦ ἐνταῦθα (= Oxyrhynchus) μυλοκόπου. Possibly these persons are the same and Serenus followed his father in the same trade.

7 For the restorations cf. XVI 1896 14–15 χαίρειν. ὁμολογοῦμεν διὰ ταύτης ἡμῶν τῆς ἐγγράφου ἀϲφαλείαϲ ἑτοίμωϲ ἔχειν . . . διδόναι. Bad grammar appears below, see 19 n., so that ἔχω as a mistake for ἔχειν is credible, and ὁμολογ]ῶ suits the remains very well, but we might have expected to find traces of the large initial chi as we see it in χρυϲοῦ at the beginning of 14.

8 We might expect ἀπὸ τοῦ νῦν, ἀπὸ τῆς ϲήμερον, *vel sim.*, cf. P. Cair. Masp. I 67001. 21; 67006. 101; 67007. 22; 67110. 15, 20. The last letter before ἐπί looks like iota.

μυλαίους. Apparently μυλιουϲ was written at first, and alpha inserted later, but the result is blotted and smeared, so the process may have had the reverse intention. The neuter form of the adjective, μυλαῖον, became the standard word for 'mill' in the papyri. Otherwise it hardly exists, except in the epigram ἴϲχετε χεῖρα μυλαῖον, *AP* 9. 418. μύλιος is attested in Procop., *Aed.* 2. 6. 7, 8. 18.

8–10 On *strobilus* and *calathus* see 6 n. and especially 3639 10–11 n. This passage states clearly that mills with these parts were used in bakeries, that is, for grinding grain, and in oil factories, that is, for grinding vegetable seeds.

9 The first τε seems to be a mistake, by anticipation, for τῷ.

14 ἰδιωτικῷ ζυγῷ. See L. C. West, A. C. Johnson, *Currency* 140–5.

15 λίθους. This makes it doubly clear that the *strobilus* and *calathus* are made of stone, cf. 6 n.

After the gap]ωϲ might be read, i.e. μή + adverb + ἀποϲτῆναι. In I 140 24–5 we read μὴ ἐξεῖν[αί] μοι . . . ὑπαναχωρῆϲαι ἀπὸ [τ]ῆϲ ὑμῶν χρείαϲ καὶ παραμονῆϲ. χρείαϲ is useful here as a stopgap at the end of the line, but μὴ [ἐξεῖναί μ]οι will not suit.

19 αὐτή. Correct probably to αὐτή⟨ν⟩, understanding ⟨ἐπὶ τῷ⟩ ὑποκεῖϲθαι καὶ αὐτή⟨ν⟩, cf. εἰ . . . ποιήϲω, ἐπὶ τῷ με δοῦναι (15).

ὑποθέμενος. Instead of the hanging participle we should prefer καὶ ὑπεθέμην, as elsewhere, e.g. I 138 37, cf. 136 39.

21 [ὅϲα ἄλλα]: a stopgap, which could be varied in several ways, especially as ἐπικτήϲομαι might be a phonetic spelling of ἐπικτήϲωμαι.

26 The same notary appears in XVI 1985 32 (AD 543). The hand appears to be the same. Here as there

the writing after *etelioth*(*e*) has resisted decipherment. It might be tachygraphy, as suggested there in the note. The initial chi-rho monogram is complicated by a flourish at the top and a second chi underneath the first on the stem of the rho.

A Justus *diaconus* appears as notary to two later documents, one of 553 (XXXVI **2780** 32), the other of 569 (I **134** 30, where a photograph shows that Ἰϲατοϲ should be corrected to Ἰοῦϲτοϲ, 32, where for *Isat*(*u*) read *Iust*(*u*)—*iust̊* pap., cf. XLVIII, p. xv under **134**). These two are probably the same as each other, to judge from the hands, which are, it must be remembered, years apart in date. The hand of the earlier Justus does not look very similar, but again the intervals are large. Unfortunately the meaning of *apo diacon*(*on*) is not sure. It might possibly mean 'with the honorary rank of deacon', rather than former deacon or simply deacon.

27 At the beginning of the line there was probably some form of Christian cross, followed by a word for 'contract'; ϲυνάλλαγμα is the likeliest, cf. 22, with I **136** 41, 51; **140** 29, 33.

III. PRIVATE LETTERS

3642. Phanias to Harthonis

33 4B.83/B(3–8)a   7 × 16.5 cm   Second century

The interest of this letter is chiefly lexicographical. The form δισακκία, feminine instead of neuter, has a rarity value, see 4–5 n.; a new word or name possibly occurs in line 16, λοχιαδα[; and the expression ἡ πλαγία (sc. θύρα), 'side door' or 'back door', is again rather rare. The door in question belongs to a Serapeum, which is probably the Serapeum in Oxyrhynchus, cf. 10 n.

The address is written across the fibres of the back. With respect to the front it is upside-down and near the foot. This indicates that the letter was rolled up from the top, cf. L **3560, 3591, 3592** introductions, and then pressed into a flat spill on which the address was written half on each side of a ligature which closed the letter.

Φανίας Ἀρθώνι τῶι
        φιλτάτωι χ(αίρειν).
μέμφομαί σε λείαν χ[άριν
τῶν σάκκων καὶ τῆς [δι-
5   σακκίας. ῑβ̄ ἠνέχθη[σαν
οἱ σάκκοι καὶ μέχρι τού-
του οὔπω ἠνέχθη ἡ δι[σακ-
κία. πάντως οὖν διὰ α[
λου. πέμψεις. ἐρεῖς [
10   ρωι 〚ἐλθεῖν〛 καταβῆν[αι
εἰς Νεμέρα χάριν τοῦ
ὁρίου τῇ κ̄, ἐπὶ σπείρονται
οἱ τόποι αὐτοῦ. ἐπισκέ-
ψαι τὴν μητέραν μ[ου
15   καὶ τὴν οἰκίαν καὶ τ[ὸν
ἰατρὸν καὶ λοχιαδα[
τὸ συνηλιγμένον [δί-
πλωμα ἐπαναγκας[..
τὸν ἰατρὸν ταχέω[ς

1 l. Ἀρθώνει   2 χ̅ϛ̅   3 l. λίαν   12 l. ἐπεί   16, 19 ἰατρον

20   cφραγίcαι αυτ[. . . . .
     ψειc εὐθέωc. κ[αὶ cύν-
     τυχ{υχ}ε τῇ μητρί [μου
     καὶ εἰπὲ αὐτῇ εἰ ἐκ[τε-
     νίcθη τὰ ἔρια τῆc μη-
25   τρόc cου. εἰ δὲ μή, ἐπανα[γ-
     κάceιc αὐτὸν κτενίc̣αι̣.
     καὶ cύντυχε τῷ cακκο-
     ποιῷ τῷ πρὸc τῇ{c} πλα-
     γίᾳ τοῦ Cαραπείου καὶ ἐ-
30   ρεῖc αὐτῷ ἢ γέγονε
     ἡ διcακκία Φανίου. καὶ
     περὶ τούτων μοι πάντων
     δηλώcειc. ἔρρω(co). Ἀθὺρ ῑδ̅.

Back.   Ἀρθώνι (design) φίλωι

30 l. εἰ   33 ερρ^ω   34 l. Ἀρθώνει

'Phanias to Harthonis his dearest friend, greeting. I blame you very much over the sacks and the saddlebag. On the 12th (?) the sacks were delivered, and so far the saddlebag has not yet been delivered. So send (it) without fail . . . Tell Horus (?) to go down to Nemera about the boundary on the 20th, because his pieces of land are being sown. Look to my mother and the house and the doctor and . . . When (?) you have compelled the doctor to seal the enclosed double document quickly, . . . immediately. And visit my mother and ask her if your mother's wool has been carded. If not, compel him (?) to card (it). And visit the sackmaker at the side door of the Serapeum and ask him if Phanias' saddlebag has been made. And let me know about all these matters. Farewell. Hathyr 14.'

Back. 'To Harthonis, (my) friend.'

4–5 [δι]cακκίαc. Cf. 7–8, 31. For the rarer feminine form see P. Coll. Youtie II 84. 12 (δειcακεία) and n., and the supplementary note by H. C. Youtie, *ZPE* 35 (1979) 108. The common forms are neuter, διcάκκιον and variant spellings. See also G. Husson, *Atti del XVII Congreso . . . Napoli* (forthcoming).

5 ῑβ̅. The letter was written on Hathyr 14 (33), so this seems to stand for τῇ δωδεκάτῃ, 'on the twelfth', and it is possible that we should actually emend it to ⟨τῇ⟩ ῑβ̅, cf. τῇ κ below (12). It is much harder to make the numeral 12 or 12th apply to the sacks or the saddlebag.

8–9 The doubtful letter in 9 appears as a round blot and may have been deliberately cancelled, like ⟦ἐλθεῖν⟧ in 10. If so, restore perhaps διὰ ἄ[λ]λου ⟦ . ⟧. A name such as Ἁ[ρπά]λου or Ἁ[κύ]λου would also suit and other possibilities could be imagined. If the doubtful letter is not intended to be cancelled, διὰ ἀ[cφα]λοῦc, 'by a safe messenger', is a strong possibility, cf. e.g. XLVII 3357 15–17 πέμψον μοι διὰ τῶν ὀνηλατῶν ἢ διὰ ἄλλου ἀcφαλοῦc.

9–10 Restore probably a name, such as [Ὡ]ρωι.

10 καταβῆν[αι. Compounds of κατά are often used of journeys from a nome capital into the countryside, see H. C. Youtie, *Scriptiunculae* ii 493 n. 36. This reinforces the suggestion of the find-spot that the Serapeum mentioned below (29) is the one in Oxyrhynchus itself.

11 Νεμέρα. Cf. P. Pruneti, *I centri abitati* 114–15. The form Νεμέραc in I 76 12 is not well supported by a

photograph supplied by the Cambridge University Library. If there is any ink in that place, it is probably there by accident.

12 Probably cπείρονται is future in sense, cf. B. G. Mandilaras, *The Verb* §214, pp. 102–3, because boundary questions ought to be settled before sowing begins.

14 μητέραν. For the superfluous final nasal see F. T. Gignac, *Akten XIII. Intern. Papyrologenkongresses* 142.

16 λοχιαδα[. The last letter is virtually certain, though damaged. Above the last two letters are some very faint traces, which might be stray ink, but could be a short addition between the lines. It may be that λόχια (n. pl.) is to be recognized. If this were right, it would mean presumably, not 'afterbirth', but 'requirements for the confinement' or simply 'the confinement'. This seems to be the sense in the fragmentary PSI VIII 895 (= M. Naldini, *Cristianesimo*, no. 27) καὶ πάντα τὰ εἰωθότα π[οι]|¹⁰ῆcαι τῶν λοχίων. οἶδεν γὰρ ὁ θε[ὸc ὅτ]ι (ε]ἰ edd.) ἐβουλόμην . . . |¹¹ πάν[τα] τὰ πρὸc τὴν χρίαν τῶν λ[ο]χίων ἀποcτῖλαι κτλ. However, the absence of the article is rather against this interpretation, and the end of the line remains intractable. Hesychius has the entry λοχιάδεc· αἱ ὗλαι. There is room to restore a sigma here, if required. Λοχιάc is the name of a promontory which bounded the eastern side of the great port of Alexandria, cf. P. M. Fraser, *Ptolemaic Alexandria* i 22–3. A magical papyrus uses λοχιάc as an epithet of Hecate, apparently in the sense of 'aiding birth', cf. *LSJ* Suppl., s.v., where P. Par. Mag. I. 2285 is the equivalent of PGM IV 2285. Here the association with the doctor might suggest that it means 'midwife', cf. λοχεύτρια and the entry λοχία· μαῖα in Hesychius. If so, the usage is new; μαῖα occurs in the papyri twice, ἰατρίνη once, see **3620** 17–18 n. The absence of the article may be against this interpretation too and may imply that Λοχιάc is an unattested personal name, though Dr Holford-Strevens points out that there could be a contrast between the known particular doctor and a midwife yet to be found.

17–21 The sentence probably begins with 17. It is not possible to read καὶ Λοχιάδο[c in 16, see note. The diploma rolled up with the present letter ought strictly, according to that description, to be a papyrus document rather than a wooden or bronze tablet. The word is used of various kinds of document, including some relating to taxes, cf. S. L. Wallace, *Taxation* 91–2, 186–7, 207, 222, 309, and official arrests, cf. XXXVI **2730** 3, XLII **3061** 9, but very likely this was a document with an interior text designed to be rolled up and sealed for the sake of security and with an exterior text left hanging from below the seals, see H. J. Wolff, *Das Recht der griechischen Papyri Ägyptens* ii 78–9, add P. Turner 22.

Only about five letters can be missing at the end of 20, which hardly leaves room for καί vel sim. Therefore, in spite of ἐπανα[γ]κάcειc in 25–6, and even though this writer does not use participles elsewhere and is particularly fond of connecting his sentences with καί, we should probably restore a participle, ἐπαναγκάc[αc, in 18. The subordinate clause looks as if it ought to end after cφραγίcαι (20). If so and if αυτ[is part of αὐτόc, it must bear some stress. Perhaps restore αὐτ[ὸν—or αὐτ[ὸc—πέμ]ψειc εὐθέωc. The whole would then mean, 'When you have compelled the doctor to seal the enclosed double document, send the man himself—or 'send (it) yourself—'immediately'. But αὐτ[ό, picking up the initial phrase, is also quite possible in colloquial language, see E. Mayser, *Grammatik* ii 1. 63–4, and we should probably punctuate after it, 'The enclosed double document, when you have compelled the doctor to seal it, send (to me) immediately'.

26 The run of the sentence tempts us to correct αὐτόν to αὐτήν, picking up τῇ μητρί [μου (22). However, it is quite possible that the work of carding the wool was to be done by a man under the orders of the mother of Phanias.

28–9 For ἡ πλαγία (sc. θύρα) 'side door' or 'back door' cf. CPR V 17. 8 n. This is the first mention of a back door to the Oxyrhynchite Serapeum, to judge from the references collected in G. Ronchi, *Lexicon Theonymon* s.v.

29–30 ἐρεῖc, cf. 9. This is a standard expression in private letters, see P. Mich. VIII 476. 24 n., and is virtually equivalent to an imperative, cf. B. G. Mandilaras, *The Verb* §396, but it means 'tell, say to'. Here the run of the sentence requires the translation 'ask . . . if', a sense which I have not found elsewhere. I would attribute it to poor drafting rather than to memories of ἐρέω (A) and ἔρομαι.

34 On the purpose of the design in the middle of the address see XLVIII **3396** 32 n. It is very much damaged, but was probably the common interrupted saltire pattern as described there, cf. **3644** 31.

3643. LETTER OF RECOMMENDATION

5 1B.38/J(a)   8 × 11.5 cm   Second century

The damage to this letter, which has lost its foot and the end of ll. 1–4, 14–17, and has suffered other minor losses and abrasions, is tantalizing. As it is, the letter gives us only an obscured glimpse of scholarly contacts with Oxyrhynchus. The writer may have been Valerius Diodorus, an Alexandrian known to us as a student of Attic oratory, see 1 n. The person introduced was the nephew of a philosopher of the Epicurean school, whose name is damaged, see 10 n. A fragmentary papyrus letter mentioning Epicurean books has been published by J. G. Keenan in *The J. Paul Getty Museum Journal* 5 (1977) 91–4. Dr Keenan remarks (p. 92 n. 7) on the scarcity of evidence from Egypt for an interest in Epicureanism. For a collection of the epigraphic evidence on Epicureanism see M. N. Tod, *JHS* 77 (1957) 136–7, with J. and L. Robert, *RÉG* 71 (1958) 198.

The handwriting is a rounded cursive, making no great use of ligatures. It is written carelessly with a tendency to change from upright or even slightly backhand letters to a pronounced forward slope. In this and other respects it is somewhat like the third hand of XVIII 2192, illustrated in E. G. Turner, *Greek Manuscripts*, no. 68, and, like that, gives the impression of being the hand of a private individual writing for himself, cf. op. cit., p. 114, rather than that of a professional scribe. It may be the hand of Valerius Diodorus, who is mentioned in 2192 24–5 (οἱ περὶ Διόδωρον). The best evidence for his date is given by P. Mert. I 19, which dates from some time in the sole reign of Marcus Aurelius, 169–76, perhaps from 173.

For documentary letters of recommendation in general see C.-H. Kim, *Form and Structure of the Familiar Greek Letter of Recommendation*, H. Cotton, *Documentary Letters of Recommendation in Latin from the Roman Empire*, with additions to Kim's list of Greek examples, pp. 53–4.

The back is blank.

Οὐαλέριος . . . . . [. . . . .
Ὀφελλιανῶι τῶ[ι . . . . .
        ἀδε[λ]φῶι [. . . . .
πάντες ἴcαcιν [. . . . . .] . [
5   . εις. διόπερ ἐπιcτέλλω
       cοι ὑπὲρ Διογένου[c] . εῳ . ος,
       ἀδελφιδοῦ ὄντος [ἀνα]γκαιο-
       τάτου μοι φίλου, ἀνδρὸς
       φιλοcόφου γενομένου τὰ

2 οφελλιανωϊ   3 αδε[λ]φωϊ

10 'Επικούρια, Θε. [.] . ς
 τοὔνομα. διχόθ[εν] . [. .] . ν
 τὸν νεανίσκον, καὶ δ`ι″ ἐκεῖ-
 νον καὶ δι' αὐτὸν ἐπάξιον
 ὄντ[α τῆς] παρ' [.]μεῖν . . [. .
15 ϲεωϲ [. . . .]ϲ δὴ ουκε[. . .
 αυτ . [. . . .]ϲθᾳ . [. . . . . . .
 ϲοι[*c.* 16 letters

· · · · ·

10 l. 'Επικούρεια 14 l. ἡμῖν or ὑμῖν

'Valerius Diodorus (?) to Ofellianus his brother, greeting. All men know . . . Therefore I write to you on behalf of Diogenes son of . . ., who is the nephew of a very close friend of mine, a man who was a philosopher of Epicurean doctrines, called The . . . (Loving ?) the young man on both counts, since for that man's sake and for his own he is worthy of . . .'

 1 The traces at the end of the line suit Διόδω[ρος very well, although the damage is too great to allow complete certainty. The persons called Harpocration, Pollio, and Diodorus in XVIII **2192** have been identified by Sir Eric Turner with the author of the surviving lexicon to the Attic orators and two other Alexandrian scholars, father and son, Valerii, who are mentioned in Photius (*Bibl.* 149, 150) and in the *Suda* as students of Attic oratory, see *JEA* 38 (1952) 91–2; cf. Turner, *Greek Papyri* 87–8, *Greek Manuscripts* 114. B. Hemmerdinger pointed out in *REG* 72 (1959) 107–9 that the lexicographer was also a Valerius according to the *Suda*. Diodorus has appeared in a contract from Oxyrhynchus dated to the sole reign of Marcus, see introd. The *Suda*, though describing Pollio and Diodorus as father and son, appears to date both to the reign of Hadrian. Perhaps, therefore, γεγονώς in the entry for Diodorus should be emended to γεγονότος, as follows: Διόδωρος, ὁ Οὐαλέριος ἐπικληθείς, φιλόσοφος, μαθητὴς Τηλεκλέους, Ἀλεξανδρεύς, υἱὸς Πωλίωνος τοῦ φιλοσόφου, τοῦ γράψαντος τὴν Ἀττικὴν λέξιν, γεγονότος (γεγονώς codd.) ἐπὶ τοῦ Καίσαρος Ἀδριανοῦ. In his own entry Pollio is described as φιλόσοφος γεγονὼς ἐπὶ Ἀδριανοῦ.

 1–3 The layout is doubtful. My impression is that 1 and 2 would have been blank after Διόδω[ρος and τῶ[ι and that χαίρειν would probably have been abbreviated to χ⌐ in 3, but there might have been a very short *nomen* (Λουκκηΐωι, cf. 2 n., is too long) in 1, κυρίωι in 2, and χαίρειν in full in 3, or any combination of the three.

 2 Ὀφελλιανῶι. The only person of this name known from the papyri is Lucceius Ofellianus, epistrategus of the Heptanomia *c.* 166–9, see J. D. Thomas, *The Epistrategos in Ptolemaic and Roman Egypt* (Pap. Colon. VI), Part 2, 189, 201. In spite of the rarity of the name and the proximity of the dates the recipient of this letter is likely to be a resident of Oxyrhynchus and not the epistrategus.

 4–5 The articulation ἴσασι ν[seems unlikely. The last trace in 4 is from the foot of a long descender with a hook to the left, e.g. ι, ρ, φ, ψ. The first letter of 5 looks like alpha with part of the loop worn away on the left, or it might possibly be a botched lambda. We expect something like, 'All men know (that you do something praiseworthy), therefore . . .'. It might be a quotation from poetry with an uncontracted verb with a stem in alpha. Or possibly εἰς should be recognized. Or φ[ι]λεῖς might do, e.g. [ὅτι ἡμᾶς] φ[ι]λεῖς.

 6 The patronymic might well be Θέωνος. The remains of the first letter show a curve cut by a medial crossbar and are entirely suitable for theta. The fourth letter is represented by a foot which slopes and curves to the right in a way which is not characteristic of nu, but could suit a backhand version of it. It is close to the preceding letter and would be the first upright of nu. It looks as if another member of the family was also called Theon, see 10 n.

 9 I take it that γενομένου means that the philosopher was dead, though there may be the possibility that φιλοσόφου γενομένου is the equivalent of φιλοσοφοῦντος.

10 Θε. [.]. ϛ. The final horizontal at the level of the tops of the letters makes sigma and a third declension genitive virtually certain. Θέω[ν]ος or Θέων[ο]ς would fit the very meagre traces and there is good reason to read this name also in 6. Since ἀδελφιδοῦς can mean 'sister's son' as well as 'brother's son', the putative Theons need not be brothers, but it is not uncommon to find Egyptian families with two sons of the same name, often distinguished by πρεϲβύτεροϲ and νεώτεροϲ. There was also a prominent Alexandrian family with Oxyrhynchite connections in which brothers were called Theon, see P. J. Sijpesteijn, *The Family of the Tiberii Iulii Theones* and XLIV **3197**, but so far there is no Diogenes known in that family or any attested connection with philosophy. Theon is such a very common name that there is very little hope of identifying these men. No Epicurean philosopher of suitable name, origin, and date has been located.

11 .[..]. ν. Mr Parsons suggests φ[ιλ]ῶν, which is very convincing, to be followed at some point by a main verb in the first person singular. The first trace is the foot of a long descender, which suits phi, and omega is quite possible.

14 Restore [ἡ]μεῖν, 'us', meaning either 'you and me' or 'us and our friends', or [ὑ]μεῖν, 'you', meaning 'you and your friends'.

14-15 ..[..]¹⁵cεωc. The traces suggest the tops of two rounded letters, and these might be the last of the line, but probably some papyrus has been stripped away near the edge.

15 On the extreme left-hand edge of the sheet opposite this line there is some ink which looks like deliberate writing and might be read as]ω or possibly]ν. Presumably it has little to do with this document. Two letters may have been written originally on the same sheet which was then divided clumsily. Or the piece for this letter may have been cut from a piece that already had writing on it.

3644. Heras to Papontos

14 1B.202/F(b)　　　　13 × 22 cm　　　　Third century

Here is a story of a woman who struck another with a heavy key and injured her so badly that she was still in bed at least four days later when the letter was written. The attacker had by then fled to another district.

The writer's vulgar Greek is fluent, but his spelling is phonetic and unfamiliar, so that it is best interpreted by printing a version in orthodox spelling alongside. All the unorthodox spellings can be matched by page-references to F. T. Gignac, *Grammar* i, as follows:

171	μ ⟩ ν	3
213	ο ⟩ ου	3
277	ο ⟩ ω	3, 4, 7, 9 (*ter*), 10, 15, 17 (*ter*), 24, 25 (*bis*), 26 (*bis*), 27, 30 (*bis*), 32
276	ω ⟩ ο	4, 6, 9, 30, 31
90-1	χ ⟩ κ	7
192	αι ⟩ ε	9, 30
190-1	ι ⟩ ει	14, 17, 22, 25
204	υι ⟩ η	15
93	φ ⟩ π	18
112	{ν}	18 (*bis*)
86	τ ⟩ θ	19
226-7	αυ ⟩ α	19
189-90	ει ⟩ ι	20, 26

159	c ⟩ cc	23, 26, 30
197	οι ⟩ υ	26
192–3	ε ⟩ αι	28
155	λλ ⟩ λ	30
140	ξ ⟩ κξ	11–12

The writing shows the influence of the severe or mixed style, especially in the angular epsilons, and belongs probably to the third century. It runs along the fibres of a piece which shows no sheet joins.

Ἡρᾶς Παποντῶ[τι τῷ
πατρὶ χαίρειν. [
  ἔπενψά σοι Ἀρπουχρᾶν τὼν
ἡμέτερον ὥπος λάβῃ παρὰ
5 τοῦ ἀδελφοῦ μου γράμμα-
τα ἐπιθηκὸν ¯ ξ̄ᾱ . . . . , [ἐ]πιδὴ
συνεσκέθην ὑπὼ Κερ. [.]ος
τοῦ φίλου καὶ ἀνήκας[έ] με
ὠμώσε αὐτῷ ὥπος ἐντὸς
10 τῆς κ̄ ἀναδωθῆναι αὐτῷ
μετὰ πολλῆς ὕβ[ρε]ως. ἐκ-
ξη. ησῃ δὲ ε[. . Ἀρπ]οχρᾶς
. . . . [. .]. [.]. .[. . . .].
  καὶ εὗρον τὴν Σαβεῖναν πεπλη-
15 χῆαν τὴν Cύραν καὶ ἐπυθώμην
αὐτῆς πῶς ἐπλήγη καὶ ἔμα-
θον ὑπὼ πάντων ὥτει διὰ τὼ
μὴ ἀπεθῆναι τὴν Σαβεῖναν
ἄρθι ἃ εἶχε ἐντὸς ἀτῆς ἦ κα-
20 τίχε κλειδεὶ τῆς ἐξέδρας ἔπλη-
ξε αὐτὴν καὶ μέχρι τῆς cήμε-
ρον ἡμέρας κατακλεινῆς
ἔccτιν. ἡ δὲ Σαβεῖνα ἀπὸ τῆς
δεκάτης ἀνεύρετος ἐγένετω
25 καὶ ἤκουσα ὥτει ἐν τῷ Ἡρακλεω-
πωλείτῃ ἔccτίν. ἐρῖ cυ δὲ Ἀρπω-

Ἡρᾶς Παποντῶτι τῷ
πατρὶ χαίρειν.
  ἔπεμψά σοι Ἀρποχρᾶν τὸν
ἡμέτερον ὅπως λάβῃ παρὰ
τοῦ ἀδελφοῦ μου γράμμα-
τα ἐπιθηκὼν . . . , ἐπειδὴ
συνεσχέθην ὑπὸ Κερᾶτος (?)
τοῦ φίλου καὶ ἠνάγκασέ με
ὀμόσαι αὐτῷ ὅπως ἐντὸς
τῆς κ̄ ἀναδοθῆναι αὐτῷ
μετὰ πολλῆς ὕβρεως.

  καὶ εὗρον τὴν Σαβῖναν πεπλη-
χυῖαν τὴν Cύραν καὶ ἐπυθόμην
αὐτῆς πῶς ἐπλήγη καὶ ἔμα-
θον ὑπὸ πάντων ὅτι διὰ τὸ
μὴ ἀφεθῆναι τῇ Σαβίνᾳ
ἄρτι ἃ εἶχε ἐντὸς αὐτῆς ἦ κα-
τεῖχε κλειδὶ τῆς ἐξέδρας ἔπλη-
ξε αὐτὴν καὶ μέχρι τῆς cήμε-
ρον ἡμέρας κατακλινῆς
ἐccτιν. ἡ δὲ Σαβῖνα ἀπὸ τῆς
δεκάτης ἀνεύρετος ἐγένετο
καὶ ἤκουσα ὅτι ἐν τῷ Ἡρακλεο-
πολίτῃ ἐcτίν. ἐρεῖ σοι δὲ Ἀρπο-

χρᾶς ἃ ἤκουςεν ἐν τῇ πώλει ἃ ἔπρα-   χρᾶς ἃ ἤκουςεν ἐν τῇ πόλει ἃ ἔπρα-
ξεν πράγματα. ἐρ[ρῶς]θέ ςε εὔχ(ομαι).   ξεν πράγματα. ἐρρῶςθαί ςε εὔχ(ομαι)
   Φαῶφι ιδ΄.   Φαῶφι ιδ΄.
                                  ἀλλ᾽ ὅρα μὴ κατάςχῃς Ἁρποχρᾶν διὰ τὸ
Left margin, downwards: ἐπείγεςθαι περὶ τῶν ἐπιθηκῶν.

30 ἀλ᾽ ὥρα μὴ κατάςχῃς Ἁρποχρᾶν διὰ τὼ ἐπίγεςςθε περὶ τὸν
ἐπιθηκόν.

Back, downwards:

].. ( ) Παπ[ο]ν[τῶτ]ι [τῷ] πα-⟩ ⟨ τρὶ π[αρ]ὰ Ἡράτως.

'Heras to Papontos his father, greetings. I have sent you our Harpochras so that he may get from my brother letters of credit for . . ., since I was detained by Ceras (?) my friend, and he compelled me with great violence to swear to him that they would be delivered to him by the 20th. . . . Harpochras . . . . . . and I found that Sabina had injured Syra and I asked Syra how she got injured and learnt from them all that because the things which Syra had in her possession were not immediately released to Sabina she struck Syra with the exedra key which she was holding and Syra is confined to bed up to the present day. Sabina disappeared since the tenth and I heard that she is in the Heracleopolite nome. Harpochras will tell you what he heard in the city of the things she did.
  'I pray for your health.
  'Phaophi 14.
Margin: 'But see that you don't detain Harpochras, because there is a rush for the credits.'
Back: 'Deliver (?) to Papontos his father, from Heras.'

  1 There would have been room for Παποντῶ[τι τῷ κυρίῳ, but the wide spacing in 1–2 suggests that no more than τῷ was written.
  6 For the little that is known about the term ἐπιθήκη, 'letter of credit', see XLIII 3146 8 n. Before ξᾱ stands something with another horizontal bar over it. It might be φ̄ = 800, or there might be two figures, e.g. ς̄. = 200 + (?). The plural in ἐπιθηκόν, cf. 31, suggests that we should look for two separate figures here, i.e. not 861, but 800 and 61 *vel sim.*, though the absence of any indication of the units, e.g. drachmas, is disquieting. After ξᾱ the size of the illegible writing seems much reduced. One might guess ἐις μ[ε] (or με), 'in my name', but this is highly uncertain.
  7 Perhaps Κερᾱ[τ]ος. Κέρδ[ων]ος, even spelt Κέρδ[ον]ος, seems too long.
  8 ἀνήκας[ε] = ἠνάγκαςε. See XXXVI 2783 29 n., B. G. Mandilaras, *The Verb* §268.
  9–10 For ὅπως with the infinitive cf. B. G. Mandilaras, *The Verb* §776.
  11–13 Perhaps understand ἐξηγήςῃ δὲ ἐ[ὰν Ἁρπ]οχρᾶς . . ., 'You will have explanations to make if Harpochras . . .'; 13 might begin ἀποδημ-, just possibly. See the injunction not to detain Harpochras in 30–1. But this has very little chance of being right, especially since ἐξηγεῖςθαι is not attested with this special shade of meaning.
  17–19 The interpretation is doubtful. The translation supposes that την Caβειναν stands for τῇ Caβίνᾳ, as it could easily do, see F. T. Gignac, *Grammar* i 111–12. Possibly it might be better to take την Caβεῖναν as the subject of ἀπεθῆναι (ἀφεθῆναι) and ἃ εἶχε as an internal accusative, translating, 'because Sabina was not immediately released (from responsibility for) the things which she had in her possession'.
  19 For the sense of ἐντός, 'in a person's hands, in his possession', see C. H. Roberts, *Harvard Theological Review* 41 (1948) 1–8, esp. 5–6.
  20 κλειδεί. As implied by the story, a key of the period might be a very substantial piece of wood or metal. For illustrations see W. M. Flinders Petrie, *Tools and Weapons*, pls. lxxv, lxxvi, with the text of pp. 59–60.
  ἐξέδρας. Usually thought of as an arcade or portico, the exedra in the papyri appears rather as a barn or outhouse, see e.g. BGU III 981 ii 26 ἐξέδρας, εἰς ἣν ἐνκλείςι (= ἐγκλείςει) χόρτο(ν), cf. G. Husson, *Ktema* i (1976) 15–16.

29 Phaophi 14 = 11 October, or 12 October before a Roman leap year.

32] . . ( ). The last trace is well above the line in a manner which suggests an abbreviation. We should expect ἀπ]όδ(ος), 'deliver', written απ]ρδ, and this may be right even though it is difficult to see the remains in that way. The sense must certainly have been the same.

For the interrupted saltire pattern in the middle of the address cf. **3642** 34 n.

3645. DISCREET LETTER

9 1B.170/J(b)   13 × 7 cm   Third century

'No names, no pack drill' is a motto that would have appealed to this writer. He suggests that he and another, probably the recipient, can now be protected by a person who has been appointed to a magistracy, by the magistrate's brother, and by a friend of the two brothers. When this friend arrives, the recipient is supposed to make himself known to him.

All four margins survive and, except for wear, the slip of papyrus seems complete. The pattern of folds shows that the sheet was rolled up with the right edge inside and that there was not another column to the right; otherwise the folds would have been wider apart. There is no proof that there was not a preceding column on the left, but there is nothing to suggest that there was. Probably, therefore, the absence of prescript, farewell formula, and address, is deliberate and was part of the same marvellous discretion which forbade the mention of names and makes it so difficult now to understand what the writer's predicament was.

The writing is a good sloping cursive, showing some influence from the severe or mixed style of book hand. This is especially noticeable in the last line and a half (from καὶ cὺν αὐτῷ), which are written in a blacker ink and much more compactly. They look as if they were written at a later time but by the same hand.

The back is blank, except for offsets left by the text of the letter while it was rolled up.

εἰ, ὡς ἀκούω, κατὰ τὰς εὐχὰς ἡμῶν ὁ κύ-
ριος ἡμῶν φίλος εἰcαῦθις ἄρχει, δύνανται ἐκ ταύτης τῆς προφάcεως ἀμφοτέ-
ρους ἡμᾶς καὶ αὐτὸς καὶ ὁ ἀδελφὸς ῥύcα-
5   cθαι παρὰ τῷ φίλῳ αὐτῶν, τῷ εἰς Ὄαcιν
ἀναβάντι ὁπότε καὶ ἐπεδήμει ὁ βρα-
χύτερος αὐτῶν καὶ cὺν αὐτῷ ἐκεῖ ἐγέ-
νετο. ἐπιδ[ὰ]ν παρ' ὑμῖν γένηται, γνωρίcθητι αὐτῷ.

8 l. ἐπειδάν; ὑμιν

'If, as I hear, our prayers are answered and our lord and friend is to be holding a magistracy in the future, he and his brother can as a result of this give both of us protection with their friend, the one who went up to the Oasis at the time when the shorter (?) of them was also here and went there with him. Whenever he arrives among you, make yourself known to him.'

2 εἰcαῦθιc ἄρχει, δύνανται. Possibly divide εἰc αῦθιc, see *LSJ* Suppl., s.v. εἰcαῦθιc. The sense of this word, 'for hereafter, for a future time', shows that the present tense of ἄρχει has a future meaning, cf. B. G. Mandilaras, *The Verb* 102–3 (§§214–5). The same may apply to δύνανται, but need not.

4–5 ῥύcacθαι. From this word one might guess that the difficulty here was, as so often, over public service, cf. XII **1424** 9–10 cπούδαcον τοίνυν, ἄδελφε, τοῦτον ῥύcacθαι τοῦ λειτουργήματοc.

5 παρὰ τῷ φίλῳ. The meaning might be that the friend was to provide a hiding-place for the two who were in need of protection, or perhaps he was simply the person on whom the magistrate's influence was to be exerted.

Ὄαcιν. This is probably the Small Oasis, now Bahariya, in the desert west of Oxyrhynchus, cf. *Rech. de pap.* iii, p. 28, P. Merton III 106. 3 n., R. Pintaudi, *Miscellanea papyrologica* 325, 18 n.

6 ἀναβάντι. In this case ἀνα- refers to 'the ascent from the valley to the desert plateau', see H. C. Youtie, *Scriptiunculae* i 493 n. 36.

6–7 βραχύτεροc. Of the meanings recorded in *LSJ* only 'shorter' or 'less important' would apply to persons. I suspect that 'littler' i.e. 'younger' is a more likely meaning, cf. H. Stephanus, *Thesaurus* ii, col. 403B, citing Artemidorus, *Onirocritica* 1. 50 παιδίον βραχύ, 3. 27 νήπιοι καὶ βραχεῖc; Schol. Aristoph., *Vesp.*, 570 βραχεῖαν τῶν παίδων ἡλικίαν (cf. βραχυῆλιξ).

3646. HARSONTHOÜS TO FLAVIANUS

29 4B.48/H(7–8)a   10.5 × 25 cm   Third/fourth century

The mention of a strategus called Heracleides gives this private letter a little more than routine interest. He might be the Oxyrhynchite strategus of 288–9, see J. E. G. Whitehorne, *ZPE* 29 (1978) 182, no. 106, but the handwriting suggests rather a date in the early fourth century. He supplied hay for animals belonging to the recipient of the letter and this too suggests the fourth century, when the strategus was a member of the local curial class and no longer an appointee from another nome, cf. J. Lallemand, *L'Administration*, 123. Lallemand writes here of the later fourth century, but this seems to have been true also in the earlier part. For example, Aurelius Dioscurides alias Julianus, Oxyrhynchite strategus of 311, see *ZPE* 29 (1978) 183, no. 114, is virtually certain to be the same as the ex-prytanis of Oxyrhynchus addressed by the same names in 315 in XXXI **2585** 3–4, cf. J. G. Keenan, *ZPE* 13 (1974) 297. It is, of course, not entirely certain that our strategus held his post in the Oxyrhynchite nome, since the letter was found at Oxyrhynchus and may have come from somewhere quite outside that district. The writer, an older person but an inferior, seems to be reporting the situation at home to a man who is away.

κυρίῳ μου πάτρωνι καὶ
υἱῷ Φλαβιανῷ χαίρειν
Ἁρϲωνθωοῦϲ ὁ πατήρ᾽.
ὃν ἕγ᾽ ἐπροϲδοκᾶϲ προϲέχιν

5   τοῖϲ πράγμαϲί ϲοι καὶ τοῖϲ
κτῆ[ϲ]ι οὕτωϲ δὲ ἠμέληϲεν
καὶ οὐ προϲέχιν ὅλλωϲ αὐτοῖϲ.
ὁ δὲ Ἡρακλίδηϲ ὁ ϲτρατηγὸϲ
γνηϲίωϲ ἠπηρέτηϲέν ϲου

10   τὰ κτήνη, δοὺϲ ἤδη χόρτου δέϲμαϲ διϲχιλλίαϲ καὶ
ἴ τινοϲ ἐὰν χρήζῃϲ λαμ-
βάνω. οὕτωϲ γάρ μοι λέγι,
‘περὶ πάντων τῶν πραγμά-

15   των ϲοι διαφερόνθων ϲοι,
μὴ ὄχνι ἔρχεϲται καὶ
λαμβάνι⟨ν⟩.᾽ καὶ ἐπίϲτιλον
Ἐλουρᾶτι περὶ οἴν[ο]υ Ϲαΐτια
δέκα, ἐπιδὲ χρία ἐϲτὶν

20   εἰϲ τοὺϲ γάμουϲ τοῦ υἱοῦ
μου. καὶ ὃ ἂν ποιήϲῃϲ
τῷ προφήτῃ, ἐμοὶ ποιεῖϲ.
οἶδα γὰρ ὅτι ϲὲ ἔχω⟨ν⟩, οὐδίϲ μοι
μέλλι καταπατῖν. ἐρρῶ⟨ϲ⟩θαί

25   ϲε εὔχομαι, κύριέ μου πάτρων
καὶ υἱέ.

Back, downwards:

κυρίῳ μου Φλαβιανῷ (vac.) Ἁρϲονθωοῦϲ ὁ πατήρ.

2 υἵω   2–3 l. Φλαβιανῷ Ἁρϲωνθωοῦϲ ὁ πατὴρ χαίρειν   4 l. ὃν ἕνα προϲεδοκᾶϲ προϲέχειν
6 l. οὗτοϲ   7 l. προϲέχει ὅλωϲ   8 l. Ἡρακλείδηϲ   9 l. ὑπηρέτηϲεν; ϲου corr. from ϲοι
11 l. διϲχιλίαϲ   12 l. εἴ   13 l. λέγει   15 l. διαφερόντων   16 l. ὄκνει ἔρχεϲθαι
17 l. λαμβάνειν, ἐπίϲτειλον   18 l. Αἰλουρᾶτι; ϲαΐτια; l. Ϲαΐτίων   19 l. ἐπειδὴ χρεία   20 υἱου
23 l. οὐδείϲ με   24 l. μέλλει καταπατεῖν   26 ὑιε

‘To my lord patron and son Flavianus, Harsonthoüs your father, greetings. The one man whom you expected to attend to the business and to the animals for you—this is the one who has been neglectful and pays no attention to them at all. Heracleides the strategus has loyally served your animals, having already given two

thousand bales of hay, and anything you need I take. This is what he says to me: 'In all the affairs which concern you do not hesitate to come and take'. And write to Aeluras about ten Saïte jars of wine, because they are needed for my son's wedding. And whatever you do for the *prophetes*, you do for me. Indeed I know that, while I have you, nobody is going to trample on me. I pray for your health, my lord patron and son.'
Back. 'To my lord Flavianus, Harsonthoüs your father.'

1 πάτρωνι, cf. 25. The title is probably a mark of respect rather than a technical term, cf. CPR V 19. 18–19n.

2 Flavianus is not identifiable; the name occurs in this spelling in I **43** verso v 10, VI **939** 1, 32, XLIII **3124** 1, 13, XLVIII **3386** 3.

3 Ἁρϲωνθοῦϲ, cf. 27 Ἁρϲονθωοῦϲ. The name is not recorded in F. Preisigke, *Namenbuch*, or D. Foraboschi, *Onomasticon*. It appears to be related to Ϲοντωοῦϲ, cf. Ϲαντωοῦϲ, Ϲεντωοῦϲ, Ϲενϲεντωοῦϲ, Ταϲοντωοῦϲ, Ϲενϲοντωοῦϲ. For theta in place of tau cf. 15, διαφερόνθων for διαφερόντων.

This line was added later in a smaller version of the same hand. It stands below 2, but it belongs before χαίρειν. In the margin to the left there is ink which seems to be accidental.

4 ὅν ἔν᾽ ἐπροϲδοκᾶϲ. The damaged nu is split in two, but seems certain. The elision is a little unexpected, cf. F. T. Gignac, *Grammar* i 315. For the misplaced augment see Gignac, *Grammar* ii 252 d(2), B. G. Mandilaras, *The Verb* 117 (§252).

6 For κτῆ[ϲ]ι = κτήνεϲι see F. T. Gignac, *Grammar* ii 67.

οὕτωϲ (= -οϲ) δέ. Cf. E. Mayser, *Grammatik* ii 3. 132–3, but possibly δέ is for δή, cf. 19 and note on ἐπιδέ = ἐπειδή.

9–10 The alteration of ϲοι to ϲου may indicate that the writer was aware that ὑπηρετεῖν takes a dative and ˏmeant to write ϲου τοῖϲ κτῆϲι.

13 It is possible, but perhaps less likely, that ουτωϲ stands for οὗτοϲ again, as in 6.

15 For the repetition of personal pronouns cf. E. Mayser, *Grammatik*, ii 1. 63–4.

19 ἐπιδέ = ἐπειδή. Cf. F. T. Gignac, *Grammar* i 244.

19–22 It appears that the *prophetes* is to be identified with the person the writer calls 'my son' in 20–1, who may actually be his son, though it is fairly clear that the recipient, whom he also calls his son (2, 26), is not in fact his son. For the customary loose use of terms of blood relationship see P. Mich. VIII, pp. 16–17, with no. 468. 46–7n.; cf. H. C. Youtie, *Scriptiunculae* i 393 (= *TAPA* 95 (1963) 341) and n. 39.

On προφήτηϲ in Egyptian contexts see E. Fascher, *ΠΡΟΦΗΤΗΣ. Eine sprach- und religionsgeschichtliche Untersuchung* 76–101. It is usually the equivalent of an Egyptian title, ḥm-ntr, Demotic ḥm-ntr, Coptic ϩοντ, which means merely 'servant of the god'. The Greek term may originally have been applied to priests at Egyptian oracles and spread gradually to others. At this comparatively late date, however, there may be some connection with the worship of Hermes Trismegistus, see Fascher, op. cit. 98–100, and cf. P. Herm. Rees 3. 21–5, 26. The writer of that letter is an ἀρχιπροφήτηϲ called Anatolius and he ends his letter with the wish that Hermes Trismegistus and all the gods may grant that the recipient be happy for ever. Two other letters from Anatolius are preserved, P. Herm. Rees 2 and SB XII 10803. On the whole religious context of the archive of Theophanes, with which those letters are associated, see E. A. Judge, S. R. Pickering, *JAC* 20 (1977) 53–4.

23–4 The 'correction' of εχω to ἔχω⟨ν⟩ assumes that the writer intended a hanging nominative participle, which is well known in the colloquial language, see B. G. Mandilaras, *The Verb* §879, H. C. Youtie, *Scriptiunculae* i 305 and n. 76. The omission of a final nasal is an even more common phenomenon.

INDEXES

Square brackets indicate that a word is wholly or substantially restored by conjecture or from other sources, round brackets that it is expanded from an abbreviation or a symbol. An asterisk denotes a word not recorded in *LSJ* or Suppl. The article and *καί* are not indexed.

I. RULERS AND REGNAL YEARS

Septimius Severus
Καῖϲαρ **3614** 2
No titulature: **3601** 31 (year 3)

Septimius Severus, Caracalla, and Geta
Αὐτοκράτορεϲ Καίϲαρεϲ Λούκιοϲ Ϲεπτίμιοϲ Ϲεουῆροϲ Εὐϲεβὴϲ Περτίναξ Ἀραβικὸϲ Ἀδιαβηνικὸϲ Παρθικὸϲ Μέγιϲτοϲ καὶ Μᾶρκοϲ Αὐρήλιοϲ Ἀντωνῖνοϲ Εὐϲεβήϲ, Ϲεβαϲτοί, καὶ Πούβλιοϲ Ϲεπτίμιοϲ Γέτα Καῖϲαρ Ϲεβαϲτόϲ (year 11) **3601** 35–9

Caracalla
Αὐτοκράτωρ Καῖϲαρ Μᾶρκοϲ Αὐρήλιοϲ Ϲεουῆροϲ Ἀντωνῖνοϲ Παρθικὸϲ Μέγιϲτοϲ Βρεταννικὸϲ Μέγιϲτοϲ Γερμανικὸϲ Μέγιϲτοϲ Εὐϲεβὴϲ Ϲεβαϲτόϲ (year 24) **3602** 26–9   **3603** 27–30   **3604** 25–8   **3605** 17–21
Μᾶρκοϲ Αὐρήλιοϲ Ϲεουῆροϲ Ἀντωνῖνοϲ Παρθικὸϲ Μέγιϲτοϲ Βρεταννικὸϲ Μέγιϲτοϲ Γερμανικὸϲ Μέγιϲτοϲ Εὐϲεβὴϲ Ϲεβαϲτὸϲ ὁ κύριοϲ (oath formula) **3602** 2–6   **3603** 5–8   **3604** 3–7 (om. ὁ κύριοϲ)
ὁ κύριοϲ ἡμῶν ἀήττητοϲ Αὐτοκράτωρ Μᾶρκοϲ Αὐρήλιοϲ Ϲεουῆροϲ Ἀντωνῖνοϲ Εὐϲεβὴϲ Εὐτυχὴϲ Ϲεβαϲτόϲ (*adventus* of) **3603** 12–15
ὁ κύριοϲ ἡμῶν Αὐτοκράτωρ Ϲεουῆροϲ Ἀντωνῖνοϲ (*adventus* of) **3604** 12–13   [**3605** 4–6]
ὁ κύριοϲ ἡμῶν καὶ θεῶν ἐμφανέϲτατοϲ Ἀντωνῖνοϲ (*adventus* of) **3602** 10–12

Elagabalus
Αὐτοκράτωρ Καῖϲαρ Μᾶρκοϲ Αὐρήλιοϲ Ἀντωνῖνοϲ Εὐϲεβὴϲ Εὐτυχὴϲ Ϲεβαϲτόϲ (year 4) **3638** 32–3

Severus Alexander
No titulature: **3606** 2 (year 8), 17 (year 9), 20 (year 10)
ὁ κύριοϲ ἡμῶν Αὐτοκράτωρ Μᾶρκοϲ Αὐρήλιοϲ Ϲεουῆροϲ Ἀλέξανδροϲ Καῖϲαρ ὁ κύριοϲ (*natalis* of) **3606** 6–10

Gordians I and II
. . . Μᾶρκοϲ Ἀντώνιοϲ Γορδιανὸϲ Ῥωμανὸϲ Ϲεμπρωνιανὸϲ Ἀφρικανόϲ . . . καὶ . . . Μᾶρκοϲ Ἀντώνιοϲ Γορδιανὸϲ Ῥωμανὸϲ Ϲεμπρωνιανὸϲ Ἀφρικανόϲ . . . (fragmentary) **3607** 5, 9–12, 16–18

Decius and Herennius
Αὐτοκράτωρ Καῖϲαρ Γάϊοϲ Μέϲϲιοϲ Κυῖντοϲ Τραϊανὸϲ Δέκιοϲ Εὐϲεβὴϲ Εὐτυχὴϲ Ϲεβαϲτὸϲ καὶ Κυῖντοϲ Ἑρέννιοϲ Ἐτροῦϲκοϲ Μέϲϲιοϲ Δέκιοϲ ὁ ϲεβαϲμιώτατοϲ Καῖϲαρ Ϲεβαϲτοί (year 2) **3608** 1–7   **3609** 11–15
Γάϊοϲ Μέϲϲιοϲ Κυῖντοϲ Τραϊανὸϲ Δέκιοϲ Εὐϲεβὴϲ Εὐτυχὴϲ Ϲεβαϲτὸϲ καὶ Κυῖντοϲ Ἑρέννιοϲ Ἐτροῦϲκοϲ Μέϲϲιοϲ Δέκιοϲ ὁ ϲεβαϲμιώτατοϲ Καῖϲαρ Ϲεβαϲτοί (oath formula) **3609** 5–8

Gallus
Τρεβωνιανὸϲ Γάλλοϲ ὁ κύριοϲ . . . (year 1; fragmentary) **3610** 6
Αὐτοκράτωρ Καῖϲαρ . . . (year 1; fragmentary) **3610** 7

II. CONSULS

III. INDICTIONS

IV. MONTHS

V. PERSONAL NAMES

Ἰcίων, Aur., s. of Heras **3621** 22

Ἰωάννης, deacon and archimandrite of the monastery of Apa Hierax **3640** 1

Ἰωάννης, παραπομπός **3636** 8

Ἰωνᾶς, παραπομπός **3634** 9, 11, 12 **3636** 10, 12 (*bis*)

Καῖcαρ *see* Index I *passim*; II (AD 326, AD 329, AD 356); VIII s.v. ἀντιγραφὴ Καίcαρος

Καλλικλῆς: Septimius Callicles **3611** 6

Καλπούρνιος: Calpurnius (son of?) Gaius, prytanis **3606** 4

Κάcιος, παραπομπός **3634** 10

Κερᾶς [**3644** 7?]

Κερεάλιος: Neratius Cerealis, *consul*, *see* Index II (AD 359)

Κηνςώριος: Censorius Datianus, *patricius*, *consul*, *see* Index II (AD 359)

Κλᾶρος, Aur., sitologus, s. of Panechotes **3621** 15

Κλαύδιος: Aur. Claudius Lycarion alias Sarapammon, overseer of prefectural letters and other matters **3615** 1

Κυῖντος *see* Index I s.v. Decius and Herennius

Κωνσταντῖνος *see* Index II (AD 326, AD 329)

Κωνστάντιος *see* Index II (AD 326, AD 356)

Λ . . . τος (gen.), f. of Aur. Pollio **3604** 18

Λαῖτος: Maecius Laetus, *praef. Aeg.* **3601** 7

Λαῖτος: Ti. Flavius Laetus, *praef. Aeg.* **3620** 24

Λεόντιος, baker **3625** 6

Λικίννιος *see* Index I s.v. Valerian and Gallienus

Λιμένιος: Fl. Limenius, *vir clarissimus* **3639** 4

Λούκιος *see* Index I s.v. Septimius Severus, Caracalla, and Geta

Λυκαρίων: Aur. Claudius Lycarion alias Sarapammon, overseer of prefectural letters and other matters **3615** 1

Μάγνιος: Magnius Felix, *praef. Aeg.* **3611** 15

Μαίκιος: Maecius Laetus, *praef. Aeg.* **3601** 7

Μακάριος, παραπομπός **3636** 9

Μαμερτῖνος, Aur., alias Ptolemaeus, ὑπηρέτης **3602** 18 **3604** 20-1 **3605** 13

Μαξιμιανός *see* Index I s.v. Galerius and Maximinus

Μαξιμῖνος *see* Index I s.v. Galerius and Maximinus

Μάξιμος, (syndic?) **3618** 3

Μάξιμος, Theon alias, prytanis **3606** 18

Μαρῖνος **3637** 20

Μαρκίων(?): M. Valerius (Marcion?) **3609** 15-16, cf. 20

Μᾶρκος: M. Aurelius Chaeremon, s. of Hermias, m. Tayris, half-b. of Aurelia Tetseiris m. Tanetbeus **3638** 1-2, cf. 34

Μᾶρκος: M. Valerius (Marcion?) **3609** 15-16, cf. 20

Μᾶρκος *see* Index I s.vv. Septimius Severus, Caracalla, and Geta; Caracalla; Elagabalus; Severus Alexander; Gordians I and II

Μέλας, Aur., [**3624** 24?]

Μέccιος *see* Index I s.v. Decius and Herennius

Μηνᾶς, slave **3641** 4

Μοῦϊς, f. of Aur. Papnuthis in charge of meat **3621** 17

Μουςῆς, Aur., systates, s. of Theon **3622** 4 **3623** 4

Μύcθης, f. of Aur. Hermias, s. of Petenuphis **3602** 14 (Μύcτου), 22

Μύcτης *see* Μύcθης

Νεῖλος, Aur., **3603** 26

Νεράτιος: Neratius Apollonides, *magister privatae* **3618** 7

Νηράτιος: Neratius Cerealis, *consul*, *see* Index II (AD 359)

Ὄλυμπος: Junius Olympus, *praef. Aeg.* **3627** 8

Ὀννῶφρις, Aur., s. of Sarapion **3602** 16, 20, 24

Ὀννῶφρις, f. of Aur. Thonius **3620** 6

Ὀνώριος *see* Index II (AD 412)

Οὐαλεριανός *see* Index I s.v. Valerian and Gallienus

Οὐαλέριος: M. Valerius (Marcion?) **3609** 15-16, cf. 20?

Οὐαλέριος: Valerius Diodorus(?) **3643** 1

Οὐϊκτωρά, slave-girl **3620** 9

Οὐϊκτωρῖνος *see* Index II (AD 200)

Ὀφελλιανός **3643** 2

Π. . ., Aur., (s. of?) Silvanus **3622** 7

Παελένης, Aur., in charge of tunics and cloaks, s. of Amoitas **3621** 17

Παελένης, f. of Aur. Pettiris (or Petseiris) *tesserarius* **3621** 5

Πακλῆς, Aur., **3604** 22

Πάμμαχος, f. of Aur. Paysiris sitologus **3621** 14

Πανεχώτης, Aur., comarch, s. of Heracles **3621** 6, 21

Πανεχώτης, f. of Aur. Clarus sitologus **3621** 15

Παπνοῦθις, Aur., in charge of meat, s. of Muis **3621** 17

Παποντῶς, f. (?) of Heras **3644** 1, 32

Παταῦρις, f. of Aur. Paysas in charge of chaff **3621** 15

Παυcᾶς, Aur., comarch, s. of Besas **3621** 6, 21

Παυcᾶς, Aur., in charge of chaff, s. of Patayris **3621** 15

Παυcῖρις, Aur., sitologus, s. of Pammachus **3621** 14

Πέκυλλος, alias Theon, prytanis **3606** 20

Πελῶρις, Aur., son of . . . **3605** 10, 16

Περτίναξ *see* Index I s.v. Septimius Severus, Caracalla, and Geta

Πετενοῦφις, gd.-f. of Aur. Hermias, f. of Mysthes **3602** 14, (22)

Πέτρος, Aur., oil-manufacturer **3639** 5

VI. GEOGRAPHICAL

(a) Countries, Nomes, Toparchies, Cities, etc.

Ἀδιαβηνικός *see* Index I s.v. Septimius Severus, Caracalla, and Geta
Aegyptus Iouia **3619** 7, 10–15, 17–21
Ἀθριβίτης (nome) **3617** 2
Αἰγύπτιος **3617** 1
Αἴγυπτος [**3611** 15] **3613** 2, 7 **3620** 24
Ἀλεξάνδρεια **3614** 2 **3634** [2], [4], 13, [16], [18?] **3637** 8
    ἡ μεγαλόπολις Ἀλεξάνδρεια **3635** 2 **3636** 4, 17
Ἀλεξανδρεύς **3611** 9, 11 **3612** 2
Ἀλεξανδρέων· ἡ λαμπροτάτη Ἀ. πόλις **3613** 4, cf. 6, 17
Ἀντινοεύς **3611** 13
Ἀντινόου πόλις **3611** 5
Ἀραβικός *see* Index I s.v. Septimius Severus, Caracalla, and Geta
Ἀρσινοΐτης (nome) (**3632** 1) **3635** 7 (**3636** 2)
Ἀφρικανός *see* Index I s.v. Gordians I and II
Ἀφροδιτοπολίτης (nome) (**3633** 1) (**3635** 6) (**3636** 2)
Βρεταννικός *see* Index I s.v. Caracalla
Γερμανικός *see* Index I s.v. Caracalla
Διοπολίτης Μικρός (nome) **3601** 4, 12, 21
Ἑλληνιστί **3617** 3
Ἑρμοπολίτης (nome) (**3615** 5)
Ἡρακλεοπολίτης (nome) (**3635** 8) (**3636** 2) **3644** 25–6

Θεοδοσιοπολίτης (nome) **3636** 2, 16
Θηβαΐς **3601** 5, 21
Iouia *see* Aegyptus Iouia
κάτω τοπαρχία **3638** 6
Κυνοπολίτης (nome) **3628** 5 (**3635** 8) (**3636** 2)
Λητοπολίτης (**3635** 6) (**3636** 2, 15)
μεγαλόπολις *see* s.v. Ἀλεξάνδρεια
Μεμφίτης (nome) **3635** 6 **3636** (2), 15
Νιλοπολίτης (nome) (**3636** 2)
Ὄασις **3645** 5
Ὀξυρυγχίτης (nome) **3601** 18 **3610** 1, [5] **3612** 4 **3623** 3 **3624** 2 **3625** 2 [**3626** 2] **3629** 1 (**3636** 2)
Ὀξυρυγχιτῶν· ἡ Ὀ. πόλις **3638** 1–2 **3641** 6, 27
Ὀξυρυγχιτῶν· ἡ λαμπρὰ Ὀ. πόλις [**3641** 3–4]
Ὀξυρυγχιτῶν· ἡ λαμπρὰ καὶ λαμπροτάτη Ὀ. πόλις [**3618** 4–5] [**3620** 5] **3622** 4–5 [**3639** 4–5]
Ὀξυρύγχων πόλις [**3610** 3]
πάγος **3621** 4, 7 (3rd)
Παρθικός *see* Index I s.vv. Septimius Severus, Caracalla, and Geta; Caracalla
Πηλούσιον **3602** 9
Ῥωμανός *see* Index I s.v. Gordians I and II
Σαΐτιον *see* Index X(a)
Ταρσικός **3626** 17

(b) Villages, etc.

Θεαδέλφεια (Arsinoite) [**3604** 2?]
Κυνῶν πόλις (Arsinoite) **3602** 23
Νεμέρα **3642** 11

Σενεκελεύ (3rd pagus) **3621** 7
Σιναρύ **3638** 6, 37
Χενρῆς(?) or -χενρῆς (Athribite) **3617** 2

(c) Miscellaneous

Ἄνω (or Ἱππέων or Λυκίων) Παρεμβολῆς (ἄμφοδον) [**3639** 9–10]
Δρόμου Γυμνασίου (ἄμφοδον/φυλή) **3622** 6 **3623** 5–6
ἔξω τῆς πύλης (προάστιον) **3640** 2
Εὐτρυγίου (locality?) **3640** 3
θερμά (in Alexandria) **3613** 8
Ἱππέων (or Ἄνω or Λυκίων) Παρεμβολῆς (ἄμφοδον) [**3639** 9–10]

κλῆρος· Ῥοδίππου κ. **3638** 6, 37–8
Λυκίων (or Ἄνω or Ἱππέων) Παρεμβολῆς (ἄμφοδον) [**3639** 9–10]
μοναστήριον Ἄπα Ἱέρακος **3640** 1
πύλη· ἔξω τῆς πύλης (προάστιον) **3640** 2
Σαραπεῖον **3642** 29
Τῶμις ποταμός **3638** 12

VII. RELIGION

ἄπα **3640** 1
ἀρχιερεύς *see* Index VIII
ἀρχιμανδρίτης (**3640** 1)
διάκονος (**3640** 1) **3641** 26 (*diacon*( ))
θεῖος *see* Index I s.v. Justinian; VIII
θεός· θεῶν ἐμφανέστατος (Caracalla) **3602** 11
—: Αὐρηλιανὸς ὁ ἐν θεοῖς **3613** 5

ἱερεύς **3610** 4
ἱερονίκης *see* Index VIII
ἱερός *see* Index VIII
μοναστήριον **3640** 1
προφήτης **3646** 22
Σαραπεῖον **3642** 29
τύχη (*genius*) **3602** 6 **3603** 8 [**3604** 7] **3609** 8

VIII. OFFICIAL AND MILITARY TERMS AND TITLES

IX. PROFESSIONS, TRADES, AND OCCUPATIONS

X. MEASURES

(a) WEIGHTS AND MEASURES

(b) MONEY

XI. TAXES

ἀρουρατίων *see* ναῦλον
βοῦς *see* ὄνος: ὄνων καὶ βοῶν
γαλαθηνός? [**3634** 15]
δημόσια **3638** 26, 28
εἶδος **3638** 24
ἐπιμερισμός **3638** 26
ἐρέα **3635** 1

κηρός **3635** 9
μιςθός: μιςθ(οῦ?) ἀρτοκόπ(ων?) **3636** 17, 20, 21
ναῦλον: ναῦλα ἀρουρατίωνος **3634** 1
ὄνος: ὄνων καὶ βοῶν **3636** 17, 20, 21
πλατυπήγιον (= πλατυπύγιον?) **3636** 1
τέλος **3609** 10 **3614** 5 **3638** 30

XII. GENERAL INDEX OF WORDS

ἀγορά **3628** 1
ἀγορανομεῖν *see* Index VIII
ἀγράμματος [**3624** 25 n.?] **3641** 25
ἄγροικος **3619** [25?], 35
ἀγωγή **3641** 5
ἀγών **3611** 12
ἀδελφή **3638** [2], 35
ἀδελφιδοῦς **3643** 7
ἀδελφός (**3609** 9) **3638** 11 **3643** 3 **3644** 5
  3645 4
ἀήττητος *see* Index I s.v. Caracalla
ἀθροίζειν **3603** 2
ἀΐδιος [**3607** 18?]
αἱρεῖν **3638** 25
αἱρεῖςθαι **3602** 7 **3603** 4 [**3604** 8] [**3605** 1-2]
  3638 21-2, 29
αἰτεῖν **3627** 8
αἰτία **3641** 19
αἰώνιος *see* Index VIII
ἀκαταγνώςτως **3641** 11
ἀκολούθως **3601** 14 **3628** 2
ἀκούειν **3644** 25, 27 **3645** 1
ἀκρίβεια **3627** 3
ἀκρόδρυον **3638** 7
ἀλήθεια **3627** 8
ἀλιαδίτης *see* Index VIII
ἀλλά **3613** 6 **3614** 7 **3620** 13 **3627** 8 **3644** 30
ἀλλήλων **3638** 13
ἄλλος **3614** 2 **3615** 3 **3622** 6 **3623** 6 **3638** 12,
  20 [**3641** 21?]
ἅλς **3628** 17, 31, 45 **3629** [13], 17 **3630** [13], 27,
  40 **3631** 4, 16 **3632** 12, 21, 33 **3633** 12, 25, 38
ἅμα [**3603** 3?] [**3604** 7?] [**3620** 9?]
ἀμέλεια **3641** 11
ἀμελεῖν **3646** 6
ἀμπελικός **3638** 7, 14, 20, 38
ἄμφοδον **3622** 6 **3623** 6; cf. Index VI(*c*) s.v. Δρόμου
  Γυμναςίου **3639** 9; cf. Index VI (*c*) s.vv. Ἄνω
  Παρεμβολῆς, Ἱππέων Π., Λυκίων Π.
ἀμφότεροι **3620** 4 **3645** 3-4
ἄν **3612** 7 [**3627** 3 n.?] **3646** 21

ἀναβαίνειν **3645** 6
ἀναβολ( ) **3626** 21
ἀναγινώςκειν [**3614** 4]
ἀναγκάζειν **3644** 8
ἀναγκαῖος [**3643** 7]
ἀναγκαίως **3613** 12-13
ἀναδιδόναι **3644** 10
ἀναιςχυντεῖν **3627** 6
ἀναπέμπειν **3601** 5
ἀναπόγραφος [**3613** 15]
ἀναφαίρετος **3638** 17
ἀναχώρηςις? [**3613** 11, 18-19]
ἀνδρεῖος *see* Index II (AD 356)
ἀνεύρετος **3644** 24
ἀνήκειν **3609** 9
ἀνήρ [**3627** 3 n.?] **3641** 5 **3643** 8
ἀντί **3640** 3
ἀντιγραφή *see* Index VIII
ἀντίγραφον **3601** [16-17?], 17, (22) [**3610** 5-6]
  (**3611** 22)
ἀντικνήμιον (**3603** 26) (**3604** 23, 24?) (**3605** 15?)
ἀντίχειρ **3605** 16
ἀντλεῖν **3640** 2
ἀξία *see* Index VIII
ἄξιος **3637** 20
ἀξιοῦν **3620** 17 (**3641** 25)
ἀόκνως **3641** 10
ἅπα *see* Index VII
ἀπανθρωπία **3627** 2
ἀπαντᾶν **3620** 18
ἅπας **3613** 6-7 **3638** 5 **3641** 20
ἀπεργαςία **3638** 24
ἀπέχειν **3638** 16, 39-40
ἀπηλιώτης **3638** 12
ἀπό **3601** 7 **3602** 15, 23 **3603** 18 **3604** 2, 18
  3613 4 **3616** 4 **3617** 1 **3618** 20 **3620** 6
  3621 19 **3622** 4, 7 **3623** 4 **3634** 1, 2, 15, 16
  3635 1, 2, [9] **3636** 1, 4, [17] **3638** 2, 3, 5,
  17-18, 23 (*bis*), 24, 25, 26, 27, 28 **3639** [4], 6, 7,
  [8] **3641** 6, 8, 15, 16, 26, 27 **3644** 23
ἀπογράφεςθαι **3606** 15, (19), [24]

XIII. LATIN

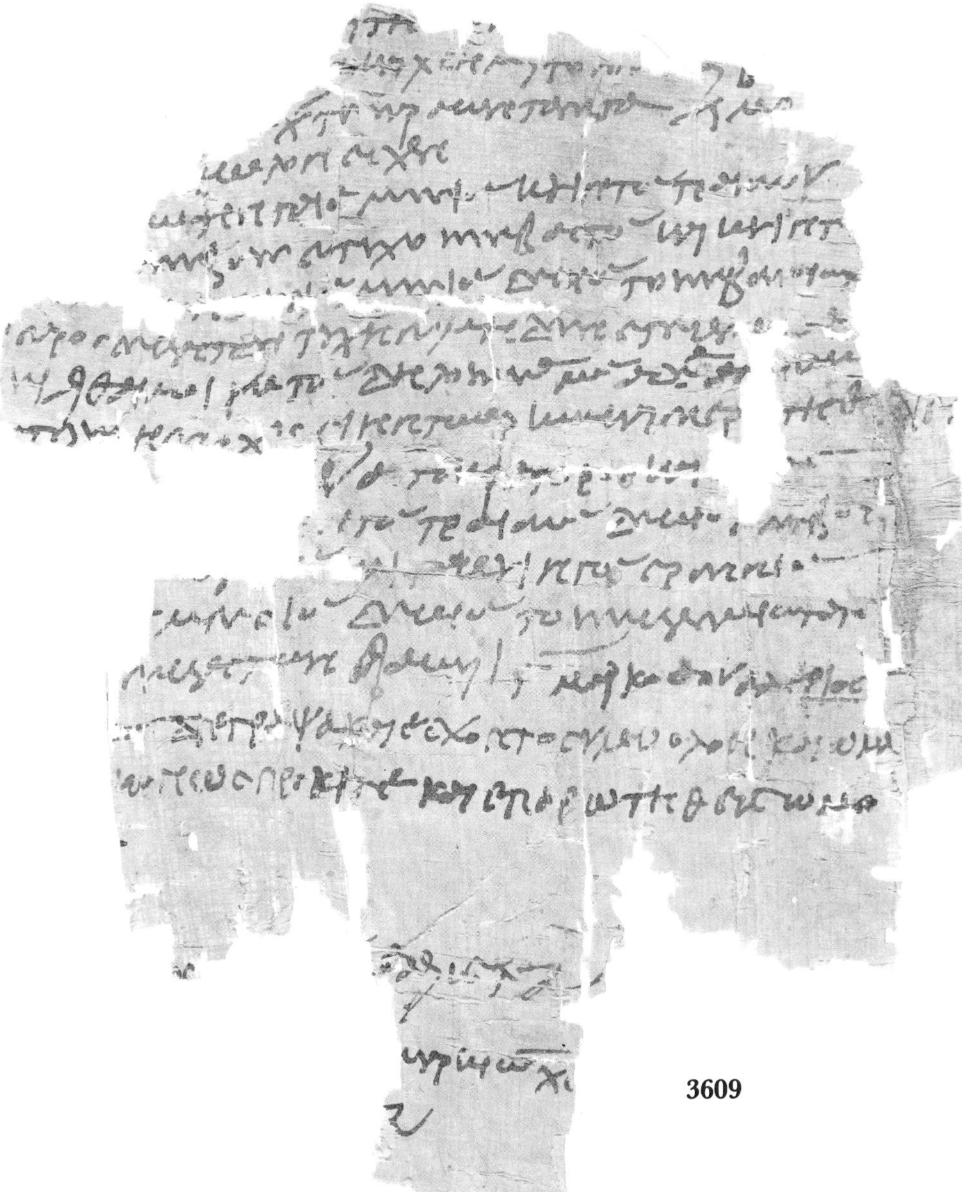

PLATE I

3609

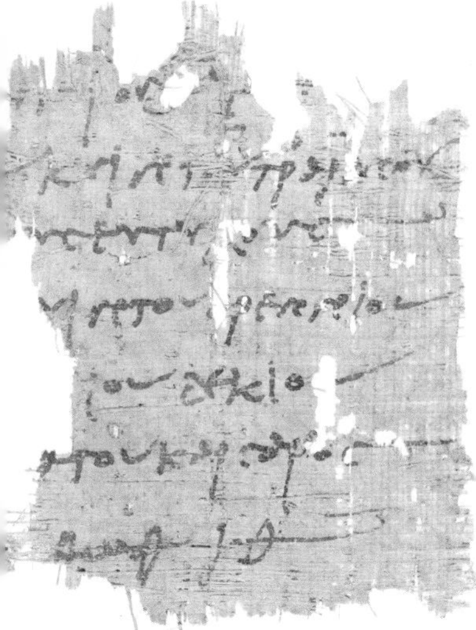

3608

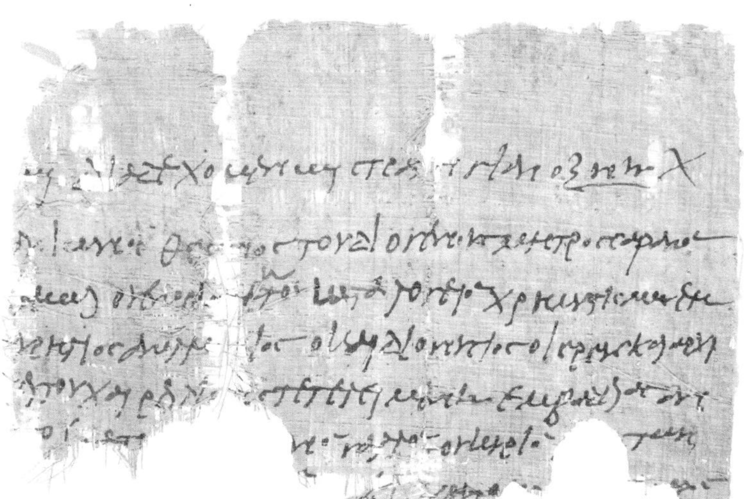

3610

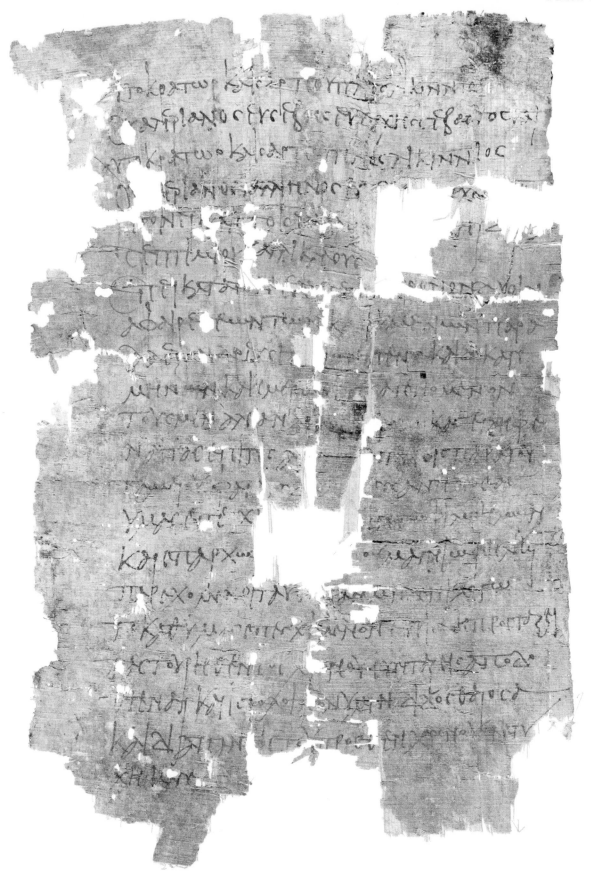

PLATE II

PLATE III

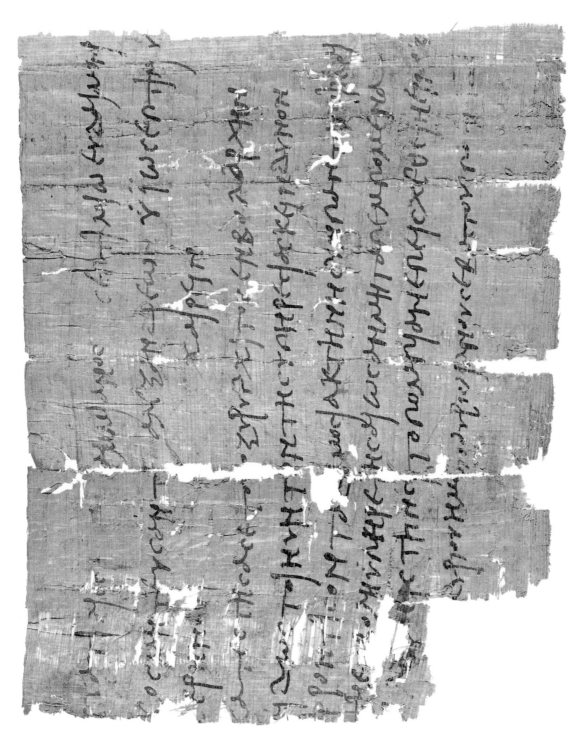

3612

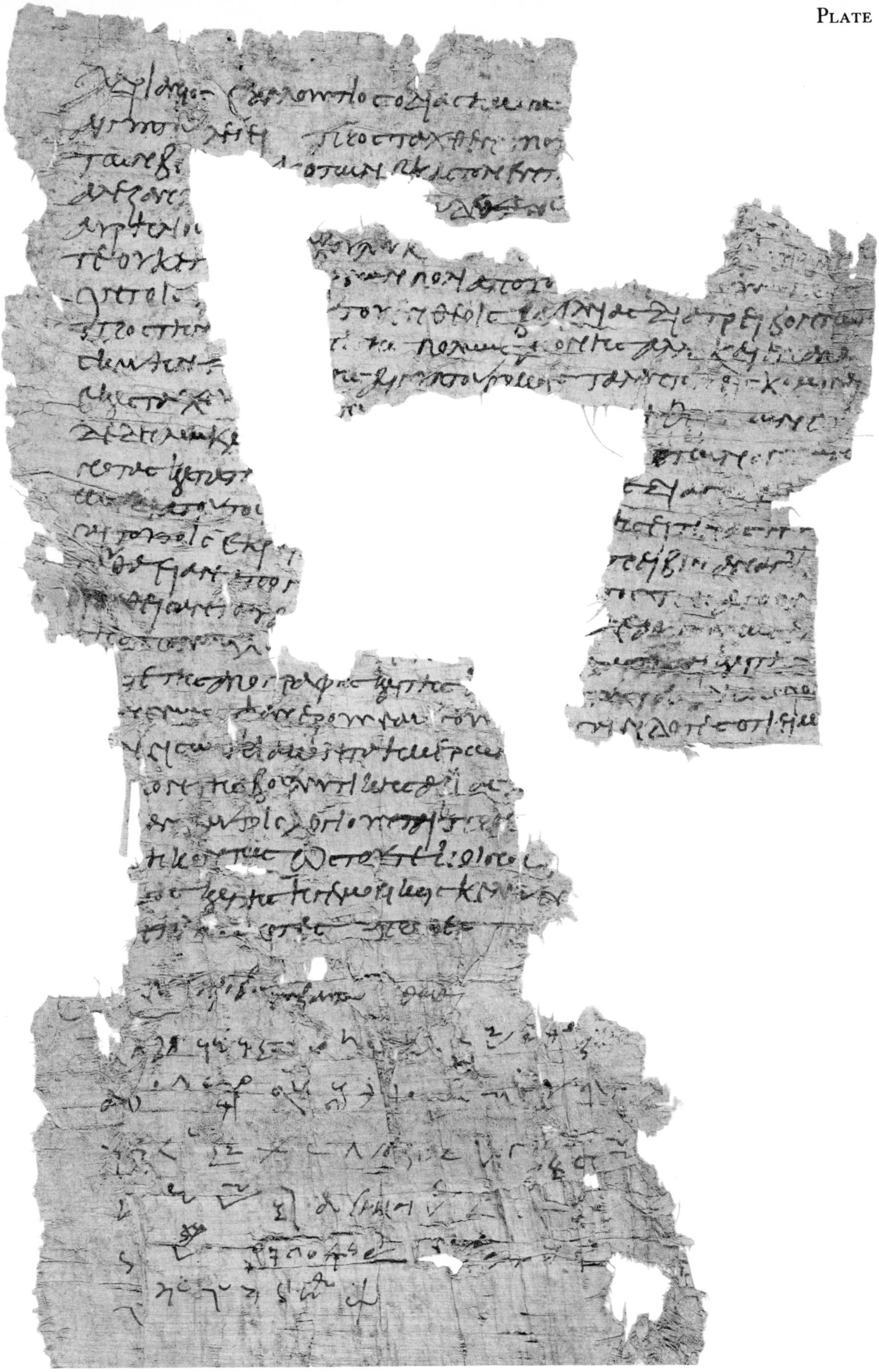

3613

PLATE V

3614

3616

PLATE VI

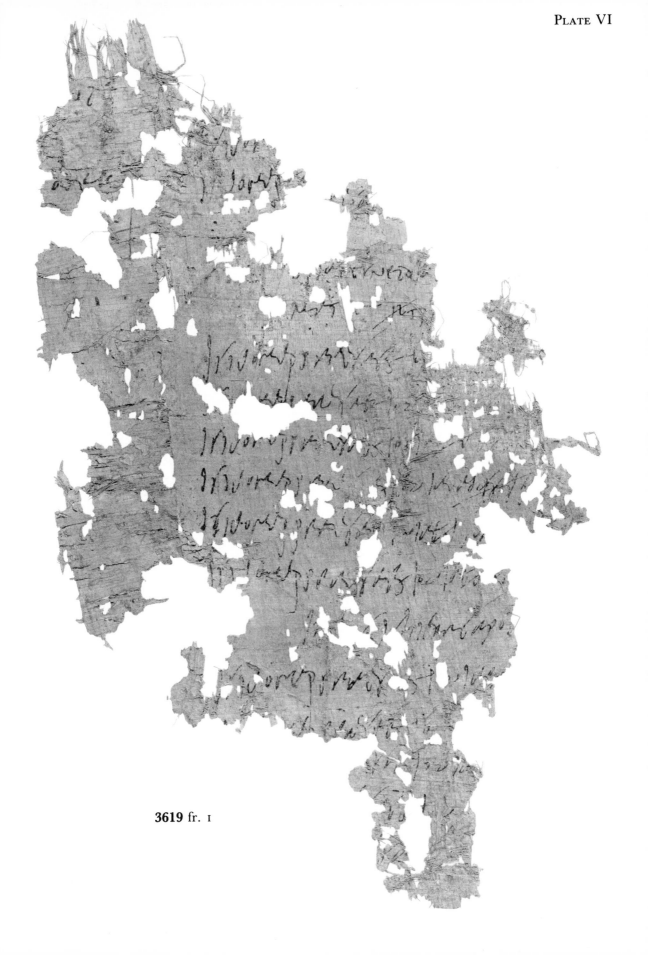

3619 fr. I

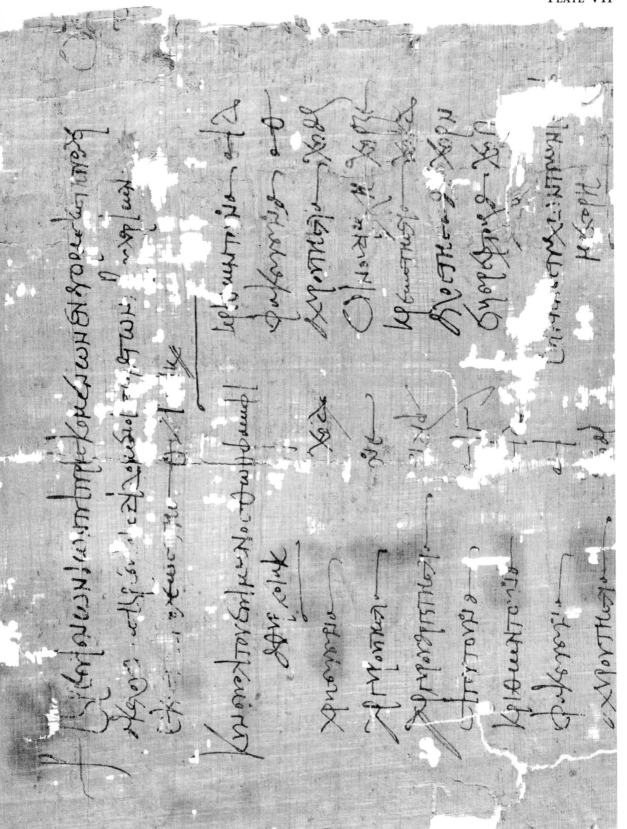

PLATE VII

PLATE VIII

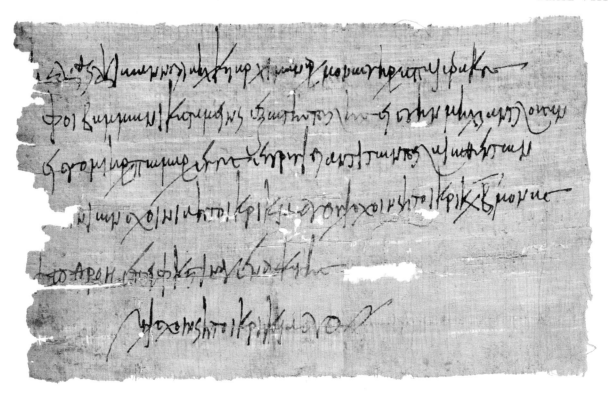

3640

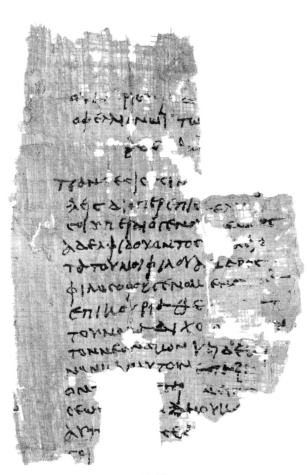

3643

DATE DUE

GAYLORD			PRINTED IN U.S.A.